Profit and the Pursuit of Energy

Also of Interest

Oil Strategy and Politics, 1941–1981, Walter J. Levy, edited by Melvin A. Conant

Resource Management and the Oceans: The Political Economy of Deep Seabed Mining, Kurt Michael Shusterich

International Dimensions of the Environmental Crisis, edited by Richard N. Barrett

U.S. Foreign Economic Strategy for the Eighties, Timothy W. Stanley, Ronald L. Danielian, and Samuel M. Rosenblatt

Soviet Economic Planning, Fyodor I. Kushnirsky

Oil, Money, and the Mexican Economy: A Macroeconometric Analysis, Francisco Carrado-Bravo

Critical Energy Issues in Asia and the Pacific: The Next Twenty Years, Fereidun Fesharaki et al.

OPEC and Natural Gas Trade: Prospects and Problems, Bijun Mossavar-Rahmani and Sharmin B. Mossavar-Rahmani

Transitions to Alternative Energy Systems, edited by Thomas Baumgartner

Solar Energy and the U.S. Economy, Christopher Pleatsikas, Edward A. Hudson, and Richard J. Goettle IV

Alcohol Fuels: Policies, Production, and Potential, Doann Houghton-Alico

* *Energy Futures, Human Values, and Lifestyles: A New Look at the Energy Crisis,* Richard C. Carlson, Willis W. Harman, Peter Schwartz, and Associates

* *Living with Energy Shortfall: A Future for American Towns and Cities,* Jon Van Til

Technology and Soviet Energy Availability, Office of Technology Assessment

Technology, International Economics, and Public Policy, edited by Hugh H. Miller and Rolf R. Piekarz

OPEC: Twenty Years and Beyond, edited by Ragaei El Mallakh

* Available in hardcover and paperback.

Profit and the Pursuit of Energy:
Markets and Regulation

edited by Jonathan David Aronson
and Peter F. Cowhey

Routledge
Taylor & Francis Group
LONDON AND NEW YORK

First published 1983 by Westview Press, Inc.

Published 2019 by Routledge
52 Vanderbilt Avenue, New York, NY 10017
2 Park Square, Milton Park, Abingdon, Oxon OX14 4RN

Routledge is an imprint of the Taylor & Francis Group, an informa business

Library of Congress Cataloging in Publication Data
Main entry under title:
Profit and the pursuit of energy.
(Westview special studies in international economics and business)
Includes index.
1. Energy industries. I. Aronson, Jonathan David. II. Cowhey, Peter F., 1948–
III. Series.
HD9502.A2P763 1983 338.2′728 82-13424

ISBN 13: 978-0-367-28441-1 (hbk)

Westview Special Studies in International Economics and Business

Profit and the Pursuit of Energy: Markets and Regulation
edited by Jonathan David Aronson and Peter F. Cowhey

Among the books on the world energy crisis, on technological possibilities for self-sufficiency, and on various energy sources, this is one of a very few to address the practicalities of government regulatory responsibilities versus the pursuit of profit in the private sector and to look at the processes, logistics, and complex interactions among private energy companies, financial sectors, and national governments.

The authors provide answers to such questions as: How do oil company operations influence government policies? What kinds of energy projects can be financed by existing financial institutions? How does the availability of insurance affect innovations in energy? They also examine how major investors and governments make decisions about the management of the volatile mix of political, economic, and technological risks that buffet the energy sector; critique the conventional wisdom concerning the major fuels; and project the likely evolution of the world energy market over the next decade.

Dr. Aronson is an associate professor in the School of International Relations at the University of Southern California and for 1982-1983 is on leave as a Council on Foreign Relations International Affairs Fellow in the Office of the U.S. Trade Representative in Washington, D.C. He is the author of *Money and Power: Banks and the World Monetary System* (1978) and the editor of *Debt and the Less Developed Countries* (Westview, 1979). **Dr. Cowhey** is an assistant professor of political science at the University of California in San Diego. In addition to acting as a consultant to the U.S. Department of Energy, the State of California, and many independent organizations, Dr. Cowhey is author of *The Problems of Plenty: Energy Policy and International Politics* (forthcoming).

It is more interesting to be provocative than right.

To three who have been both:
Wanda Jablonsky, Edith Penrose, and Susan Strange

Contents

Part 3
Market Competition and Risk

Tables and Figures

Tables

Chapter 1

Chapter 2

Chapter 3

Chapter 5

Chapter 6

Chapter 7

Figures

Chapter 3

Foreword

The 1970s was a difficult decade for the United States in energy policy. At the beginning of the decade, the United States imported 3.5 million barrels of oil a day, about a quarter of our needs, at roughly $2.00 per barrel. We were the world's largest producer, at 11.3 million barrels per day. In 1967, our surplus capacity had allowed us to easily defeat an Arab oil embargo triggered by the June war. By the end of the decade, we were importing 8.5 million barrels per day, or nearly half our needs, at fifteen times the nominal price, and our home production was declining. The painful experience of the 1973 Arab oil embargo did not save us from repeating mistakes when the Iranian Revolution curtailed production in 1979. The president called the situation a "clear and present danger to our national security."

Our national energy policy debate in the 1970s was frequently confused and poorly focused. There was often a failure to distinguish the long-term (i.e., thirty-to-forty-year) transition from fossil fuels to new sources of energy from the short-term (i.e., within ten years) problem of coping with increased dependence upon Persian Gulf oil. Ironically, given our fascination with high technology and the power of lobbies for research and development, energy was one of the rare cases in which government could be criticized for overemphasizing the long run at the expense of the short run. It was far easier to find funds for breeder reactors and fusion research than to launch an adequate strategic petroleum reserve or to fund research for conservation.

Ostensibly, the United States always considered energy as a security problem involving significant risks. In reality, however, U.S. policies focused more heavily on price and economic effects than on the security dimensions of the issue. In 1959, President Eisenhower created a mandatory quota program to reduce oil imports, allegedly for national security reasons, but its real political roots were in trade protectionism. As a security measure, the program was a failure, for it stimulated artificially high production levels that eroded domestic reserves rather than creating stockpiles and spare capacity. Ironically, in 1970 a cabinet task force recommended the gradual elimination of these quotas on the grounds that they did little for national security while imposing high prices on our economy. This occurred just at the time that U.S. domestic oil production was peaking. Imports had risen to 30 percent of our oil consumption by the time of the 1973 oil embargo.

Looking back at our energy policies in the 1970s, one is struck by two strong ironies. First, we talked about risks and security but instituted policies such as domestic price controls that had the effect of subsidizing oil imports—which increased 25 percent between the first and second oil shocks of the decade—despite President Nixon's official goal of energy independence by 1980. Second, the United States acted as though government controls at home and market forces abroad would solve its energy security problems when the opposite was closer to the truth. That view failed to recognize the changing realities of the world politics that underlay the laissez-faire regime governing international oil trade. At the interstate level decolonization and Britain's withdrawal from the Persian Gulf and at the transnational level the eroding bargaining power of the multinational oil companies combined to change the international regime quite dramatically over the course of the decade.

Another interesting feature of the 1970s was the unreliability of energy projections. They grossly exaggerated the demand for energy because they failed to take into account slackening GNP growth rates and responsiveness to rising prices. Forecasts on the supply side were even worse. The supply side is hard to predict because it depends more heavily on political factors than it does on demand. For example, political and environmental factors have tended to undercut projections of nuclear and coal supplies. The largest supply factor continues to be oil, particularly the rate of OPEC production. In the early 1970s, it was common to find buoyant projections of OPEC production in the range of 40–60 million barrels per day by 1980. The original Saudi Arabian development plan called for raising production to a level of 20 million barrels per day. Now there are uncertainties about whether the Saudis will produce 6 to 8 million barrels per day.

The current conventional wisdom is that oil markets will be soft in the 1980s, and consumers are benefiting from a glut. But there have been three political interruptions of Persian Gulf oil in the past eight years, two of which produced enormous price spikes in 1973 and 1979. It is such political surprises that pose the central and unpredictable problems in the future. In the face of risk and uncertainty in production decisions, it behooves us to be skeptical of all projections on the supply side as well as on the demand side. We may be lucky, but the current glut has not solved the energy security problem.

What should we learn from our experiences in the 1970s? The lessons for analysis and strategy are the importance of integrating economic and political factors and instruments—both domestic and international—and the importance of government and corporate strategies for dealing with political risk.

Such a focus is shared by the chapters in this book, and it is one reason why this book makes an important contribution to the current debates on energy policy. Rather than trying to provide yet another cloudy crystal ball projecting supply and demand, Jonathan Aronson and Peter Cowhey have persuaded the authors to focus on the more lasting and more important task of understanding how specific government and private actors behave in the face of uncertainty and risk. Their analysis of markets is not in terms of hidden hands but in terms of the particular strategies and responses of key actors.

There are no magic solutions or quick fixes to energy problems promised in this book. As a result, the essays focus on the major energy sources of the next decade: oil, gas, and coal. The authors come from both practical and academic backgrounds, and their discussions of the energy trade, government intervention, and public and private risk management are sensitive to both economic and political considerations. It is a work of political economy that helps to clarify and lay the foundations for better energy policy than we have seen in the past decade.

Joseph S. Nye, Jr.
Harvard University

Profit and the Pursuit of Energy

Introduction

Everyone knows that the energy market is undergoing a profound transition. Unfortunately, no one is quite sure where it is heading. Everyone agrees that unless changes in the prevalent patterns of supply and demand occur in a prompt and prudent manner, all the major participants in the world market will suffer. Unfortunately, deep divisions exist about what constitutes the proper mix of market incentives and government policies to propel change.

This book examines some of the risks and rewards, the incentives and disincentives at work shaping the search for and the production and utilization of oil and other energy sources within an increasingly complex energy market. We explore some of the trade-offs, inequities, and bureaucratic insanities (and occasional inspirations) that drive and retard "rational" energy developments and energy transition. In particular, we are concerned with trying to understand some of the factors shaping the evolving balance between market forces and government regulation. How is the balance determined? How is the balance likely to change?

Unlike many who study the world energy market, the authors of this book do not emphasize the question of what constitutes the best guess on the future distribution of supply and demand for specific fuels for specific nations or regions. We do not concentrate on the prediction of the dynamics of pricing. Neither do we advocate an optimal policy designed to achieve particular energy outcomes.

Our collection tries to shift the focus away from crystal-ball gazing. Instead we explore how and why major public and private participants in the energy market make their choices about energy strategies. Thus, we seek to illuminate how major investors and governments make decisions about the management of the volatile mix of political, economic, and technological risks that buffet the energy sector. Given an understanding of the nature of the risks and rewards for major players, we can criticize the conventional wisdom concerning the major fuels and identify probable future turning points. We have reluctantly limited our discussion to the realm of oil, natural gas, coal, and to some extent the synthetic fuel derivatives of coal and natural gas. We have excluded any systematic discussion of the prospects for either solar or nuclear energy, not because they are not potentially of great importance, but because we do not expect them to challenge the dominance of the oil, gas, and coal triad in this century. Similarly, we do not have separate coverage of conservation, but all our chapters assume that there has been a fundamental revolution in the utilization of energy.

Even though one recurring theme of this volume is that the future is largely indeterminate, we adhere to several key assumptions about the parameters for change. First, we assume that there will be a substantial shift in the relative market shares of fuels and a steep decline in the overall growth of demand for energy, particularly in the industrial world. But the precise shifts, especially which fuels will profit most from a declining share for oil, may be full of surprises. Second, we assume that the central players in the marketplace and the relationships among them will change significantly over the rest of this century. For instance, the growth in market share and expertise of the national oil corporations of oil-exporting countries has already toppled the large Anglo-American firms from their unquestioned dominance of the world oil, and thus energy, markets. Other public and private actors have grown and will continue to grow in importance as the energy market becomes more complex. Third, we assume that governments and private companies often will clash on such fundamental issues as who should develop energy resources, which pricing system should prevail, how best to manipulate markets in order to advance political and national security interests, and how much regulation of environmental and economic risks will be necessary to safeguard and satisfy the public. We expect that the overall thrust of governments' actions will produce more intervention in and attempts to control energy markets domestically and internationally. Rollbacks of selected regulations, such as decontrol of oil and natural gas prices, are not likely to reverse this general trend. Fourth, we assume that there will be no "definitive solution" for the energy crisis during the rest of this decade or the rest of this century. Even with lower oil prices and more ample supplies during the early 1980s, problems for oil importers seeking to avoid repeating earlier cycles of falling prices and deteriorating energy balances will persist.

Perhaps no problem is more difficult for the editors of a collection than to translate their questions and assumptions into guidelines to unite the different chapters. Too often the only thing that holds them together is the book's binding. We followed a twofold approach. We solicited contributions from experts outside the university who deal with these issues on a regular basis. In effect, we asked these collaborators from the "real world" to reflect on the patterns of risks that shaped their choices. To complement these views, we asked our academic contributors to theorize more broadly about the factors that shaped these patterns. The results of these labors unfold in three parts.

Part 1 surveys the changing trade in world energy. Its three chapters are designed to probe the dynamics of the three major fuels in the world energy trade: petroleum, natural gas, and coal. The authors adopt three complementary approaches. In Chapter 1, on the major international oil companies, Peter F. Cowhey provides an overview of the debate over the shifting patterns of world energy trade by examining one set of corporations' plans to become diversified energy producers. He shows how the aggregate pattern of contemplated changes for each individual fuel substantially alters the overall mix of political and economic risks confronting governments and corporations in the 1980s. In contrast to Cowhey's emphasis on corporate strategy as a road map to change, Jonathan David Aronson and Christopher Cragg's analysis in Chapter 2 of the developing international trade in natural gas stresses the detailed regulation of this trade by both importing and exporting governments. They demonstrate that technology and economics reinforce the importance of government policy because there is no integrated market for gas. As a result, prices and market opportunities vary substantially around the globe, yet governments face political and economic pressures to bring more uniformity to market practices. The future of the gas trade will, at least in part, depend on whether governments decide to seek a more thoroughly integrated market. In Chapter 3, Michael Gaffen's examination of the world coal trade shows that there are rivalries between nations but commonalities of interest for particular classes of market participants that cut across national boundaries. As a result, the types of institutions dominating the coal market are changing, and governments must confront a complex series of choices about how to allot responsibilities for the development of infrastructure and to ensure fair and efficient trading practices.

Part 2 focuses on governmental incursions into domestic regulation of energy markets that have a major impact on world trading. Its chapters concentrate on the ability of governments to formulate policies that can allocate risks and profits successfully. It begins by showing that the classic question is always, "Who benefits?" Sometimes the answer is very surprising. The first vehicle for this argument is discussed in Chapter 4, Merrie Klapp's study of how the British and Norwegian governments have worked out their policies on the exploration and production of North Sea oil and gas. Her work demonstrates that conventional analyses of optimal cost-benefit policies, on the "absorptive capacity" of national economies, and on the changing characteristics of the international oil industry cannot adequately account for the differences between the policies of the two nations. Instead, one must turn to the broader picture of national political competition and industrial structure in businesses that are affected strongly by the development of oil fields. Her analysis serves as a warning that political factors put substantial constraints on energy policy, and it spells out some of these parameters in the North Sea.

Yet even if government is free to be relatively Solomonic in its deliberations, Kermit R. Kubitz's study of the utility industry (Chapter 5) argues, appealing solutions may not be readily available for one of the largest segments of the energy industry. He shows that changes in the marketplace have produced a revolution in thinking about how to regulate the utility industry; both industry and government agree that the ancien regime is dead. But the alternatives to the traditional modes of regulation differ radically in terms of who would bear the risks and appropriate the profits from supplying electricity. Each alternative has supporters and each would yield substantially different mixes of energy supply and demand. Finally, in Chapter 6 Zvi Adar and Tamir Agmon reexamine the frustrating and seemingly quixotic effort to launch a synthetic fuels industry in the United States. They argue that there may be sound reasons for a large, sustained commitment by the U.S. government to such an undertaking, and they develop a model that helps to choose the optimal strategies for support through subsidy. They suggest that the debate over policy has suffered because we have failed to distinguish adequately between the types of risks confronting entrepreneurs and the types of subsidies that will encourage development of large-scale technological projects that employ innovative design or technology. In their analysis of how qualitative variations in risks shape the incentives for efficiency and innovation, they suggest some surprising alternatives open to governments. For example, they urge that in some situations more serious attention be given to the possibility of "prizes" that would, in effect, provide bonuses to successful projects, while bearing little responsibility for ill-fated ventures.

Part 3 provides a more general reconsideration of how private investors manage risk or in some instances fail to do so in the heat of competition. Chapter 7, by Jonathan David Aronson and Charles Rudicel Proctor, explores a frequently neglected aspect of the management of risk in energy projects, the role of private insurers. The authors examine the incentives provided to developers of energy projects in terms of pricing and available capacity. They argue that in providing a boost to smaller projects on both dimensions the interests of society and indeed the long-term interests of the insurance industry may suffer. For example, there may be so much insurance available at reasonable rates to the owners of oil tankers that they have no incentive to take special precautions against accidents. Aronson and Proctor suggest that government intervention to protect society may actually be less necessary for large and innovative projects than for smaller undertakings. In Chapter 8, Peter F. Cowhey argues that all parties in economic transactions have temptations to deceive or rewrite the terms of their agreements on more advantageous grounds whenever possible. By pinpointing the conditions that make such behavior more likely, one could predict when risk increases and when energy investments will slow down because of risk. Cowhey applies this argument to a number of issues concerning oil, coal, and synthetic fuels. The chapter concludes by speculating about ways in which government policies could alter the situation.

It is clear that governments will never allow a pure market solution to energy problems. It is equally clear that even the governments most interested in the use of the tools of a "command economy" do not advocate a total reliance on regulation and national control over energy investments. These chapters explore the variations between these two extremes and suggest likely paths for balancing private profit and public authority.

Part 1

World Trade in Oil, Natural Gas, and Coal

1 The Engineers and the Price System Revisited: The Future of the International Oil Corporations

Peter F. Cowhey

"What we have here is a battle of nerves between the OPEC producers and the companies," says a London oilman. . . . "Someone is bound to crack, and I fear it will be on the company, not the producer side."
—*Business Week*, December 22, 1980, p. 17

During the first three-quarters of this century the major international oil companies transformed the world's energy system by finding, developing, transporting, refining, and distributing oil on the basis of a strategy geared to providing secure supplies at prices low enough to ensure continued growth of the world economy (and, thus, an increased and rapidly growing demand for oil).[1] Even though these companies still control a very large share of the investment capital available for energy projects, as well as formidable logistical and engineering resources, their role in the next transformation of the energy sector is in doubt today.

Any assessment of the future role of the majors in the energy sector must begin by recognizing that their control of the world oil industry eroded substantially during the 1970s and that the change has forced the majors to adjust their corporate strategies accordingly. This chapter examines the new strategies of U.S.-based majors with two questions

The author's two chapters in this volume have profited from the comments of Peter Gourevitch, Gary Jacobson, Peter Katzenstein, David Laitin, Joseph Nye, Dennis Smallwood, Susan Strange, Serge Taylor, and Miguel Wionczec.

in mind. First, what logic ties together their moves to become more diversified energy companies? Second, do strategies that focus on providing security for the majors actually provide security for consumers in the industrial nations, as they once did?

The answers to these questions are rooted in two guiding premises for this chapter. The first is that analyzing "strategic bargaining" by oil companies—vis-à-vis other firms, host countries, and Organisation for Economic Co-operation and Development (OECD) governments—is critical to solving the puzzle of corporate strategy. To understand how oil firms respond to the changing market and the political forces in their environment, we must examine closely how managers change their mix of investments and their basic relationships with governments and corporations in order to strengthen bargaining positions. I call this mix of investments and basic relationships a *bargaining strategy*.[2] I shall argue that the history of the oil industry prior to 1970 can provide us with a clear understanding of how a vertically integrated company can successfully manage risk in a world commodity market. I will then examine the less successful alterations in strategy from 1970 through 1978 and the latest round of adjustments after 1979. My first premise leads me to seek to identify a coherent bargaining strategy from a wealth of small, often intuitive moves by senior oil executives who are trying to maximize both profit and security. Put differently, firms seek to maximize profit and reduce risk; they intuitively recognize that the two ambitions may clash and therefore they weave back and forth between these goals, often in a manner more clearly discernible to the observer than to the participants. Understanding this bargaining strategy allows me to go beyond predictions of corporate behavior based on models of optimal investments given certain projected resources and costs.

My second premise is that the major oil companies affect the security of consumers in two ways that go beyond their direct contribution to the balance of supply, demand, and price. First, how well companies have positioned themselves for bargaining is as important as any specific level of global supply and demand for ensuring consumer security. The companies' strengths and weaknesses as bargainers may put them in very different circumstances than might be expected given existing international energy balances.[3] For example, for a long time after the international positions of industrial nations weakened, the Seven Sisters' global diversification and supply base shielded the industrial world from many of the coercive bargaining ploys of the Organization of Petroleum Exporting Countries (OPEC). Second, the majors alter the security of consumers by influencing the coherence and direction of government policies in the industrial nations. Particularly in the United States, the ability of government to orchestrate an international oil policy varies depending on relations between government and industry.

In summary, we ultimately want to know the relationship between corporations' vulnerability or strength and the degree of consumer security. In this chapter I articulate the implicit outline and logic uniting the many specific changes in corporate strategy by which the majors hope to reduce their own vulnerability. I then show how these developments change the risks confronting consumers in OECD nations in the future. Throughout the chapter I assume that the strategy of the majors is basically feasible, even though I examine the consequences of different levels of success in executing the strategy by individual firms. In contrast, in Chapter 8 I step back and critically question the fundamental premises of the companies' plans. I conclude that the majors may confront risks that their strategies cannot easily resolve. This possibility suggsts that the governments of industrial nations, and especially the U.S. government, may have to reassess some key aspects of their energy policies.

The Classic Multinational Strategy: The Majors as Global Engineers

Until 1970 the multinational corporations (MNCs) operated in a comparatively secure and profitable world. They faced many risks, but they also enjoyed a wider array of "permissive support" from governments than is normally thought.[4] This support, however, depended on finding and marketing ample supplies of oil at predictable prices. If the majors faltered, governments would expand their power in oil markets. This challenge was formidable because, with the skyrocketing demand for oil and gas, primitive regions had to be opened up for many of the production projects, and the smooth meshing of global supply and demand required many massive infrastructure development projects scattered throughout the oil-importing and -exporting nations. To succeed the majors had to think of themselves as architects and logistical engineers on a global scale, dedicated to ensuring that each step from production to the gas pump was completed in a timely manner. One country's withholding of production, local disruptions of pipelines, or failure to build sufficient refining capacity to meet demand posed serious risks. Yet, the majors made the system work. Support from the U.S. government helped. So did the numerous political obstacles to formulation of effective energy policies by oil-exporting and -importing nations. But these factors do not suffice to explain why the majors succeeded.

The majors succeeded because, in their golden years, they played five crucial roles with panache.[5] To begin with, as *experts,* they were exclusive repositories of technical and managerial know-how. As is often the case early in an industry's history, expertise was highly concentrated. Subcontractors could not easily replace the large firms. Beyond this know-how was a second key role: The companies were *strategic risk takers.* They made their money by betting heavily on various production and distribution opportunities. The entire ethos and financial organization of the industry were geared for self-financing, which facilitated large speculative investments that no financial institution would accept. The companies' ability to phase big investments over a number of years, reserving many of the heaviest expenditures until relatively advanced stages of a project, greatly facilitated this strategy.[6] Besides giving the majors a large edge on developing gigantic oil fields, risk taking also paid off in the realm of distribution. Companies spent lavishly on holding and expanding their market shares by saturating targeted markets with refining capacity and service stations even though they often had to risk long periods of slender returns on their outlays. As a result, even in the late 1960s many experts believed that the majors would continue to dominate oil markets because their expenditures on distribution had made them the key to moving the large volumes of production that countries like Saudi Arabia wanted to sell.

Third, the majors were *commercial diplomats.* Supporters of multinationals long ago argued that these firms keep conflicts about economic interests between nations within a framework of market competition, thus preventing such conflicts from escalating into the realm of high diplomacy. But these supporters missed the companies' crucial role as the coordinators of infrastructure projects and the catalysts of sectoral policies. The majors' global operations forced them to coax the governments of their suppliers and customers to enlarge the "right" ports, to formulate "appropriate" tax policies, and to ensure that operations meshed globally. Such wide-ranging prodding of governments was not easy (as shown by the delicate diplomacy entailed by the current expansion of the coal trade). But the major oil firms were willing to pay the costs of being the lobbyists and brokers for their preferred public policies in order to protect the operations of their global networks. In short, as theories of collective goods suggest, some group had to invest to coordinate choices of sovereign parties in order to achieve reasonably efficient solutions.

Commercial diplomacy, however, would not have sufficed if the leading oil companies had not played the role of *insurers* who spread risks over a wide portfolio of productive facilities. With a complex sequence of steps necessary to hold world markets in balance, the majors were highly vulnerable to blackmail or other disruptions in many parts of their operations. A global spread does not automatically reduce vulnerability to the disadvantages of bargaining with small numbers of partners in particular projects, so the companies developed multiple options for each step in their global network.[7] Surplus productive capacity distributed around the world, flexible transportation possibilities, and diversity of refining investments meant that no one country or partner could easily disrupt the entire network. Thus the insurance principle in developing a project and choosing the optimum level of global capabilities reduced the vulnerability of firms to local threats.

Finally, the majors were able to mesh global operations because they served as *agents of interdependent interests of governments.* The majors tried to preempt governmental choices by making governments aware that the fate of a project in a particular country depended on the fortunes of other operations in the global networks of the majors. A pipeline closed anywhere in the Middle East threatened the interests of several producing countries.[8] A disruption in production from Iran hurt the interests of European partners of the majors in the refining industry. Thus the troubles of the majors often could evoke the support of many countries beyond their parent governments. In short, multinational firms with integrated, interdependent operations were protected by a range of governments and associated companies that varied according to the particular project at stake. Their parent governments were not the only ones with vested interests in their success.

The old synthesis collapsed in the 1970s, partly a victim of its own success. Numerous new entrants—large and small domestic firms from the United States, state-supported firms from Europe and Japan—made the skills of the majors more dispensable, while national oil companies (NOCs) of oil-exporting nations grew in technical competence and could reasonably hope to direct subcontractors on projects. Moreover, the new entrants were sufficiently large (e.g., such enormous firms as Continental Oil and Standard of Indiana) or well subsidized by their governments (as in the case of European firms) to be able to gamble on large investments in expanding their retail operations. Thus the newcomers gave the OPEC nations more latitude in selecting commercial partners for selling their oil. At the same time, the oil exporters established greater autonomy in production. High oil prices and the comparatively simple technical problems posed by the fields of the major OPEC members made it possible for exporting countries to finance their oil and gas operations without relying on finance by foreigners. Projections of rising demand in the 1970s threatened to squeeze capacity sufficiently to endanger the ability of any company (particularly smaller ones) to meet supply requirements while maintaining its market share in the 1980s. Even if adequate capacity existed in the short run, the threat of a shortage removed the protection once provided by spreading risks through insurance. Meanwhile, rising political attention to oil problems in both importing and exporting nations crowded the majors' central role in the policy arena, thereby diminishing their ability to succeed as commercial diplomats. As countries grew more nervous about oil crises, oil-importing governments willingly paid premiums to move in and take the place of the major private firms if the majors faced difficulties in their relations with host governments. The majors' old role as agents of interdependent interests was thus weakened.

After 1973: The Majors as Honest Brokers

Between 1973 and 1978 the majors' holdings were nationalized in OPEC nations; simultaneously they had to weather many adverse decisions by OECD nations concerning pricing, production, and antitrust policy. In reaction to these changes the large companies experimented with many new tactics to shore up their position. In essence, from 1973 through 1978 the companies moved incrementally from emphasizing their ability to serve as "global engineers" of world energy markets to being "honest brokers" between importers and exporters.

The majors observed the dip in the demand for oil starting in 1974 and the influx of oil from new sources (Alaska, the North Sea, and Mexico) and concluded that oil prices would not climb very rapidly in real (that is, adjusted for inflation) terms. A price range of $12 to $16 per barrel (in 1976 dollars) was a common estimate for 1985. This estimate had two implications. First, OPEC nations would still have to expand production over the next few years in order to obtain the revenue desired for ambitious development projects. Thus, these countries were the logical source of much of the necessary new production for the coming decade, and the companies had to stay on good terms with them. Second, a large number of long-term possibilities for energy supply were commercially risky. Even if prices were just high enough to make these new sources viable, competitors might obtain higher rates of return by concentrating on conventional sources of oil and gas produced at lower prices.

The effects of the majors' price forecasts on new energy supplies were soon evident in the field of synfuels. While rounding up leases and designing small prototype plants for synthetic fuels, the companies decided that synfuels were not yet economic. By late 1974 most had concluded that the necessary selling price of synthetic fuels would range from $8 to $16 per barrel.[9] Moreover, they foresaw that intricate regulatory battles would delay the launching of a major expansion of the coal synthetics, shale oil, and tar sands industries. Even conventional coal mining had only limited appeal because many big oil firms doubted that the low price and limited demand for coal, compounded by regulatory and labor problems, could yield the 13 to 15 percent minimum rate of return that they required. As late as 1978, only Conoco, Exxon, Occidental, and Kerr-McGee planned to become leading coal producers by 1985.[10]

The companies settled on offshore and "frontier" (such as Alaska) fields as their areas of "technical expertise" and "strategic risk taking." As a measure to build a new domain of superiority in the oil business, this was a successful tactic. Simultaneously, they tried to increase their "insurance" by putting most of their offshore investments in OECD countries, especially by tapping the United States Outer Continental Shelf (OCS). The subsequent failure of the OCS to yield large new discoveries was a sharp setback for corporate hopes.

To augment their insurance function companies also reorganized to shift their profit mix to downstream activities (where they retained a large share of the market). But the expense of refinery modernization, government price controls, and slowly declining demand limited the contribution of this move to profitability. However, a number of the majors found the results of their expanding role in the petrochemical industry very encouraging. They concentrated largely on high-volume plants producing basic petrochemicals that could be built in association with refineries. By 1979, for example, the ten largest U.S. oil corporations owned 55 percent of the ethylene capacity of the United States. In a few cases (notably the U.S. affiliates of Shell, Mobil, and Exxon) the majors pursued an important role in the building of petrochemical export plants in Saudi Arabia. This decision promised to expand their market share overseas and, as a side-payment by the Saudis, boost their supplies of crude oil.[11]

Because the oil crisis was a political revolution, the major responses of the firms came in regard to their political roles as "commercial diplomats" and as "agents of interdependent interests." The primary theme of the majors' agenda for global diplomacy was that governments should restrain their impulse to expand their role in energy markets. For example, the majors tried to dissuade OPEC nations from investing in downstream refining and marketing by arguing that these were less lucrative tasks for NOCs. Within the OECD, the corporations campaigned for expanded leasing of public lands for oil exploration and against price controls, government allocation of oil supplies, and subsidies for state energy firms. They also discouraged talk about grand deals between OECD and OPEC governments.[12] They justified their opposition on the reasonable grounds that realities of supply and demand were likely to prove more important than global social compacts between the "Northern" and "Southern" nations, especially with no resolution to the Middle Eastern conflict. Had the corporate preferences been accepted, the industry would have remained dominant in representing OECD oil interests. The companies succeeded to some extent in the United States in regard to price controls, allocation programs, and government diplomacy; elsewhere they settled for more freedom on pricing in return for greater government roles in oil diplomacy.

The heart of the corporate strategy was trying to define a new set of "interdependent interests" between OPEC and OECD nations. This approach reflected a combination of strengths and weaknesses. The companies knew that they would be nationalized in OPEC countries but wanted to retain access to large amounts of oil on preferential terms so that they could meet projected demand. In return the companies offered OPEC producers assured disposal of large amounts of crude during periods of surplus capacity. Although the companies sometimes canceled purchase commitments if price differentials charged by a particular supplier moved out of line with international standards, the companies steadfastly sought to remain the indispensable buyers of last resort for major producers. This strategy ingratiated them with sellers and let the companies argue to importers that they could still negotiate reasonable prices and continue to manage security of supply.[13] The majors warned that stripping them of their power would reduce a nation's ability to switch and match crude oil during an emergency. (Oil importers remained dependent on the large firms for handling the smaller, more probable disturbances, although they had instituted a collective system for rationing oil during large shortages.) Even Japan encouraged further investment by the majors in Japanese refineries as a measure to increase national security.

The companies' limited redeployment of resources as of 1978 amounted to a rather muddled, and ultimately precarious, shoring up of their position. The majors were very unhappy with the situation. Neither their profits nor their market shares in production and marketing had been buoyed by the oil revolution. (See Table 1.) They also largely failed to retain purchasing terms markedly better than those available to other oil companies.[14] There was certainly no conspiracy between OPEC and the majors. But the firms had retained their dominant role in downstream marketing and were still by far the largest sources of crude oil.[15]

Despite their careful redeployment of resources, the oil companies had underestimated the potential for change. This was partly because Western countries did not permit the expansion of supplies envisioned by corporate planners and partly because the companies had not

TABLE 1
Shares of Eight Major International Oil Companies in World Markets Outside Communist Countries (Shares outside North America in parentheses)

Type of Firm	Share of World Production		Share of World Refining	
	End of 1970	End of 1975	End of 1970	End of 1975
International Majors	64% (75%)	57% (63%)	55% (59%)	50% (51%)
OPEC National Oil Companies	2% (3%)	12% (17%)	2% (2%)	3% (5%)
Others	34% (22%)	31% (20%)	43% (39%)	47% (44%)

Source: Computed from Petroleum Economics Limited, Technical Analysis of the International Oil Market (Washington: GPO, 1978).

appreciated how tenuous their influence over supplies could be. In mid-1978 the majors faced gigantic new challenges when the revolution in Iran fundamentally altered the oil industry's future.

The following facts underscore the degree of change. During 1979 the total spot market around the world hovered around 10 percent, double the average level of the previous five years. Meanwhile the fifteen largest firms' share of the world market in oil shrank from more than 90 percent to 60 percent, and the Seven Sisters' share of OPEC oil declined from 70 percent in 1973 to about 33 percent in 1980.[16] Even the partners in Aramco hoped only to maintain about 6 million barrels per day in contracts from Saudi Arabia, conceding the rest to other majors or direct sales by Petromin to other nations. The Seven Sisters had to give up their sales to independent refiners in Japan and other important countries, and oil sales consummated directly between governments rose from 11 percent in early 1978 to 19 percent of the world market by the first quarter of 1980. OPEC also revived its claim for a share of the profits from refining, a development that threatened to weaken the majors' standing in world markets.[17]

In summary, the majors finally conceded that their day as the clearly dominant force in the world oil trade was over. The national companies of OPEC had taken over the majors' role in the initial disposition of OPEC crude sufficiently to make the majors' role as balancers and honest brokers of the world energy system no longer viable.

After 1978: The Majors as Diversified Energy Corporations

Even though individual variations in approach are substantial, the companies have responded to the Iranian revolution by undertaking a much more fundamental alteration of their strategies than they did after the oil price rises of 1973–1974. To show the commonalities and variations of the changes, I have collected data on the operations of the five U.S. members of the Seven Sisters and three of the major U.S. independents. Although the two Anglo-Dutch giants, British Petroleum (BP) and Shell (or their U.S. subsidiaries), are not included in my sample, I have taken account of them in the more general line of analysis. In general, BP and Shell's strategies were closer to that of Gulf than the other U.S. Sisters. These three companies had only limited access to Saudi oil. Therefore they came to rely more on the spot market for supplies.

The change in strategy was feasible only because higher oil prices fundamentally lowered demand growth and made other sources of supplies profitable. At the same time, much higher levels of profit and investment were made possible by the appreciation in value of the firms' existing oil and gas reserves. As Tables 2 and 3 show, revenues of the eight companies jumped from $210.3 to $376.4 billion between 1978 and 1981, while corporate investment rose from $17.7 in 1978 to about $31 billion in 1980. My sample of firms accounted for about 27 percent of all capital investment in the oil and gas industry and about one-third of production in the noncommunist world in 1979.[18] This financial muscle made it conceivable to convert the pronouncements of yesterday into the financial commitments of today and tomorrow.

After these plans emerged in 1979–1980, the forecasts concerning the global energy market again shifted. In general, continued recession and unanticipated gains in conservation slashed projections of demand. OPEC production plunged below 19 million barrels per day by early 1982. And analysts revised their projections to suggest that the OECD countries' consumption of oil might well never equal the levels of demand of 1980. As the evidence of these changes accumulated, predictions concerning prices changed, beginning late in 1981. Most experts foresaw a decline in the real price of oil through 1982 and perhaps a de facto freeze in its level through 1984. Demand would then rise sufficiently to permit a small average increase in the price of oil for the rest of the decade. Late in 1981 the mid-range forecast of a sample of predictions about oil prices (in 1980 dollars) in 1990 was about $40 per barrel.[19] By spring 1982 forecasters had lowered their predictions to between $35 and $40 (in 1980 dollars).

TABLE 2
Corporate Profits and Revenues of the Eight Largest U.S.-Based Oil Companies: 1978 - 1981

Company	Total Revenues[a] (% U.S. in parentheses) 1978	1979	1980	1981	Profits as a Percentage of Shareholder Equity 1978	1979	1980	1981
Exxon	$64.9 (26.7)	$85.0 (25.6)	$110.4 (25.5)	$108.1	14.0	20.1	23.6	19.5
Mobil	$37.4 (41.8)	$48.2 (39.2)	$63.7 (36.6)	$64.5	13.0	20.5	23.9	16.6
Texaco	$29.1 (33.4)	$39.1 (31.5)	$52,4 (30.8)	$57.6	9.0	17.7	19.7	16.8
Standard of California	$24.1 (40.7)	$30.9 (42.8)	$41.5 (44.9)	$44.2	13.6	19.2	22.6	18.7
Standard of Indiana	$16.3 (73)	$20.2 (77.7)	$27.8 (79.5)	$29.9	15.8	19.4	21.6	18.0
Gulf Oil	$18.4 (53.4)	$26.1 (52.4)	$28.8 (58.5)	$28.3	10.5	16.3	15.3	12.3
Atlantic Richfield	$12.7 (86.7)	$16.7 (88.1)	$24.1 (89.8)	$27.8	16.2	20.5	24.4	19.3
Phillips Petroleum	$7.4 (75.3)	$9.7 (79.6)	$13.7 (77.9)	$16.0	22.2	23.3	23.8	16.0
Total	$210.3	$275.9	$362.4	$376.4				
Average					14.3	19.6	21.9	17.2

Source: Annual reports.

a. Revenues in billions of dollars

The change in outlook about demand and price led the companies to review their investment plans. For the purposes of this analysis I have accounted for these modifications according to two rules of thumb. First, because the basic vision of the long-term future remained intact, albeit subject to changing dates (perhaps set back between six to ten years) for the feasibility of some options, I stress the basic idea of the diversification strategy as it was sketched out through 1981. Second, throughout the analysis I shall note specific departures from the long-run plan made necessary by the weakening of prices. These generally meant that synthetic fuels and liquefied natural gas (LNG) received lower priorities, while exploration for petroleum slowed somewhat and

TABLE 3
Corporate Investment Practices of the Eight Largest U.S.-Based Oil Companies: 1978-1980[a]

		Exxon	Mobil	Texaco	SoCal	Standard of Ind.	Gulf	ARCO	Phillips	Total
Total Corporate Investment	1978	5.3	2.175	1.906	1.692	2.239	2.129	1.358	.940	17.739
	1979	7.4	3.812	2.025	2.258	3.027	2.513	1.823	1.454	24.312
	1980	8.0	4.185	3.075	3.599	4.175	3.001	3.370	1.666	31.071
Of Which:										
Oil and Gas Exploration and Production	1978	3.468	1.117	1.073	1.163	1.738	1.279	.666	.721[b]	11.23[b]
	1979	4.808	2.572	1.199	1.603	2.397	1.612	1.058	1.237	16.48
	1980	5.291	3.000	2.043	2.230	3.376	2.085	1.832	1.318	21.18
Refining, Marketing, and Transport	1978	.985	.464	.361	.291	.257	.391	.290	not separated out	
	1979	1.185	.590	.322	.385	.354	.466	.342		
	1980	1.360	.927	.416	.734	.430	.600	.529		
Chemical	1978	.510	.104	.109	.026	.228	.139	.104	.125	1.34
	1979	.484	.146	.086	.057	.247	.065	.104	.114	1.30
	1980	.487	.248	.061	.091	.234	.082	.454	.181	1.84
Other (Includes Mineral, Coal, Non-energy)	1978	.629	.378	.047	.212	.014	.327	.363	.093	2.06
	1979	1.753	.504	.034	.213	.027	.338	.404	.103	3.34
	1980	1.333	.641	.170	.544	.132	.170	.612	.167	3.77

Source: Annual reports and Forms 10-K.

a. All figures in billions of dollars.
b. Includes investment in refining by Phillips Petroleum.

work on expanding coal production continued. In general, companies delayed exploration and development of smaller onshore fields because they could revive these efforts quickly when prices climbed. Work on the most expensive offshore fields did not lag immediately because it takes a long time to develop such projects, but continued soft prices were thought to hurt the prospects for offshore development at a later date.[20]

Insurance by Geographical Spread

The heart of the new corporate strategy is the reestablishment of "insurance" by diversifying sources of energy and achieving more flexibility in switching fuel imports from one energy product to another. In practice, the companies continue to focus most of their attention on oil and gas operations, as the figures on capital investments in Table 3 attest. (And only about 5 percent of large oil companies' revenues came from other than oil, gas, and petrochemical operations in 1980.[21]) The total amount allocated for other forms of energy and nonenergy investment, shown under the category of "other," remains less than 10 percent in most cases; only Exxon, Arco (Atlantic Richfield), and Mobil regularly exceed this level.

Even though spending on the "other" category is a small percentage of total investment, the majors account for the lion's share of the investment by the oil and gas industry in other fuels. Moreover, part of the refining investment is also relevant to synthetic fuels and a large share of energy reserves in other than oil and gas was accumulated at lower prices over many years. In addition, only a few of the larger acquisitions of coal and mineral firms by oil companies were reflected in my sample.[22] Most assuredly, if the companies are to succeed in their plans, spending on new forms of energy will grow sharply.

The much-publicized diversifications into nonenergy investment were a long-term hedge and perhaps a way of stabilizing annual earnings by being in several lines of business; the companies remained basically energy concerns.[23] The chief short-term implication of nonenergy investments was that they provided the companies with a plausible alternative to disbursing more money to stockholders, repurchasing their own stock, or making marginal energy investments. Particularly important in this regard were the purchases of major mineral companies. These acquisitions provided an outlet for heavy capital investments and involved a business that demanded expertise comparable to the kind already commanded by the majors. Thus aggressive spending was possible at an earlier date because management thought that it understood the new business better than such new ventures as information systems.[24]

Yet the continued drop in global demand for minerals and unexpected problems in managing mineral holdings cut profits sharply.

To understand the companies' direction we have to examine their projections about the future of the energy sector. In essence, they believed that the world's energy trade was beginning a long switch away from petroleum. In 1979, about 31 million barrels per day (mbd) of oil moved in trade, compared to about 3 mbd of coal and 2 mbd of natural gas. But in 1980, company forecasts envisioned that the volume of oil traded in 2000 could be somewhat lower while coal could rise to 8 mbd and natural gas could account for between 6 and 10 mbd. In addition, the sources of oil and gas could alter as OECD nations shift increasingly to synthetic fuels to supplement diminishing reserves of oil and gas. Estimates differed, but Exxon's optimistic scenario of 1980 suggested that the U.S. supply of very heavy oil and synthetic fuels could reach roughly 5 mbd in 2000 and that the rest of the world could contribute another 3 mbd.[25] (Other companies suggested that a U.S. total on the order of 2 to 3 mbd was more realistic.[26]) Whatever the precise numbers on supplies, forecasters agreed that global demand in the free world would grow at less than 2.5 percent annually (and even more slowly in the industrial world, less than 1.5 percent annually), while the use of oil outside the Third World would slowly decline.

The revised forecasts of 1982 again reduced the projected increase in the demand for energy, to less than 1.8 percent annually in the free world. Petroleum might contribute only 6 percent of all new energy supplies, while global oil demand might grow at a pace of only 1 percent and the use of oil in industrial nations decline below its 1981 levels. Even though total OPEC output had plunged to less than 18 mbd in early 1982, the companies believed that it would climb again to as high as 23 mbd in 1983. But even their forecasts suggested that OPEC countries would contribute as little as 23 to 26 mbd to world supplies in 2000, a drop from about 57 percent of free world supplies to about 46 percent. Substantial new discoveries of oil would be necessary to achieve even these much-reduced demands on the oil industry, perhaps as much as the equivalent of 25 mbd worth of reserves for the world (including the socialist nations). Synthetic fuels would provide a maximum of 2.5 to 4 mbd to world supplies by 2000, while estimates of the potential coal trade remained unchanged.[27]

Thus, the oil companies still must expand their supplies of oil outside OPEC countries through new discoveries, the development of synthetic fuels, or selective purchases of other companies' reserves if they are to retain a substantial share of the future market for oil in the industrial world and some lucrative markets in the non-OPEC developing nations.[28] But they no longer assume that sharply increasing supplies of crude from OPEC countries in the 1980s are indispensable to their success. Moreover, in a number of developed and developing nations they are voluntarily (or involuntarily) withdrawing from refining and marketing, contenting themselves with the discovery and production of crude oil for a set fee by the local NOC. (Gulf, BP, and Shell were especially aggressive on this score.) This is a sharp reversal of earlier strategies that tried to use OPEC oil to meet rapidly growing demand and maintain market shares. Herein lies the first revolution in insurance. The companies can concentrate on the most profitable segments of the OECD market, in terms of both production and marketing, where their political risks are lowest. Although they obviously will remain active in profitable markets outside of OECD countries, they are no longer as concerned about retaining their world market share and no longer as dependent on OPEC countries for future growth in revenues and profits.

(The principle of insurance does not exclude the pursuit of profit. Rather it endorses looking for more security within a profit-seeking strategy. For example, if a company is willing to take larger risks on exploration and production, it can win higher profits per barrel from output in OECD countries than in the Middle East.)

Outside the OECD countries the priority is to reduce exposure to any one group of suppliers. To begin with, the majors are diversifying sources of OPEC supplies. Each major is working toward a wider spread of entrée into OPEC suppliers. This alters the classic pattern, in which each major specialized in a few OPEC members. Most of the Seven Sisters (BP and Gulf less so than the others) have worked furiously to hold onto their Middle East supplies by taking equity shares in major refining and petrochemical projects, the areas for which OPEC members still want their capital, marketing, and management resources.[29] But in regard to most OPEC nations the companies are more reluctant to make themselves hostages of the governments. This means that they will not pledge to absorb surplus production in return for longer supply contracts.[30]

The principle of diversification, like most rules, also has some crucial exceptions. The most important is the world's foremost producer of oil, Saudi Arabia, where Mobil and Shell have been the most aggressive majors in expanding their shares of supplies. To a lesser extent, some of the majors also have secondary "regional anchors" for their supply strategies. For example, Gulf, Shell, and Mobil bank heavily on Nigeria as an anchor for their efforts in developing a supply system in West Africa. Standard of California and Texaco rely on Indonesia for their extensive Asian networks. However, the majors have generally proved less willing to make major sacrifices for these regional anchors than they have, for the sake of goodwill, in Saudi Arabia. Witness the dramatic cuts in purchases of Nigerian oil from the last quarter of 1981 to the first quarter of 1982.

(It should be noted that Saudi Arabia, more than other OPEC members, values the majors' continuing ability to guarantee purchases during soft markets. This strengthens the Saudis' bargaining position vis-à-vis other OPEC nations. For example, Aramco members took hefty losses on their liftings of Saudi oil early in 1982 as they helped to keep Saudi production up at least temporarily. Their purchases permitted the Saudis to reinforce their power within OPEC. When Aramco members later reduced their purchases, British Petroleum entered into its first long-term contract with Saudi Arabia.)

A second measure to improve the security of oil supplies outside the OECD countries is to explore for oil and gas in non-OPEC Third World countries. Although every company looks for exclusive rights to "elephants" (giant fields), such as Socal (Standard of California) may have found in the Sudan, ventures in non-OPEC nations are being hedged by seeking oil on a widely distributed basis. Except for a few cases these countries' resource bases and policies make them unlikely to provide much more than 0.06 to 0.11 mbd to a company. This makes it easy to make a virtue out of building a portfolio to reduce exposure in any country.

If this interpretation of the majors' strategic interest is correct, companies with either the smallest percentage of U.S. supply or little overseas marketing that has to be supplied by non-U.S. production should be concentrating the most on developing U.S. supplies. It also means that the overseas activity of oil firms ought to center on OECD countries. The evidence in Table 4 concerning exploration basically confirms this hypothesis. With only about one-seventh and one-eighth, respectively, of their crude coming from the United States, Texaco and Socal are in an especially delicate position. If Saudi Arabia rapidly changed its oil policies, they would be in deep trouble. Thus their drilling programs were lopsidedly concentrated in the United States. Exxon (with about one-fifth of its supplies from the United States), Mobil (one-quarter), and Gulf (one-third) were a bit better off. As a result, they have more evenly balanced their portfolios between the United States and the rest of the world. Standard of Indiana is a domestic corporation that has become a major international firm since the late 1960s. Arco has always viewed itself as basically a domestic company. These two companies' drilling records again reflect their basic strategies; Standard has a much bigger overseas program.[31]

(Of course, spending decisions are not automatically reflected in discoveries. Of the five U.S. Sisters, Exxon and Socal were traditionally considered to have the best exploration groups, but Standard of Indiana has the best exploration record of big U.S. companies in recent years,

TABLE 4
Production and Exploration by the Eight Largest U.S.-Based Oil Companies: 1978-1980

		Exxon	Mobil	Texaco	SoCal	Standard of Ind.	Gulf	ARCO	Phillips	Total
World Crude	1978	4.69	2.12	3.55	3.29	1.032	1.82	.643	.444	17.589
and NGL		(.829)	(.320)	(.595)	(.320)	(.525)	(.400)	(.527)	(.259)	(3.805)
Production	1979	4.48	2.18	3.63	3.20	.849	1.73	.560	.436	17.065
MMB/D		(.791)	(.321)	(.539)	(.343)	(.494)	(.382)	(.537)	(.269)	(3.676)
(U.S.	1980	4.01	1.99	3.32	3.01	.836	1.17	.589	.452	15.378
Production)		(.787)	(.318)	(.481)	(.386)	(.464)	(.364)	(.556)	(.283)	(3.639)
Natural Gas	1978	8,062	3,270	3,894	1,423	3,263	2,153	1,517	1,549	25,131
Production	1979	8,044	3,649	3,646	1,732	3,328	2,176	1,486	1,558	25,619
MMCF/D	1980	7,137	3,598	3,103	1,739	3,057	2,032	1,388	1,497	23,551
Exploration	1978	115	100	31	71	148[a]	171	78	6[b]	716
Wells Drilled		174	155	43	38	84	45	21	20	565
(Net Wells	1979	153	94	83	82	154	176	59	10	803
including		164	116	34	21	97	80	6	32	527
dry wells)	1980	155	125	98	119	198	162	65	21	929
- U.S.		150	143	25	29	103	140	2	21	615
- Rest of World										

Source: Annual reports and Forms 10-K.

a. Figures for net wells exclude extensions drilled on unproven acreage.
b. Phillips figure for net wells excludes share of "farmouts" thus lowering its totals.

and Shell [USA] has the best record of offshore discoveries in the United States. Moreover, Mobil has shown surprising acumen since 1980, while Exxon has discovered comparatively less for its expenditures.[32])

Moreover, the insurance principle has led the corporations with the highest volume of drilling outside the United States—Exxon, Mobil, Gulf, Standard of Indiana—to site much of their new exploration in Europe and, especially, Canada (at least until the dispute with the Trudeau administration in 1980). In 1980 their percentages of "rest of world" wells drilled in these two areas were 66 percent, 86 percent, 90 percent, and 91 percent respectively. Nonetheless, even though expenditures for exploration outside the OECD countries was a small percentage of their total, the majors' coverage of the Third World was very broad because of numerous joint ventures and because even a small percentage of the majors' budget constituted large sums in poor nations. Thus, my analysis of thirty-five leading oil and gas prospects among the non-OPEC developing nations showed that the overwhelming majority of countries relied primarily on the majors for exploration and production.[33] Only the geographic specialization of these ventures was not predicted by the insurance principle. Large companies typically spend most of their exploration money in the non-OPEC developing countries in a few regions. For example, Gulf specializes in West Africa and Texaco works primarily in Latin America. These clusterings apparently are partly a consequence of luck, partly a result of the economies of scale from several operations in a single region, and partly a function of specialized regional expertise.

Lower oil prices further complicate the efforts to diversify oil sources. For example, if proved correct, the 1982 forecasts of smaller and slower increases could mean a decrease in the rate of growth of total drilling by the late 1980s. Moreover, some new oil fields become marginal prospects if prices do not increase substantially. (The Hibernia field in Canada may fall into this category.) This poses an especially serious problem for the majors because, even though exploration and production in the United States were the most profitable in the world by 1982, only a few have had enough success in U.S. exploration to maintain or expand their production levels. However, low oil prices also tend to depress the stock prices of oil companies. This makes it attractive to purchase smaller firms in order to obtain oil reserves and exploration acreage. Another possibility is the creation of new partnerships designed to provide funding by the majors for the exploration of the smaller firms' acreage. Texaco has made substantial efforts along this line, and smaller independents in the United States and Australia reportedly were seeking such partnerships by early 1982.[34] The choices of individual firms about these matters reflect management's confidence in their exploration departments, their fears of antitrust sanctions, and their predictions about oil prices.

Despite all their efforts to reduce vulnerability to OPEC, the position of the majors, especially the Seven Sisters, remains very uncertain. In 1981 BP only drew 18 percent of its oil from OPEC, while Shell relied on OPEC for 36 percent of its supplies and Gulf required 50 percent from OPEC. To understand their future prospects, consider the situations of Gulf and Socal. The former has already shrunk its market share substantially as a result of cuts in supply from Iran and Kuwait. In early 1981, an optimistic reading of Gulf's production prospects at the decade's close would have projected the following: United States, 0.300 mbd; Nigeria (and other West Africa), 0.440 mbd; Canada, 0.360 mbd; global synfuels, 0.050 mbd; and North Sea, 0.075 mbd. At the same time it would have increasingly switched from an international production company to a regional marketer (primarily in North America). Assuming a smaller sales volume due to a smaller world market for oil and a smaller share of the market for Gulf (say, about 1.2 mbd in 1990), Gulf would rely on North Africa and the Middle East for only about 4 percent of its supplies. This would be a highly favorable situation, but it could easily be reversed by new difficulties in either Nigeria or Canada. (Certainly, the synfuels will not materialize by 1990, and U.S. production may fall short of the estimate here.)

A similar situation pertains with Socal, which is highly dependent on Saudi Arabia to maintain its market share. If everything went extremely well, in the early 1990s it might produce oil as follows: continental United States, 0.390 mbd; North Slope (Alaska) and Canada, 0.350 mbd; Sudan, 0.300 mbd; Nigeria, 0.100 mbd; Indonesia, 0.400 mbd; and North Sea, 0.150 mbd—a total of 1.69 mbd in crude before having to rely on Saudi Arabia. If Socal's worldwide product sales shrank slightly to 2.2 mbd by 1990, it would rely on the Middle East and North Africa for only 23 percent of its refining needs. In theory, Saudi crude could cover this demand and still provide the oil necessary for Socal to maintain its 1980 level of sales to third parties, about 0.7 mbd. Obviously, troubles in Indonesia or disruption of the flow from Saudi Arabia would be a large setback for Socal.[35]

The very speculative projections about Gulf and Socal are less important for their specifics than for their larger message: The security of the major oil companies may vary markedly by the early 1990s. For example, Arco will have virtually all of its crude requirements filled by its own production in the United States. Even if some firms do very well, the share of private oil companies in the world oil market is unlikely to expand, and some companies may be very vulnerable to strategic bargaining ploys by exporting nations.

A final step to build insurance in petroleum is the drive to recalibrate refineries. By investing heavily in refining, the companies can produce medium and light distillates from a much wider range of crude oil, especially heavier and higher-sulfur crudes, which will be relatively more abundant in the future. The new refineries are crucial to using heavy crudes produced by very expensive processes of secondary and tertiary recovery, which Shell Oil (USA) has projected will provide one-half of U.S. output by 2000. (The biggest users of tertiary recovery are currently Getty, Socal, and Shell. It differs from secondary recovery in that more complex methods of forcing oil out of a reservoir are employed.) More important, tertiary recovery gives the large firms a major advantage over smaller rivals because the majors have tax bills large enough to make the tax breaks earned from tertiary recovery highly attractive. In addition, the windfall profits tax on oil production in the United States provides all companies with an incentive to sell crude cheaply to their refineries and boost efficiency in refining. A final implication of easier use of heavy, dirty oil is less vulnerability to the volatile North African suppliers of light, low-sulfur crude.[36]

Despite its many advantages, the modification of refining capabilities may slow as a result of two problems. First, the decline in oil prices has prompted some OPEC nations to subsidize refining operations in Europe (especially Italy) in order to attract buyers of their oil. This development compounds the already dreadful economics of the refining industry and the particularly serious difficulties of European refiners. Second, if demand is weak, the creation of a large export refining capacity for OPEC countries (projected at roughly 3.5 mbd by 1985) makes forecasts of necessary new (or upgraded) capacity more risky.[37] Accordingly, the industry may proceed more promptly with refining investments in the North American market than in Europe.

Insurance by Diversification of Energy Sources

The changes in refining are part of a larger move to change the world's pattern of energy use. In general, the companies are pressing customers, especially large-scale users, to become more flexible in their choice of fuels. This can occur in two ways. Large industrial users and electric utilities, which may account for nearly 25 percent of energy consumption of the members of the International Energy Agency in the year 1990, may actually reduce their consumption of oil.[38] And the oil companies can invest heavily in technology to convert fuels from one form to another. Synfuels come immediately to mind; more immediate applications may include mixing coal and oil (a priority of

Arco and BP research) and converting medium-Btu gas into liquid fuels (Mobil is building a plant to convert methanol from natural gas into gasoline in New Zealand and has offered to build one in Malaysia). If the companies can succeed in getting more flexible use of fuels by large consumers (by installing the capacity to burn more than one fuel) and can build the capacity to alter products from energy inputs more freely, then a second revolution in the insurance principle will have taken place. Instead of depending on diversity of location and enormous surplus capacity of a single inexpensive fuel, the companies could offer diversity of fuels, each with a wide spread in sources of origin, and a sophisticated capacity to convert fuels more easily from one end product to another.

The large oil companies have already carved out a profitable niche in world markets for natural gas. The majors are actively involved in the LNG trade, but they often content themselves with a minority share equal to those of other foreign investors in the project. Most frequently, they are involved only in the production and liquefaction of the gas. Shell and British Petroleum probably have the biggest commitment to LNG, partly because of Shell's relatively small production of oil in the early 1970s, partly because of the legacy of British colonial rule in Brunei, and partly because of the two companies' interest in preparing to service the European gas trade. However, Exxon and Mobil also have prominent roles in the trade, and most major firms have some role in at least one current or planned LNG project.

As a group, the majors hold a very large share of the foreign equity in ongoing or possible LNG undertakings in Libya, Brunei, Indonesia, Abu Dhabi, Malaysia, Qatar, Nigeria, Australia, and Chile. They are also developing options for LNG in Cameroon and several other new producing nations.[39] However, lower oil prices could weaken the incentive for customers to switch to LNG from oil, thereby slowing several of the new projects (such as the one in Nigeria). Moreover, the majors have no role in several plans announced in 1981, such as LNG plants for the Indonesian–South Korean or the Canadian-Japanese trade.

Pipelines handle about 80 percent of the world gas trade, and by far the most important market for gas (54 percent of world imports), Western Europe, is serviced largely by pipeline. Due to their prominence in the North Sea, the majors have a strong position in Europe, which was further bolstered by the success of Exxon and Shell in controlling the new gas gathering system in the British North Sea fields. At the same time they lobbied for a pipeline from Norway to Great Britain in order to build greater flexibility into the European market. Moreover, the majors (especially British Petroleum) have a strong position in the

West German natural gas industry, which is perhaps the most important one in Europe.[40]

The European market may be only the beginning, however, of a drive to expand the pipeline trade elsewhere, especially in Latin America. For example, Exxon and Shell are working with the NOC of Argentina on a pipeline; and Occidental is a partner with the Bolivian NOC in the production of gas that will be pipelined to Brazil. Making gas into a more common item of trade would discourage developing nations from subsidizing gas prices for domestic use. This, in turn, would promote the commercial feasibility of many smaller gas fields and would end delays in developing oil fields due to governments' fretting over squandering large amounts of associated gas that might have to be flared for lack of a proper economic return.

The plans for natural gas confront many snares that are discussed by Aronson and Cragg in Chapter 2. However, the Japanese challenge deserves special note. As the largest purchaser of LNG, Japan usually obtains a share of the ownership of production facilities. It has, therefore, built expertise in production, which is now being matched by that of its shipbuilders. This development may reduce the commercial portfolio of the majors, although it would not hinder the diversification of new supplies.

Gas is one rung for diversification, but the coal industry may prove the largest step on the ladder during this century. At the start of 1982, steam coal was selling for about half the price of its principal competitor, fuel oil. As with other energy sources, a decline in energy prices could slow the growth of the coal market, discourage the entry of the oil companies into the market, and cause existing holdings to be reduced.[41] Yet even a substantial cut would still allow considerable expansion.

The oil companies differed a great deal in their enthusiasm for coal—Shell, Exxon, and Arco were more enthusiastic than Socal or Standard of Indiana, for example—but they owned 25 percent of U.S. production and reserves and could command a 40 percent share by the mid-1980s. Fairly typically, in 1980 the companies predicted that coal demand in the noncommunist world would go from about 17.5 mbd (1.3 billion metric tons per year) to 40 mbd (3 billion metric tons) in 2000, or about 24 percent of world energy demand. This would entail the coal trade's growing from 50 million metric tons (0.66 mbd) in 1980 (about one-third metallurgical coal) to 250 to 500 million metric tons (or 3.33 to 6.66 mbd, primarily in steam coal) by 2000. Conoco, which had the largest coal subsidiary, already produced more than 50 million metric tons annually in the early 1980s. British Petroleum, Exxon, Arco and Sun each looked toward production sales of about 30 to 35 million metric tons annually in 1985. Shell stated that it wanted a share of the coal market equal to its share of the oil market (about 10 to 19 percent). British Petroleum wanted a market share equal to Shell's.[42]

The companies are introducing their standard techniques for organizing markets. To begin with, they are opening up multiple sources of coal. Although the United States leads any list of future exporters, Arco and other companies, such as Socal and BP, are pushing hard to grab a large share of the Australian fields, a key to the lucrative Japanese market, as well as new operations in Indonesia (Arco), Colombia (Exxon), South Africa (British Petroleum), and Canada (Continental Oil). In general, however, their best bet for a large share of the Japanese market was to catch Japan on the "rebound." By 1985 some analysts expect Australia to supply 80 percent (19 million metric tons) of Japanese imports of steam coal, a figure that Japan is likely to reduce for fear of undue dependence. The oil companies hope to be ready to claim the market share opened up by diversification away from Australia.[43]

Finally, the companies are moving to integrate the coal market vertically and impose higher quality standards.[44] By owning transportation (including port facilities and super-colliers for coal), making quality standards for coal and its infrastructure more strict, and becoming involved in processing coal, the companies can capture a larger value-added from coal, lower transport costs, and allow greater substitutability among coal sources. These features would prove particularly attractive to smaller purchasers of coal, such as industrial users in the glass industry, who may account for a substantial share of the new coal market. Several oil companies are also endorsing extensive "pretreatment" of coal prior to burning (for example, pulverizing and cleaning the coal) as an environmental safeguard. This requirement would further favor coal suppliers capable of making large capital investments and used to running large fuel-processing plants.

As Michael Gaffen points out in Chapter 3, numerous risks confront investors in new coal production. One subtle risk may pertain to the hopes of the oil industry more than to those of any other participant in the coal market. It concerns the terms for access to lucrative markets in Germany and Japan. To reduce resistance from Japanese and German buyers, the smaller oil companies (such as Ashland) are soliciting them as production partners.[45] Many of the larger companies are also following this path, but they are resisting any major involvement by the U.S. government in promoting direct exports. For example, some firms worried that Japan might persuade the U.S. government to institute elaborate subsidies to guarantee the reliability of U.S. coal deliveries from smaller mines. This would neutralize much of the majors' advantages as large firms that are able to spend money to build reliable networks and then charge a premium for their product. This struggle is likely to continue in various guises in the future, and it suggests that the Japanese trade may be slow to develop for U.S. exporters.

The final element of diversification is synthetic fuels. More than for any other item, the fate of synfuels hinges on government policy which will determine the level of risk and ease of entry for medium-sized or small companies. Chapter 6 examines the optimal government policy for synfuels; I wish to note what the large companies hoped to achieve.

As late as early 1981, oil industry experts generally agreed that shale oil was commercially viable at prices of $35 per barrel of oil (in 1980 dollars) and could provide much-desired, high-quality light products with no additional refining. Next, according to these estimates, medium-Btu gas from coal (which can be blended with natural gas, used for petrochemical feedstock, or converted to liquid fuel) could become viable at gas prices of more than $40 to $45 per barrel of oil. Coal liquefaction came in a distant third in terms of costs for proven technology. This technology also suffered because it was best suited for heavier distillates (such as fuel oil) that were comparatively abundant. However, studies by Bechtel suggested that more attractive liquefaction technology could emerge by the 1990s, and Texaco believed that synfuels could find a market as fuels for electricity generation.[46]

The sums of money envisioned for synfuels were staggering. Exxon suggested that an 8 mbd industry in the year 2000 would cost $400 billion in investment (in 1980 dollars). Companies calculated that a 0.050 mbd plant for shale oil, the cheapest synfuel, would cost $3 billion and would require very high capital outlays early in the life of the project. Thus, synfuels challenged any corporation's financial capacity. However, the furthest advanced shale projects did not have many partners parceling out ownership shares in small amounts in order to spread risks.[47] Two or three firms typically owned the project, with perhaps some minor share for a group of other companies. This arrangement reflected the problems of strategic risk discussed in Chapter 8. They were so severe that some giants, such as Shell, largely abstained from synfuel projects.

The alternative to private financing was government assistance. The major companies generally desired assistance for shale, but they were divided over the form and conditions that subsidies should take. For all practical purposes the very largest firms were resigned to undertaking shale oil projects in the United States without government funds. The medium-sized and small companies demanded guarantees from the government. Thus, in the two full-scale plants under way as of 1981 the Reagan administration had to put up guarantees for Union's independent venture and for Tosco's share of its joint venture with Exxon. Exxon operated without aid. Meanwhile, Rio Blanco (a joint venture consisting of Gulf and Standard of Indiana), Mobil, and Socal each planned plants without guarantees. But Rio Blanco scrapped its demonstration plant at the end of 1981 and announced plans to delay completion of its commercial plants from 1991 until 1997. Socal also set back its target until the mid-1990s while seeking out two new partners for the project.

By May 1982, only the Union Oil project, the smallest of the group, survived as a project dedicated to commercial production in the mid-1980s. The continuing downward pressure on oil prices in early 1982 reinforced the adverse impact of escalating estimates of the costs of shale oil projects. By the time the Exxon-Tosco project died, the U.S. government's Synthetic Fuels Corporation had grown increasingly skeptical of Tosco's ability to sustain its share of the bill (although the agency had continued its support to Tosco). Exxon reportedly had estimates that the price of the plant would be close to $6 billion, not the roughly $3 billion originally projected. Delaying the project in order to wait for higher oil prices would only increase interest costs. Therefore the industry greeted a Mobil proposal for an industry-wide consortium to build a major shale facility with skepticism.[48]

No company was willing to launch coal projects without government assistance. As a result, the Reagan administration had to guarantee the Great Plains project for coal gasification, a plant with a long political history that has become a symbol of the commitment to gasification. However, many oil firms thought that the technology being used was far from optimal, so the plant was unlikely to generate many imitators. The Texaco, Mobil, and Exxon prototype plants were considered more important to the future of the industry.[49] Meanwhile, the demise of the Gulf plant for coal liquefaction meant that no major demonstration plant was under way in the United States in 1982. (Prototypes are small-scale versions of the proposed production system. Demonstration plants are designed to test the technology at the scale of intended production.) Ashland and Exxon ran the two largest prototypes, and perhaps four other coal gasification and liquefaction projects may survive in the United States as a result of government funding. A coal gasification plant involving Texaco and a liquefaction prototype partly supported by Sohio (BP) were among the finalists in 1982 for consideration by the U.S. Synthetic Fuels Corporation.

As with other fuel sources, the companies sought geographic diversification in synfuels. By 1981 this meant pursuing shale oil in Australia and Morocco, tar sands in Canada, and coal projects in Europe. The most striking aspect of the global picture was the central role of Exxon, the company most dedicated to massive development of synthetic fuels. Exxon, of course, had the financial base to command an industry that depended on oceans of money. If its various ventures had all born fruit, it would have become by far the largest producer of synfuels.

In mid-1981, Exxon scaled down its commitment to its joint venture in Australia to develop shale oil. It claimed that mining conditions and the quality of the shale rock were less promising than projected.[50] Exxon also organized one of two new Canadian tar sands plants designed to expand existing output. (Shell led the other new consortium. Exxon and Sun Oil ran the two existing plants.) Here, too, a delay in development was announced in 1980. Both the Shell and Exxon groups argued that delays by the Canadian government had let inflation run up costs from Can. $8 billion to Can. $13 billion for 0.137 mbd in capacity. These costs could not be recovered under Canadian price controls and tax rates. Although existing production kept going, by early 1982 Exxon had disbanded its project team and several of Shell's partners had withdrawn. The Canadian government sought Japanese partners in addition to committing funds from state corporations to revive the Shell project. However, a solicitation of seventeen additional firms yielded no takers, and Shell finally abandoned the project in May 1982.[51]

In Europe several companies announced commitments to coal-based projects. At the close of 1981 Exxon reaffirmed its commitment to build a prototype gasification plant in the Netherlands that could supplement supplies from the declining Groningen gas fields. Because the country wishes to be a key port for coal, the regulatory climate was favorable and gas prices may exceed those in the United States. In 1980 the Schmidt government in West Germany also announced plans to develop an alternative to nuclear power and to claim a larger share of profits from the coal trade by funding fourteen coal projects. (Texaco's gas technology was to be used in one plant, and British Petroleum was to play a major role in a liquefaction plant.) However, government budgetary problems have signaled the demise of about two-thirds of the projects. Total government spending is slated at only $425 million and projected capacity will consume only 4 million short tons of coal per year by 1990. Perhaps the most important commitment elsewhere in the world was a pledge of $218 million to develop a prototype for coal liquefaction by a Japanese consortium working in Australia. If this proved successful, a 0.1 mbd plant might follow for commercial production.[52] (The South African coal liquefaction plants have limited importance in the global picture because of the unique reasons for their creation.)

Thus synthetic fuel projects at one time promised a substantial diversification of the major companies' energy portfolios in the long term. But they were characterized by strong concentration in one country (the United States) and on a single phase (shale) of the field. The setback in production due to lower oil prices has delayed all the shale projects except for the ones backed by Union. In addition, only one commercial plant for coal synfuels will emerge in the United States in the foreseeable future. Meanwhile, the Japanese government has lent considerable support to a vigorous campaign by its firms to acquire a foothold in the industry during this period of delay. Japanese firms are building up a resource base and keeping open their technological options to proceed to development. Once financial conditions become favorable, they will be well situated to claim priority rights to development and fully prepared to execute the projects. This potential for competition with the international majors on the part of Japan and other new entrants is a matter to which I shall return shortly.

In summary, the majors are trying to purchase insurance by investing according to two central guidelines. First, they are trying to shift to an OECD base of supplies to a much greater degree. To the extent that they operate outside the OECD countries they can hedge their bets by establishing a broader spread of supplies from OPEC countries and diversifying their holdings in the rest of the Third World. Second, they are building a strategy based on a multiplicity of fuels, each with maximum spread in sources of origin, and a sophisticated capacity to convert fuels more freely from one end product to another.

If an elaborately diversified, carefully hedged portfolio of energy resources is the basis for insurance, what choices are corporations making in regard to the other aspect of risk management? I shall argue that their recent successes as commercial diplomats strengthen their selective advantages as experts and risk takers. Moreover, the companies may have reinforced their bargaining position by assuming a less prominent role as agents of interdependent interests.

Risk Management by Providing Expertise

Although the majors are expert and wealthy, they are less irreplaceable as technical experts or risk takers than in the past. In general, their activities in conventional oil and gas fields and their minority shares in LNG projects have not given the majors an edge. Neither have conventional coal projects in many respects. The one attribute of coal that gives companies some unique advantage is the size of the financing needed for added capacity and the fact that banks usually demand substantial guarantees of corporate repayment. Although a coal subsidiary could be guaranteed by any wealthy parent company, the uncertain timing of development of coal markets and the completion of physical infrastructure may make coal a marginal prospect from the viewpoint of all but energy firms. Energy companies are more willing to play the game of waiting for returns because they face higher risks of bad judgment in nonenergy projects.[53]

Whatever the merits of conventional coal, extremely difficult oil and gas projects and synfuels are certainly naturals for the majors. Although rivals exist for offshore ventures, the majors are the best equipped and financed.[54] Moreover, they are spending heavily to maintain their lead. The majors sometimes invest in selected offshore ventures primarily to acquire expertise about operations in new geologic conditions. The other area of clear-cut advantage is synfuels, where only state-supported consortia from West Germany and Japan appear to be plausible rivals unless government policies in the United States change.

Risk Management by Diplomacy

The selective advantages of the majors have taken on more significance because of their recent successes as commercial diplomats. The headway on oil and gas policies was particularly important. The Reagan administration gave a powerful boost to the majors' desire to open up a large amount of new land for exploration while accelerating the end of price controls throughout the OECD countries. Greater opportunities on more generous terms in the United States allowed both U.S. and foreign companies to take a firmer line when bargaining on leasing, taxes, and prices in the North Sea and Canada. For example, in 1981 the majors openly opposed the British government's latest round of added taxes in the North Sea. And they did not rush to accede to the Trudeau government's "Canadization" program for the oil industry. Indeed, while a few Canadian companies bolstered their government's efforts, many others indirectly aided the majors by shifting investments down to the United States in order to benefit from the more generous U.S. policies on taxes and prices.[55] In short, by getting the United States to reduce controls on energy profits and exploration the majors had a much more plausible threat of "exit" from other OECD nations. This is why the U.S. oil and gas industry's failure to win rapid decontrol of natural gas prices in 1981 was an international, not just a domestic, setback. But the Reagan administration's policy of liberalizing controls by the use of administrative discretion may eventually come close to decontrol.

The connection between the domestic market and the international bargaining position, particularly in terms of the pressures of "exit" brought to bear on other nations, also suggests that the majors should not support protective legislation shutting out foreign investment from the United States in oil. Such legislation would only make foreign oil companies into a captive audience for their parent governments' production policies.[56]

The Reagan administration also contributed in an important way to the agenda for synfuels when the projects appeared profitable. By limiting the range of government support, it restricted entry to very large firms that are particularly interested in energy development. In addition, the administration's views on air pollution promised to benefit the shale oil industry, in which production could suffer substantially from rigid readings of the rules. Moreover, the Reagan tax bill made synfuels more attractive to big firms because it allowed them to generate large tax credits. Tax advantages may some day allow U.S. projects to proceed more quickly than those overseas, thereby reinforcing the leadership of the majors.

Finally, in regard to coal the industry made gains on two fronts. For one, the Reagan administration announced its willingness to impose special taxes on port users to expedite the development of the necessary infrastructure. At the same time, European governments have responded to the race to serve as middlemen for coal trading in Europe. Second, the U.S. government has refused to offer guarantees of export supplies on behalf of U.S. firms. This transfers the problem of security back to the buyers (through stockpiles) or large firms (through geographic diversification of supply), thereby strengthening the position of oil companies. Moreover, if the companies act successfully as agents of interdependent interests, they can convince OECD governments to encourage a trade geared to greater interchangeability of sources, guaranteed by an integrated supply and distribution network managed by large firms. Persuading governments to accept this viewpoint would make *all* major importing countries more sensitive to difficulties concerning the conduct of *any* major exporting nation. Conversely, it would give exporters an incentive to back the companies in pushing for all major coal-using projects, not just a few designated to use the individual exporter's coal.

Risk Management Through Acting as Agents of Interdependent Interests

Beyond specific items about leases, prices, or taxes, the majors have traditionally played a pivotal role in representing OECD interests in world oil markets. As always, the companies must decide on their overall philosophy for economic and political bargaining. The choice influences the way in which governments evaluate the firms' performances as well as their informal and formal obligations to other actors. In this way the companies build their role as agents of interdependent interests.

The companies are still too dependent on OPEC oil to emphasize their ability to favor the interests of OECD nations. Nor can they claim to be capable of being the honest middlemen protecting both importers and exporters. They also could suffer from pegging themselves as "contractors, sources of technology, and financiers" of crude (as many industry analysts now describe their role) because such a role would categorize the majors as "ordinary companies," not privileged players in the world oil arena who are entitled to special treatment in government policy.[57] Nonetheless, the majors recognize the growing power of NOCs and admit that few countries will accept the majors as their sole contact with the world oil trade. But the majors have made a virtue of necessity by building more joint ventures with state-supported firms from the OECD region in order to reestablish common interests.

Conclusion: Corporate Security and Consumer Security

Although it may seem contrary to common sense, shying away from a general profile of industrial leadership and trusteeship for their clients may be crucial to the majors' strength. A lower profile gives the majors more freedom to switch suppliers and markets, thus taking advantage of the overextension of NOCs of other countries. (Because national oil companies are growing in importance for conventional projects, global investments in these oil markets are becoming less tightly matched to one another, thus threatening sporadic waves of surplus capacity on world markets.) For example, the majors' refineries are usually more efficient and their globally integrated networks reap more economies of scale than those of their competitors. And the majors can afford to shed refining, chemical, and marketing operations that have grown unprofitable as demand stagnated and new capacity developed in the Third World.[58] In 1981, for example, British Petroleum announced plans to close more than one-third of its European refining capacity. And Gulf liquidated its holdings in the saturated European petrochemical industry while expanding its operations in the United States. Similarly, Exxon planned to shut one-third of its U.S. capacity while using its new production from Saudi Arabia to expand markets in the Third World. Meanwhile, Texaco continued to withdraw from marketing in a number of less lucrative U.S. markets.[59]

More basically, one executive of Royal Dutch Shell suggested that the era of integrated international firms may be over. In the future a few may treat production ventures as their primary business and treat distribution, refining, and marketing as smaller separate ventures. Indeed, some experts predict that only Exxon, Shell, and perhaps Mobil will remain true global companies.[60]

If the majors are freer to shed capacity than national firms charged with fulfilling certain national missions, they are able to bargain more aggressively about prices than most of their state rivals. Shell Oil, for example, argued in 1981 that government-to-government sales of crude oil ran as much as 50 cents per barrel higher than oil obtained through the majors.[61] And when bargaining with Kuwait over prices, the majors pressed for reductions sooner than did their Japanese counterparts. (However, once the Japanese firms did press for concessions, they did so vigorously.)

In short, the majors can benefit from the advantages of being the largest (albeit shrunken) globally integrated firms and enjoy comparatively large economies of scale, while having fewer specific commitments to suppliers and purchasers than in the past. Diversification into nonpetroleum fuels and minerals further enhances the credibility of the majors when they bargain on oil. Other parties cannot assume that the majors' growth will stagnate if they do not get large volumes of new oil and gas business. Instead, in each year's capital commitments the majors can switch emphasis according to political and market opportunities.

If this argument is correct, oil and gas companies would be expected to prize highly the basic autonomy of their global networks as long as the diversification strategy remains credible. This does not mean that they ought to refuse partnerships with local NOCs in oil and gas production. (They have little choice about accepting such partnerships.) Nor does it mean rejecting other oil companies as partners in oil projects, because a diversified portfolio demands joint ventures. But autonomy should demand that they reject offers that would restrict their ability to select freely among crude sources in which they do not have equity shares. They should also resist any substantial global partnership with OPEC NOCs, whether through stock transfers or joint ownership of refineries. Finally, they should discourage governments from obtaining an active equity share of synthetic fuel projects.

In fact, the companies have approximated these expectations. When Kuwait squeezed British Petroleum and Gulf badly on their crude supplies, it offered to buy either a large share of their stock or their global refining network. They refused and lost Kuwait's supplies. With the important exception of Saudi Arabia, the other majors have also refused most proposals for crude supplies in return for joint investments.[62]

Corporate choices ought to reemphasize that the major oil companies are less beholden than other segments of the industry to the immediate pressures of governments. They are global firms with some fungibility of interests in a wide array of energy and nonenergy investments. More so than in the past, they may stop doing business in any country in order to concentrate on their best opportunities.

In summary, the majors can take advantage of their lower profile to play a new commercial game. The value of this approach is highly sensitive to success in shaping policy in the United States because U.S. choices either reinforce or weaken the selective advantages still enjoyed in regard to risk taking and expertise. Advantages gained through the interplay of elements pertaining to expertise, risk taking, commercial diplomacy, and agentry reinforce insurance by allowing more projects in OECD countries.

Yet what does the new corporate strategy imply for the security of consumers? The consequences for security fall into three bundles—impacts on levels of supply, effects on flexibility of consumption, and alterations of special sources of bargaining leverage. The picture is, on balance, quite favorable but uneven.

Supply. The majors' strategy helps to promote the diversification of oil and energy supplies. Contrary to the opinions of corporate critics, such as Peter Odell,[63] the higher costs and risks of future supplies are not a deterrent to firms with global portfolios; they are an incentive for securing an assured market advantage. Indeed, the critical reality for the majors as a group is that very large projects with long lead times and substantial risk are the only commanding heights of the industry that they can hope to seize firmly for themselves. Within the constraints imposed by soft prices in the early 1980s the majors will accelerate the push to open OECD frontier regions, and if anyone ever does it, the majors are likely to be the first suppliers of synthetic fuels from shale oil. Their policy of vertical integration may also speed up the growth of world coal markets. In terms of supplies, the majors' approach may have a negative impact primarily on one area: Their tepid support for government assistance for the development of synthetic fuels may have tipped the balance against more generous support by the Reagan administration, thus dooming most projects by 1982. It certainly led to the restriction of entry into the synfuels industry by smaller firms before 1982 and possibly slowed the rate of innovation.[64] Moreover, as a group the majors are betting on expensive sources of supplies. Although the windfall profit tax gives oil companies an incentive to hold down crude prices relative to product prices at any given time, the majors are going to urge policies that accept a long-term rise in energy prices as one of their assumptions (even though they project lower prices in the short term). They also are likely to focus governments' attention on the complex linkages among fuel prices. Major oil companies, unlike suppliers of a single fuel, are likely to push for full parity in equivalent fuel prices as their best profit-maximizing strategy.

The one exception to the majors' support for higher prices may occur in regard to taxes on the use of energy. These taxes simply reduce market demand without providing profits for corporations. Imposition of a tariff on imported oil that is designed to cut demand and encourage domestic production is especially likely to split the ranks of the corporations. Such a measure would raise the cost of crude oil for those firms relying on overseas supplies, while protecting the investments of those depending on new U.S. production ventures.

Outside the OECD countries, the majors can affect supplies in several ways. Their policy of treating non-OPEC countries primarily as hedges in the quest for oil supplies is unlikely to affect the global supply of oil adversely. The majors eagerly pursue the largest production prospects. But a number of countries with relatively small oil and gas fields may suffer from neglect, particularly if the parts of the oil industry that are most critical of World Bank funding of oil projects succeed in persuading governments to curb these programs. (The majors do not agree among themselves about the merits of foreign aid for oil development.[65]) Moreover, even if the criticism of public funding proves a setback for some nations, the majors' campaign to expand the global gas trade may prove a large benefit to some exporters and further help to diversify global energy supplies.

Consumption. The picture for flexibility in consumption is mixed. The majors bolster the security of consumers by investing massively in the capacity to switch the fuel inputs for final products. They are also encouraging users to reduce their vulnerability by becoming more flexible in their choice of fuel. But the majors' efforts to bolster profits by cutting back their coverage of markets accelerate the fragmentation of markets. They also lend impetus to a historic shift in the burden of ensuring the security of oil supplies from the private to the public sector. Fragmentation and a shift in who pays insurance costs may raise the costs of coordinating the diplomatic interests of OECD governments when they wish to harmonize their individual efforts to influence world oil markets. More independent oil traders, the shrinking of the relative importance of crude stocks of the majors for coverage of market needs, and the greater rigidity of the channels in which oil moves (due to narrower geographic coverage by the individual companies) will make it necessary for governments to establish larger public stockpiles of oil and consider other measures to coordinate oil supplies during disruptions.

On a more positive note, the majors' strategies have one general advantage for OECD consumers. The majors' emphasis on more flexible refining and conversion to end products promises to reduce the ability of individual oil exporters to bargain over price spreads as aggressively as in the past. This should help consumers throughout the OECD countries. Unfortunately, the majors may also generate differential vulnerability to OPEC pressures for individual countries. This could occur for two reasons.

To begin with, as the majors play a more selective role in national markets, some countries will become increasingly reliant on national firms using government-to-government diplomacy to secure their supplies. This trend could become especially noticeable if the refining industry in many countries remains highly unprofitable and governments relieve the financial burdens only of locally owned refiners, thus prompting fresh withdrawals by the majors. This may lead to some countries' paying substantially more per barrel than others because NOCs may have less freedom to bargain over prices. Second, government-to-government deals raise the cost of pushing advantages for consumers because they allow oil exporters to threaten export contracts of a number of industries in a particular OECD country. Of course, if the supply of oil radically dipped in the next decade, the balance of advantages between NOCs and the majors might reverse. The important point is that OECD members may differ more sharply in their market advantages than in the past. This could generate substantial tension in OECD diplomacy concerning energy. If disputes about the development of the world coal market also emerged, OECD diplomats could confront an unhappy situation concerning energy policy.

Corporate Vulnerability. The companies themselves may differ significantly in their vulnerability to OPEC pressures. For example, during the 1980s the United States may succeed in reducing OPEC imports to less than one-third of its oil needs and Middle East imports to less than one-quarter. As discussed earlier, it is reasonable to expect that the majors may have widely different levels of reliance on the Middle East in the future. Gulf, if very lucky, could rely on the Middle East for less than 4 percent of its needs; the figure for Texaco could be more than 35 percent. When compared to the aggregate dependence of the United States, the companies obviously have divergent degrees of vulnerability to disruptions in the Middle East. The question for consumers is how well their interests are reflected by companies whose levels of dependence on the Middle East vary substantially. Is the nation's bargaining position driven toward the highest or lowest level of strength of the majors? No general conclusion is self-evident. But we can speculate about two consequences of particular importance to the United States.

On the one hand, the majors can provide the benefits of diversified nuances in strategy because of differing levels of reliance on the Middle East. Some must invest more in cultivating goodwill in the Middle East than others, thereby affording the United States the benefits of having its firms pursue several tacks in regard to oil diplomacy in the

1990s. This appears to be a more promising situation than the one likely to confront most OECD nations, whose national firms are likely to show greater uniformity of strategic postures.

On the other hand, the U.S. government can expect a larger degree of discordance in the formulation of its international oil policy. Although the majors have disagreed among themselves in the past, particularly in regard to what each firm calculated was politically feasible, a growing divergence in their degrees of international vulnerability could force more splits in the future. The government may have trouble in formulating policy if it must sort out the conflicting advice from powerful companies and choose which corporate initiatives to underline through public diplomacy. In short, even though the majors are pursuing roughly comparable policies for managing risks in the 1980s, their records in implementation may vary enough to confront the U.S. government with a series of corporate interests that are much more discordant than at present. This could either paralyze policy or force Washington to articulate an independent position far more consistently than in the past.

In summary, just as the companies' new strategies may expedite a series of changes in the patterns of energy supply and demand, they can also trigger a shift in the political stances and interests of governments. The gambles being undertaken by the majors ensure that neither oil-importing nor oil-exporting countries can easily predict their respective strengths and weaknesses in the 1990s.

Notes

1. The Seven Sisters and the larger U.S. independents are the group referred to as the "majors" in this chapter. This terminology departs slightly from standard usage, which describes the major firms in the international oil industry as the "majors" or the "Seven Sisters"—Exxon, Shell, Mobil, Texaco, British Petroleum, Standard of California, and Gulf. When discussing the majors, analysts usually add one other firm, Compagnie Française des Pétroles. This firm was much smaller than the other majors and it is not included in this analysis. Although a number of independents are from Europe and Japan, including several firms of considerable individual importance, this chapter examines only the U.S. independents, which include such substantial companies as Continental Oil, Occidental, Atlantic Richfield, Standard of Indiana, and Union Oil.

One of the first analysts to recognize the technocratic engineering view of the world often found in the majors, as opposed to an ideology of short-term profit maximizing, was Thorstein Veblen in *The Engineers and the Price System.* My analysis has profited greatly from this classic work.

2. The concept of strategic bargaining is central to the work of Oliver Williamson and David J. Teece: Oliver Williamson, *Markets and Hierarchies* (New York: Free Press, 1975); David J. Teece, *Vertical Integration and Vertical Divestiture in the U.S. Oil Industry* (Stanford, Calif.: Stanford University Institute for Energy Studies, 1976). For a view somewhat similar to mine see Giacano Luciani's stimulating paper, "Oil and Security Perceptions in the Middle East," paper presented to the Rhodes Conference, September 1981.

3. I am aware that the private companies are most important for the United States, but the other industrial countries are subsidizing oil companies that have sufficient economies of scale to compete in international markets. Thus they, too, have a large degree of their security resting on the bargaining strengths of their firms. Edith Penrose, *The Large International Firm in Developing Countries* (London: Allen & Unwin, 1968).

4. Many of the ideas developed in this section are similar to those of Raymond Vernon and Theodore Moran, but I have reorganized and expanded on them for my purposes. See Raymond Vernon, *Sovereignty at Bay* (New York: Basic Books, 1971); and Theodore H. Moran, "Transnational Strategies of Protection and Defense by Multinational Corporations: Spreading the Risk and Raising the Cost of Nationalization in Natural Resources," *International Organization* 27 (Spring 1973):273–288.

5. This analysis takes vertical integration as a given. But it should be stressed that vertical integration came about as a response to the risks of dealing with unreliable partners in global operations.

6. This discussion is drawn from Ben C. Ball, "Synfuel Supply Issues from the Commercial Perspective: New Kinds of Decisions," pp. 13–28 in International Energy Agency (IEA), *Workshops on Energy Supply and Demand* (Paris: OECD, 1978).

7. The problem of small numbers occurs when only a small number of parties are available to enter into a contract. This limits the potential competition and makes both sides vulnerable to bad faith, withholding of information, and other risks normally reduced by markets comprising large numbers of buyers and sellers.

8. Edith Penrose and E. F. Penrose, *Iraq: International Relations and National Development* (Boulder, Colo.: Westview Press, 1978), pp. 390–393.

9. Interviews by author, 1974. Typical reports on expectations about markets and the costs of alternative fuels were carried in *Oil and Gas Journal,* October 21, 1974, p. 86; and *Petroleum Economist,* December 1974, pp. 442–443.

The majors believed that after 1985, increases in prices might accelerate (to increase at 5 to 10 percent per annum) because of shortages in output unless consumers took strong actions to avert a shortfall. Even if some shortages occurred, the results would not be catastrophic if the changes in price came gradually and the world could make a "rolling adjustment" to the imbalances. Thus predictions of shortages in the 1980s, which were so widely publicized around 1976, did not necessarily alarm the industry. If consumers could gradually raise prices and reduce demand, limits on supplies would not produce a disaster. I base this discussion on repeated rounds of interviewing with executives from major oil companies between 1976 and 1978.

For a sample of the pessimistic and optimistic views of the future in the industry, see Texaco, Inc., "The Role of Petroleum Through the Remainder of the Century," New York, 1977; Exxon Corporation, "World Energy Outlook," New York, April 1978.

10. Paul Ryan, Jr., and Thomas C. Ryan, *An Analysis of Petroleum Company Investments in Non-Petroleum Energy Sources, Report to the Department of Energy*, 2 vols. (Washington, D.C.: Energy Information Administration, October 1979). Mobil also had major reserves of coal, and Standard of California had a 20 percent interest in Amax, a major firm in coal. Gulf was a middle-rung producer.

11. Gulf, Shell, and Exxon also opened up new plants in Western Canada that would serve international markets. *Business Week*, March 1, 1982, pp. 108–110.

12. The general history is available in Louis Turner, *The Oil Companies in the International System* (London: Allen & Unwin, 1978). The majors cited figures showing that a barrel per day of capacity for producing oil in the Middle East cost $1,000, whereas a comparable capacity for refining oil in Europe cost $6,000.

At a more general level, the companies feared the possibilities of punitive tax measures and efforts to turn the oil industry into a quasi-public utility through extensive regulation and price controls. This discussion relies on data gathered during interviews. Many of the points about foreign policy are made in H. C. Kauffman, *Energy Independence or Interdependence: The Agenda with OPEC* (New York: Exxon, January 1977).

13. For testimony by executives of Mobil and Gulf concerning the majors' roles see U.S. Congress, Subcommittee on Energy, Joint Economic Committee, *Multinational Oil Companies and OPEC: Implications for U.S. Policy*, 94th Congress, Second Session (June 2–8, 1976), pp. 6–53.

14. The majors had lost their special discounts on purchasing oil, which had guaranteed a price advantage over their rivals, by the end of 1978.

15. Had the oil companies remained in control of the world oil industry after the quadrupling of oil prices by OPEC in 1973–1974, as the "coconspirators of OPEC," at least three developments would have emerged. Corporate profits would have reflected the profits of monopoly, in order to justify the political risk and the many changes that the industry has witnessed since 1973. In fact, except for a jump in profits due to inventory profits in 1974, profits were unexceptional (and even mediocre) from 1975 through 1978. Profit levels were often higher in primarily domestic firms. (See the 1978 figures in Table 2 for Arco, Phillips, and Standard of Indiana.) Second, the market share of the leading international oil companies would have remained substantially the same. Instead, they declined sharply. Third, the companies would not have taken such a bold gamble unless they had clear understandings with OPEC and a firm plan for the future. In fact, they were constantly caught by surprise, as evidenced by

their eroding profits on production from OPEC nations and their loss in volume of supplies throughout this period. In short, none of the prerequisites of conspiracy were clearly met.

16. The changes in the oil industry are outlined in *Wall Street Journal,* March 14, 1979, p. 5; and *Business Week,* December 24, 1979, pp. 82–88. *World Business Weekly* presented a perceptive series of reports: June 8, 1980, pp. 12–14; June 30, 1980, pp. 29–39; and July 28, 1980, p. 16.

17. British Petroleum and Gulf were particularly hurt by the changes in 1979, but all the majors gave priority to supplying their own marketing affiliates. They therefore canceled some of their most important sales contracts to third parties, particularly those to Japan, even though doing so meant creating more competitors. In some cases, such as BP, the company had to cancel for lack of supplies adequate to meet its own needs; in other cases cancellation occurred because the profit on selling Middle Eastern oil after taxes within an integrated refining and distribution system was 40 to 50 cents, compared with a profit of 10 to 20 cents on selling oil to independent refineries in Japan. (The figures on profit levels per barrel represent returns on the hypothetical typical barrel of oil. They were provided by a representative of one of the majors during an interview in October 1979.)

Figures on Saudi Arabia and on government sales of oil are reported in *Petroleum Intelligence Weekly,* March 2, 1981, and April 4, 1981.

Perhaps the biggest strategic challenge may eventually be resisting the entry of OPEC companies into the refining industry by exporting refined products from their home countries to Western markets. See the discussions in *Oil and Gas Journal,* August 11, 1980, pp. 27–31: supplement to *Petroleum Intelligence Weekly,* June 22, 1981; and *Petroleum Intelligence Weekly,* July 26, 1982, pp. 5–6.

18. My conclusion about their large share of the investment in other fuels is inferred from the following report on capital investment when compared to my own table on investments: Chase Manhattan Bank, *Petroleum Industry Investment in the Eighties* (New York, 1981). Atlantic Richfield, Exxon, and Standard of Indiana own, in whole or in part, firms that have prominent roles in photovoltaic cells. Mobil and Standard of California have also staked out positions. Atlantic Richfield has predicted commercial viability in the late 1980s for peak-load capacity in individual buildings.

19. *Petroleum Intelligence Weekly,* November 2, 1981, p. 8. One industry analyst projected oil prices at $30 per barrel at the end of 1982, but argued that they would rise to $100 per barrel by 2000. *Wall Street Journal,* April 19, 1982, p. 41; and interviews in spring 1982.

20. Naturally, if OPEC "collapsed" and prices plunged below $25 per barrel for a sustained period, a more substantial shift in strategy would be triggered. One plausible candidate is a mix of the "honest broker" and "diversified autonomy" strategies. Under such a mix the companies could rely more on traditional oil-exporting nations because these nations' market power would have declined. At the same time, they would aggressively pursue options among the lower-cost alternatives to oil, especially in the OECD region. Naturally,

such a strategy would face several inherent strains, which could be compared systematically to the ones analyzed here about "Diversified Autonomy." I have undertaken such an analysis in M. S. Wionczek (ed.), *World Hydrocarbon Markets* (New York: Pergamon Press, 1982).

21. Based on a sample of twenty-six firms developed by the Chase Manhattan Bank. *Petroleum Situation,* January 1982, pp. 2–3.

22. The table does reflect Standard of Indiana's purchase of Cyrus Anvil and Exxon's purchase of Arco's share of a Colorado shale project and of Reliance Electric. Standard planned to dispose of Cyrus Anvil in response to pressure from the Canadian government in 1981.

23. Only British Petroleum announced an intention to reduce oil investments to less than 60 percent of its assets by the early 1990s. It hoped to redeploy significantly into coal and other minerals to compensate for the decline of its only two major centers of production, the North Slope and North Sea. However, its efforts had not yielded large returns as of 1982. *Economist,* July 24, 1982, pp. 59–60.

24. When firms began to diversify outside the energy field some companies exploited their skills at marketing and distribution—Mobil's acquisitions of Montgomery Ward and real estate interests reflected its strengths in marketing. Others used their gigantic size to best advantage by developing a diverse portfolio of investments. Exxon, for instance, used its expertise at global logistics and communications as a basis for launching into data processing and telecommunications enterprises. Nonetheless, these investments constituted less than 5 percent of the industry's total investments as of 1977. Political criticism of such investments and the need to develop new organizational and managerial talents for new products both inhibited the pace of diversification. The frustration over losses from nonenergy projects explains much of the emphasis on mineral acquisitions after 1978, but even these ventures proved unprofitable. *Wall Street Journal,* August 31, 1982, p. 1.

25. Exxon Corporation, "The Role of Synthetic Fuels in the United States Energy Future," New York, 1980.

26. Standard Oil of California, *World Energy Outlook 1981* (San Francisco, May 1981). Hanns W. Maull offered the lower of the gas estimates in his study *Natural Gas and Economic Security* (Paris: Atlantic Institute for International Affairs, 1981), p. 18. The higher figure for gas trading is from Peter Walters, *The Energy Crisis* (London: British Petroleum, 1980). Also consult *Petroleum Intelligence Weekly,* March 1, 1982, p. 3.

27. Interviews in February and April 1982; *Wall Street Journal,* February 24, 1982, p. 2; and Standard Oil of California, *World Energy Outlook 1982* (San Francisco, 1982).

28. The U.S. affiliate of Shell bought Beldrige in 1978 for $3.4 billion. Mobil, of course, tried to buy Conoco and Marathon. It had earlier made a smaller acquisition of Esmark Corporation's subsidiary, Transamerica Oil. Only Exxon and Standard of California appear to have ruled out major purchases, the former on the grounds of possible political repercussions and the latter on the basis that it is cheaper to find oil using its own excellent exploration department.

29. Louis Turner and James Bedore, *Middle East Industrialization* (New York: Praeger Publishers, 1979).

30. *New York Times,* July 13, 1981, p. Y19; and *Wall Street Journal,* August 27, 1982, p. 20. However, there are occasional reports of the majors' making efforts to build goodwill by keeping up purchases beyond immediate requirements in other nations. One instance, a story from Nigeria, came immediately before major cuts in purchases by large companies. *Financial Times,* November 2, 1981, p. 4.

31. Phillips's drilling record is perhaps the one misleading sample in Table 4. The figures do not reflect the fact that in 1979 and 1980 the company spent more than 65 percent of its exploration and leasehold funds in the United States.

32. *Los Angeles Times,* July 27, 1980, p. IV-1; *Business Week,* October 13, 1980, pp. 110–118, and April 6, 1981, pp. 80–87.

33. Peter F. Cowhey, "Petroleum and the Product Cycle: The Anglo-American Companies in the Third World," unpublished paper.

34. Socal, Union, and U.S. Shell are expected to expand U.S. production between 1982 and 1985, due to larger reserves, while Standard of Indiana and Arco are the only other major companies hoping to avoid declining production. Exxon predicts expanding output for its U.S. holdings after 1985. *Business Week,* March 22, 1982, pp. 66–73; *New York Times,* February 11, 1982, p. Y34; *Wall Street Journal,* February 24, 1982, p. 2; and *Institutional Investor,* July 1982, pp. 301–310.

35. These figures represent a speculative, deliberately optimistic interpretation of the programs of the two companies made by the author. I cut U.S. production by Gulf less than most analysts while adding up the potential for Europe and West Africa based on the most favorable prognosis suggested in Gulf's 1980 corporate report. The Canadian figure assumes that Gulf is allowed to enjoy the benefits of a major find in the Hibernian field, which a low price for oil could render uneconomic. My speculation about Socal is derived from a conversation with a senior executive of the company. Needless to say, the executive underlined the difficulty of anticipating exploration successes or changing political conditions. The figures cited are my own effort to balance the numerous contingencies cited by the executive, not his own forecast.

36. Investments in the capacity to process heavier oils for light products again reflect the trade-offs between profit and security. Some companies believe that security is worth the premium of risking large amounts of money on new refining investments. Others are willing to gamble that enough light oil is going to be available in the future to cancel out the advantage of the refineries able to use heavier oils. *Business Week,* August 10, 1981, p. 34D; *Forbes,* August 3, 1981, pp. 36–38; *New York Times,* April 5, 1982, p. 21; and *Business Week,* May 17, 1982, p. 95.

37. Fereidun Fesharaki in *Petroleum Intelligence Weekly,* June 22, 1981, special supplement, "Wide Impact Seen for OPEC's Refining Push."

38. International Energy Agency, *Energy Policies and Programmes of IEA Countries, 1980 Review* (Paris: OECD, 1981), pp. 61 and 65.

39. LNG was only 2.5 percent of the world's seaborne energy trade in the late 1970s and may grow to 5 percent by 1985. Exxon had a massive project in Libya before it pulled out of that country. Phillips was to lead the Nigerian project, with BP and Shell as investors, until it withdrew in fall of 1981. BP, Shell, Chevron, and Exxon are in Australia. Mobil, Chevron, and Huffco (a U.S. independent) now are Pertamina's partners in Indonesia. Future Indonesian projects will involve Exxon, Gulf, Conoco, and Getty. Shell runs the Brunei supplies and is a leader in planned work in Malaysia. British Petroleum plays a large part in Abu Dhabi. Mobil is proposing the Cameroon project. Shell and BP may manage the Qatar supplies. Arco is the largest foreign investor in the Chile plant. Standard of Indiana recently announced a gigantic find of natural gas in Qatar that may become the basis of a LNG project. BP will participate in the feasibility study for a proposed LNG route between Canada and West Germany. However, the majors have no role in projects announced during 1981 in Canada, South Korea, and Argentina. *Petroleum Economist,* August 1979, pp. 313–316; December 1979, pp. 514–518; July 1980, p. 292; and December 1980, p. 514; and *Petroleum Intelligence Weekly,* March 2, 1981, pp. 7–8; June 1, 1981, p. 9; and August 17, 1981, p. 12.

40. For example, British Petroleum has an equity share in Ruhrgas, the dominant gas firm in West Germany. L. Grayson, *The National Oil Companies* (New York: Wiley, 1981). The *Financial Times* has reported that Shell, Exxon, and Texaco also are shareholders in Ruhrgas (June 9, 1981, p. 21). The majors have a smaller role in the more advanced system of Norway. *Financial Times,* February 9, 1979, p. 2; *Wall Street Journal,* November 24, 1981, p. 2, and November 25, 1981, p. 6; and *Economist,* July 31, 1982, p. 66. Exxon holds the largest foreign equity share in recent major finds in the northern part of the Norwegian fields. Cities Services hold a sizable share of recent gas discoveries in the Congo.

41. The delivered price of steam coal to Northwest Europe was still only about 55 percent that of sulfur fuel early in 1982. The effects of declining prices in 1982 are analyzed in the *Wall Street Journal,* February 22, 1982, p. 27, and the *Economist,* March 27, 1982, pp. 8–9.

42. Shell traded 6 million metric tons of coal in international markets in 1979 and hoped for 28 million in the mid-1980s. *Business Week,* September 24, 1979, pp. 104–108; *World Business Weekly,* May 12, 1980, p. 14; and *Forbes,* November 24, 1980, pp. 129–140.

43. I would guess (very roughly) that the majors may control about 10 to 20 percent of the steam coal trade between Japan and Australia. (General Electric's subsidiary, Utah, is the largest coal producer in Australia.) The effort of the majors to catch a larger share on the rebound may suffer from competition from growing Japanese direct investment in the Canadian coal industry. *Financial Times,* June 23, 1981, p. V; July 27, 1981, p. VI; and October 5, 1981, p. IV.

44. John Jump, *Oil Companies into Coal* (British Petroleum, June 1981); and *Wall Street Journal,* March 18, 1981, p. 22.

45. *New York Times,* May 28, 1981, p. Y39; and July 1, 1981, p. D1; *Petroleum Intelligence Weekly,* August 10, 1981, p. 9; October 19, 1981, p. 12; and *Financial Times,* January 6, 1982, p. 5.

46. Based on *International Petroleum Encyclopedia* (Tulsa, Okla.: PenWell Publishing, 1981), pp. 4–23; interviews in summer 1981; and the following accounts: *Business Week,* April 20, 1981, p. 27; *Los Angeles Times,* July 6, 1981, p. 1; and *Wall Street Journal,* August 19, 1981, p. 14; and December 28, 1981, p. 1.

47. Two of the earliest exploratory projects for shale, Parahao and Western Oil Shale, do have many participants.

48. Union and Tosco are the companies with the longest history of commitment to shale oil. It is hard to tell whether they were chosen as a type of reward for corporate virtue or because they had done the most preliminary work on the best lands. At one point Tosco also announced plans for a second plant but did not find a partner for the venture. Sohio, Sunoco, and Phillips also planned a plant designed to produce 15,000 barrels per day. Union received a government guarantee of a price of $42.50 per barrel (1982 dollars) for part of its output. *Financial World,* February 1, 1982, pp. 35–49; *New York Times,* December 3, 1981; *Los Angeles Times,* March 29, 1982, p. IV-1; May 3, 1982, p. 1; July 27, 1982, p. IV-2; and *Wall Street Journal,* May 3, 1982, pp. 3, 36.

49. Exxon's gasification system was best suited for petrochemicals, but it canceled the U.S. plant in February 1982. Texaco, which is providing the technology on a $300 million prototype project on gasification, is intent on power plants as markets. At the close of 1981, Phillips announced that it was considering building a large gasification plant. *Wall Street Journal,* January 25, 1982, p. 10. Both liquefaction plants are funded primarily by the U.S. Department of Energy. Conoco and Mobil are among the partners in the Ashland venture, which received a new federal guarantee in 1982. Japanese and German investment groups have joined Phillips and Arco in Exxon's venture. The former plant cost $300 million; the latter is costing $116 million. For an account of Reagan's policy, consult *Business Week,* November 2, 1981, pp. 50–51; and *Wall Street Journal,* June 21, 1982, p. 6.

50. Several of Exxon's competitiors initially believed that either this was an excuse to bargain over tax policy with the Australian government rather than a reaction to new data, or Exxon wanted to delay starting the project because it had moved back the date when its projected oil prices would be high enough to justify production. Because only one other syndicate (a group including BP) was close to launching an Australian project, this was the ideal time for Exxon to bargain or stall. However, little evidence exists to support this speculation. Moreover, as Exxon cut back to a maximum commitment to studies of Aus. $50 million over the next five years, a consortium of Japanese firms, assisted by the Japanese government, stepped into the breach. They committed a substantial sum to preparatory work on shale over the next five years, but they did not guarantee a demonstration plant. *Wall Street Journal,* June 11, 1981, p. 9; and *World Business Weekly,* June 15, 1981, p. 8.

51. *Petroleum Economist,* February 1980, pp. 65–71; and *Wall Street Journal,* September 3, 1981, p. 2; September 15, 1981, p. 36; and December 18, 1981, p. 8.

52. *World Business Weekly,* August 3, 1981, pp. 20–21. For developments

concerning Japan, Phillips, and Texaco, consult *Wall Street Journal,* November 25, 1981, p. 10; November 27, 1981, p. 31; and December 11, 1981, p. 15.

53. Ryan and Ryan, *Analysis of Petroleum Company Investments,* and Note 41. One company said that it was willing to accept a real rate of return of only 7 percent on coal investments, about one-third less than its return on oil.

54. Independent firms with state support, such as Dome in Canada, may whittle down the leadership of the majors on technology. The private companies' technological advantages and ability to make capital investments are outlined in *World Business Weekly,* October 6, 1980, pp. 15–16; and *Business Week,* August 18, 1980, pp. 84–87.

55. *Business Week,* November 17, 1980, pp. 162–166; and *New York Times,* August 21, 1981, p. Y31. Some signs of success for the majors were reported in 1982: *New York Times,* March 3, 1982, p. Y29; and *Wall Street Journal,* April 16, 1982, p. 49. The majors consistently pushed for some price advantage on North Sea oil in order to transfer their profits from the heavily taxed production stage of operations to the less severely taxed stage of downstream operations.

56. Continental Oil and some other firms have urged retaliation against the Canadian firms. But this is a minority position. Investments by such firms as Elf and Kuwait Petroleum Corporation are growing at a respectable rate in the United States. *Wall Street Journal,* February 4, 1982, p. 6.

57. *International Petroleum Encyclopedia* (Tulsa, Okla.: PenWell, 1981), pp. 424–429.

58. The majors are not exempt from pressure by host governments, but they can bargain for offsetting concessions. A good example appears to be the recent negotiations concerning an Exxon petrochemical plant in the United Kingdom. *Business Week,* August 24, 1981, p. 50.

59. The reports on the petrochemical industry also indicate that Cities Service planned to leave the field while Phillips was shifting from basic to speciality chemicals. *Business Week,* March 1, 1982, pp. 108–110; and *Wall Street Journal,* February 12, 1982, p. 46.

60. *Petroleum Intelligence Weekly,* October 12, 1981, supplement (on integration); a contrasting view from a Mobil Oil executive is in the supplement to *Petroleum Intelligence Weekly,* July 12, 1982.

61. *Petroleum Intelligence Weekly* reported on Shell's views on pricing: March 16, 1981 (on Kuwait); April 6, 1981, pp. 4–5; and April 27, 1981, p. 3 (on Kuwait).

62. Mobil and British Petroleum signed contracts with Saudi Arabia in 1980 to process relatively small amounts of Saudi crude in their European refineries. Most of the product returned for use in Saudi Arabia, but some was sold in Europe. In effect, Petromin rented its idle refining capacity. With the weak market in 1982 some OPEC countries, such as Libya, subsidized the processing of their oil in Italian refineries in order to boost crude sales.

63. P. R. Odell, "The Future Supply of Indigenous Oil and Gas in Western Europe," in IEA, *Workshops,* especially pp. 161–166.

64. If prices remain depressed, the retreat from massive government subsidies

for synfuels (the Carter program) could seriously impair the industry's development.

65. Aside from the issue of foreign aid, the majors argued that many developing countries demanded revenues comparable to those received by members of OPEC, which make profit margins insufficient to develop small new fields in territories requiring the installation of major amounts of new infrastructure. Moreover, the host governments may not permit conversion of earnings from local sales of petroleum into hard currencies. This discourages production and refining aimed only at domestic markets. *Petroleum Intelligence Weekly,* July 27, 1981, pp. 4–6.

2 The Natural Gas Trade in the 1980s

Jonathan David Aronson
with Christopher Cragg

The gas industry achieved massive proportions only after World War II when pipelining technology allowed long-distance transportation of gas. By 1980 worldwide production of natural gas had reached 57.8 trillion cubic feet (Tcf), the equivalent of 27.8 million barrels of oil per day. Although relatively small amounts of gas are traded across national borders, in 1980 natural gas satisfied 19 percent of world and 26 percent of U.S. energy demand. Yet, natural gas has received less attention than oil, nuclear power, coal, or solar energy, perhaps because natural gas has been considered part of the drab world of public utilities by the media.

Until recently, the international trade in natural gas was handicapped by technology and geography.[1] When gas prices were low, pipelines were economical over only limited distances. (Indeed, even today many exporters complain that the return on gas exports is unattractive due to the high cost of transportation and the relatively low price they receive per unit of energy.) Oceans were insurmountable barriers. Trade developed between contiguous nations, but because many gas discoveries were distant from possible markets, flaring was common. Today, the initial barriers to widespread global gas trade have been overcome. Although extremely expensive, liquefied natural gas carriers act as "floating pipelines." In addition, successful progress on the undersea gas pipeline from Algeria, through Tunisia, under the Mediterranean,

The authors thank Fereidun Fesharaki, Thane Gustafson, and Christina Snyder for their comments.

and up into Italy via Sicily has encouraged contemplation of other underwater gas pipelines.

Inevitably, the active entry of natural gas into world energy markets will alter trade patterns in energy in two ways. First, by creating additional complexity in the energy markets, it will give importers increasing leverage over suppliers because alternative fuels will exist. When oil markets are soft, the price of fuel oil in particular tends to dip further than the price of other petroleum products. Moreover, when African crude (the major source of low-sulfur oil) does not command a large premium, low-sulfur fuel oil becomes available at lower prices. As Chapter 1 indicates, changes in the refining industry will make it easier to use a wider mix of crude oils. All these changes may combine to limit the market for natural gas.

Second, the structure of and bargaining within the gas trade bear little resemblance to oil transactions and negotiations. The oil trade is dominated by oil companies acting as middlemen between buyers and sellers. Oil and other petroleum products are often diverted from one importer to another as prices and circumstances vary. With some limitations, oil from any source can be exported to many countries. Bargaining is multilateral. In contrast, whether oil companies are involved or not, there is little flexibility in the gas trade. Pipelines cannot be moved; liquefied natural gas (LNG) routes permit little variation.[2] Furthermore, contracts may run for two decades or more because stability and steady income streams are required to finance the gas trade.[3] As a result, gas producers and importers dominate the gas pipeline and LNG trade. Middlemen have almost no leverage. Bargaining is bilateral. One result of this separation of gas markets is that prospects for gas and for a vibrant gas trade are quite different in North America, Japan, and Western Europe.

This chapter examines the outlook for the natural gas trade during the 1980s. (The trade in liquefied petroleum gas and other natural gas liquids is not dealt with here.) We ask whether the natural gas trade will continue to expand with the same rapidity as in the 1960s and 1970s. Or will the declines in the LNG trade of 1980 and 1981 mark the beginning of a long plateau period in which major expansion in the gas trade stops? Specifically, what are the prospects for the growth of natural gas imports in the United States, Japan, and Western Europe? The chapter focuses on the different political, economic, and bureaucratic incentives and barriers to the maturation of a long-distance gas trade. The differences in U.S., Japanese, and Western European prospects are compared, and the implications of their divergence are explored. In contrast to the situation described in Chapter 1, the main political decision makers involved with the natural gas trade are nations. Energy companies are important, but they are not as central to the action in the gas trade as in the oil trade.

Prospects for the U.S. Gas Trade in the 1980s

The production and use of natural gas in the United States have not been subject to a free market since the imposition of federal price controls. Whatever their merits, price controls certainly led to faster growth in demand and less exploration, even as gas ascended to the role of the second most-used fuel in the United States. Each year since 1967, the United States has used more gas than it discovered in new resources. Although the decontrol of prices will help correct this situation, industry and government analysts believe that vast new gas discoveries are unlikely and predict that natural gas will provide only 18 percent of the United States's energy in 1990 and only 15 percent in 2000.[4] Exxon forecasts that by 2000 domestic coal will provide more U.S. energy than domestic oil or gas and that nuclear energy will provide almost as much as gas.[5] The numbers in other estimates differ, but the trend of the predictions is identical.[6] Projections reproduced in Table 1 assume that nearly 75 percent of all U.S. gas reserves have already been located because exploration and production of natural gas in the United States has been far more intense than anywhere else.[7]

If it is accepted that domestic natural gas from the lower forty-eight states will not continue to meet the U.S. natural gas demand, then three alternative strategies remain. First, the United States can allow the market to allocate supplies while restricting imports. As scarcity becomes acute and prices rise, conservation will stretch existing supplies further. Second, the United States can substitute imported gas for production in the lower forty-eight states. The United States already purchases about 1 Tcf per year of Canadian gas. Expansion is possible. Mexican and Alaskan gas could also be pipelined to U.S. users. Algerian LNG has been imported into the East Coast for more than a decade, and other nations stand ready to sell the United States LNG. Third, the United States could produce synthetic gas from coal.[8]

What can be expected for U.S. gas production and imports in the 1980s? In 1980 almost 95 percent of U.S. gas demand was met from domestic production. Most of the rest was imported by pipeline from Canada. Small amounts of pipelined Mexican gas and imported Algerian LNG made up the balance. The de facto priorities guiding U.S. natural gas policy were made explicit in early 1979 by Energy Secretary James Schlesinger. He ranked the order in which the Carter administration valued gas from different sources as follows:

TABLE 1
World Natural Gas Reserves in Trillion Cubic Feet[a]

	Reserves[b] 1/1/1982	% of Total	Reserves[b] 1/1/1978	Undis-covered	Total	% of Total
United States	198.0	6.8	211.0	80.0	291.0	4.2
Canada	89.9	3.1	95.0	350.0	445.0	6.4
Other Western Hemisphere	176.3	6.1	120.6	93.3	214.0	3.1
Western Europe	150.6	5.2	140.2	204.8	345.0	5.0
Iran	484.0	16.6	500.0	400.0	900.0	12.9
Other Middle East	278.5	9.6	197.7	402.3	600.0	8.6
Africa[c]	211.7	7.3	182.6	167.4	350.0	5.0
Asia and the Pacific	127.6	4.4	123.3	326.7	450.0	6.5
Soviet Union[d]	1170.3	40.2	875.0	2180.0	3055.0	44.0
China	24.4	0.8	28.0	272.0	300.0	4.3
Total	2911.3	100.0	2473.4	4476.6	6950.0	100.0

Sources: 1982 figures: Oil & Gas Journal, December 28, 1981, pp. 86-87; 1978 figures: B. A. Rahmer, "New Assessment of Resources," Petroleum Economist, December 1979, p. 502.

a. Estimated; excluding associated gas
b. Proven and probable
c. Including Algeria which accounts for most of these reserves
d. Small quantities of gas reserves in Eastern Europe are also included

1. Base production from the lower 48 states,
2. Alaskan gas,
3. Mexican and Canadian gas,
4. Short-haul LNG (e.g., from Trinidad),
5. Domestically produced synthetic gas (from coal),
6. Long-haul, high cost, possibly insecure LNG.[9]

To promote this agenda the Department of Energy announced its intention to intervene in markets to achieve its goals. The prospects for domestic gas producers rose; those of utilities and companies involved with LNG fell, particularly because Congress finally consented to the eventual decontrol of natural gas prices. Even with the election of a new, more free-market-oriented administration, the prospects for a booming LNG import trade into the United States during the 1980s are sinking. Despite the difficulties in launching the Alaskan pipeline that make its completion during the 1980s doubtful, these rankings appear to have remained intact.

The U.S. government's priorities emphasized security over price. It was seen as desirable to support the development of Alaskan gas despite climatic and geographic burdens destined to raise its price above world averages. In December 1981, Congress passed legislation designed to encourage the construction of the Alaskan gas pipeline. However, many analysts believe this gave insufficient incentives to ensure that the project will be built. Delays and further cost escalations are expected.[10] Energy analysts assumed that the United States would increase its Canadian purchases during the mid-1980s but that these would decline again when the Alaskan gas pipeline was operational. This assumption is already being rethought. Canada, in the eyes of the Energy Department, was little more than an extension of the Great Plains without any say in its own future. U.S. energy planners were caught unprepared by Prime Minister Trudeau's New Energy Policy designed to recapture at least 50 percent of Canada's energy production for Canadian companies. They remain uneasy that the Canadian government might be uncooperative when it comes time to renew contracts to sell gas to the United States. Some of the gas might be diverted for Canadian use and some is likely to be exported as LNG to Japan.[11] Moreover, because large U.S. energy concerns have reduced their new Canadian investment and drilling activities, the ability (as opposed to the willingness) of Canada to export gas at current levels of about 1 Tcf per year could decline much faster than previously predicted.[12]

U.S. energy officials also expected Mexico to become a major supplier of gas to the United States, but following extended bickering in the late 1970s over the plan to sell the United States about 0.7 Tcf per year, Mexico declared that a maximum of 300 million cubic feet per day (just over 0.1 Tcf per year) would be made available for export. In late 1981, however, Mexico indicated that it would be willing to double exports to 600 million cubic feet per day.[13]

Plans for short-haul LNG projects involving Trinidad, Ecuador, Colombia, and Argentina are proceeding but are unlikely to be completed rapidly unless the larger projects, based on more massive gas finds in Algeria, Indonesia, and perhaps Nigeria, are ultimately accepted and integrated into the U.S. energy picture and natural gas prices resume their upward climb. The prospects and problems facing synthetic gas developments are discussed in Chapter 6. Only long-haul LNG remains a source of great possible expansion.

To understand the problems facing LNG imports bound for the United States, some background is helpful. The United States was the first nation involved with LNG.[14] During World War II the world's first LNG peak-shaving facility, designed to store gas until it was needed to meet heavy winter demand, was built in Cleveland. In 1944 the tank failed and the LNG ignited, killing or injuring 500 people and ending all LNG development for two decades. No new LNG peak-shaving facility was opened anywhere in the world until 1965. However, by the end of 1980 almost one hundred LNG peak-shaving or satellite peak-shaving facilities were operating in twenty-six states.[15]

The transport of LNG began in earnest in late 1964 with two small carriers ferrying cargoes between Algeria and Canvey Island, near London. France, Italy, Spain, and Japan had all become LNG importers by 1971. With little commotion, the United States imported small shipments of LNG into New England ports between 1968 and 1972. On September 1, 1973, Distrigas, a subsidiary of the Cabot Corporation, began to regularly receive small LNG shipments (with a planned plateau of about 115 million cubic feet per day) at Everett, Massachusetts, from Sonatrach's Skikda, Algeria, facility. Although losses have been more frequent than profits, Distrigas has helped meet Boston's energy needs.[16] Several U.S. companies eagerly jumped into the LNG import business. General Dynamics began designing and building LNG carriers based on a Norwegian design. El Paso Natural Gas diversified from its pipeline base into LNG transport. Consolidated Natural Gas Co., Columbia Gas Transmission Corp., and Sonat Inc. (formerly Southern Natural Gas) contracted to take 1 billion cubic feet per day of Algerian gas at Cove Point, Maryland, and Savannah, Georgia. In September 1982, after long delays and pricing disputes, Algeria began shipping 460 million cubic feet per day for delivery at Lake Charles, Louisiana, to Trunkline Gas Company, a subsidiary of Panhandle Eastern Pipeline. Pacific Gas and Electric and the Pacific Lighting Company originally hoped to collaborate in importing 400 million cubic feet per day of Alaskan gas and 550 million cubic feet per day of Indonesian gas at Point Conception, California. But, even before the United States entered the import trade, U.S. LNG was exported to Japan. Since 1969, Phillips Petroleum and Marathon Oil have shipped about 135 million cubic feet per day from Kenai, Alaska, to Tokyo Electric Power Company and Tokyo Gas Company Ltd.[17]

The major oil companies have to some extent been involved in the LNG business, but usually as providers of gas, not as operators. Thus, until its recent withdrawal, Exxon's Esso Libya provided Italy with 235 million cubic feet per day of Libyan LNG. Shell owns one-third of the hugely successful Brunei-Japan operation, which supplies 755 million cubic feet per day to three Japanese companies. Mobil produces LNG from its Arun, Indonesia, fields, and Huffington Oil operates the Badak, Indonesia, facility for Pertamina. Atlantic Richfield hopes to participate in Chile's LNG plans. Still, for the most part, the oil companies are not the arbiters of the LNG trade.

The absence of the majors from a central role in the LNG traffic is in part explained by the origins of the LNG trade. The growth of the market was stimulated by low gas prices prevailing internationally, which made it possible for LNG operators to afford the expensive technology. Utilities spurred the trade by their eagerness to lock in gas supplies by signing long-term import contracts, even if they were initially more expensive than alternative energy sources. Utilities were concerned more with security of supply than with price because their profits were regulated, but they were able to roll the price of new gas and regasification facilities into their rate bases, thereby shielding them from losses. The guaranteed customers for the gas and the guaranteed cash flow that the utility and utility commission provided made these projects bankable. The projects were small enough that they did not provoke active opposition from the independent pipelines or small domestic gas producers. The U.S. public took little notice of these developments at first.

Two events changed the situation. First, on February 10, 1973, forty workers repairing the liner of a 600,000-barrel LNG storage tank on Staten Island, New York, were killed when a spark ignited the tank's flammable insulation, creating a small inferno. A public outcry followed immediately. Environmentalists began focusing on LNG safety issues, contending that an LNG leak could ignite and form a fireball that could drift over populated areas. The companies retorted that LNG was clean and difficult to set afire and that if a tank was breached the LNG would disperse into the atmosphere without polluting ocean or land. The government, however, grew concerned, forced expensive tests and safety modifications, and slowed down the licensing process. Thus, El Paso Natural Gas Company's East Coast projects were delayed an extra four years, beginning operations only in 1978.[18] In addition, in several incidents LNG was almost released into the atmosphere or blame was placed on LNG when other liquid fuels caught fire. For example, in June 1979 the *El Paso Paul Kayser* ran aground off Gibraltar, sustaining damage but not rupturing her tanks.[19] Worry increased. LNG's name was further blackened by incidents involving natural gas liquids in Qatar in 1977 and at Los Afraque, Spain, in 1978.[20] But despite the delays prompted by safety concerns and domestic opportunities promoted by oil and gas price rises, LNG project development in the United States continued through the 1970s.[21]

The second critical event discouraging the active growth of a U.S. LNG import trade was the nearly complete halt in Algerian gas imports to the El Paso projects in the United States (and for a time to France) on April 1, 1980. This halt occurred because the Algerians demanded an immediate linking of oil and natural gas prices and tripled their asking price in a single stroke. They asserted that the marginal value of their gas was not near zero and contended that they had suffered losses, not profits, on their gas exports to industrial countries.[22] The Algerians were fortified by an extra $9 billion in receipts in 1979 (as compared to 1978) derived from higher oil prices and by the impending completion of the Transmediterranean gas pipeline.

The United States, which had just completed lengthy negotiations with Mexico and Canada setting (at the time) a price of $4.47 per million Btus[23] for pipeline gas ($4.09 per thousand cubic feet), was unwilling to allow El Paso to pay $6.00 per million Btus plus shipping costs and expose the still fragile North American pricing structure to leapfrogging. El Paso's tankers and the gas importation facilities in Maryland and Georgia were idled. The smaller Distrigas operation, which relies on Algerian-owned carriers and a contract under which ownership of the gas is retained by the Algerians until it is transferred to the company in Massachusetts, continued to receive small gas shipments.[24] Although Algeria eventually lowered its asking price to $3.50 per thousand Btus and El Paso Natural Gas offered to waive 25 percent of their revenues for shipping and storing LNG, no compromise was reached in six separate negotiating rounds during 1980 and 1981. France persuaded Algeria to resume shipping LNG under an interim accord in February 1981. Beligum agreed to a record initial price of $5 per thousand cubic feet for Algerian LNG in April 1981, but the contract contained a most-favored-nation clause that entitled it to any cheaper rate that France or anyone else might be able to negotiate in the future. Finally, France agreed to pay $5.11 per million Btus (f.o.b.) in early February 1982 and to link the price to a basket of eight crude oils. Although the agreement does not provide full parity with crude oil, the price will escalate along with the full Btu equivalent of the index crudes. In 1981 El Paso Natural Gas admitted defeat, taking a $365 million write-down on its six LNG carriers that serviced the East Coast runs.[25] The three companies that owned the Maryland and Georgia import terminals began negotiating directly with Sonatrach to resume deliveries and hired former Deputy Secretary of State Warren Christopher to represent them, but as of October 1982 they had failed to come to terms with Sonatrach. Some grounds for encouragement remained, however. In August 1982 Sonatrach and Panhandle Eastern Pipeline reached accord on their price dispute and the first shipments of gas left Algeria for Louisiana in September. The price to Panhandle is about $1 per million cubic feet less than that agreed to by France and Belgium earlier in 1982, but when shipping and processing costs are included it still results in gas priced at the equivalent of $42 per barrel. Sonatrach apparently was willing to adjust its demands to the reality that the market was glutted with gas as of 1982. Panhandle has, in fact, been strongly criticized on the basis that the Algerian gas is not likely to be competitive or necessary during the early and middle 1980s at present prices. Nonetheless, the company felt it must assure its supply for the late 1980s and beyond. Two of the three heirs to El Paso's gas shared this perspective and hoped to negotiate for the resumption of gas deliveries by 1983 or 1984.[26]

Indonesia, in contrast to Algeria, was more accommodating to U.S. hesitancy. The Indonesians did not wish to rely on Japan as their sole customer, hoping to export to California as well. They were, however, unwilling to accept a markedly lower price from the United States than from Japan. After the failure of the U.S.-Algerian negotiations, Pertamina, Indonesia's national oil company, which had waited patiently through prolonged U.S. regulatory delays, announced it would redirect the gas originally intended for California to Japan. In early 1981, Pacific Gas and Electric stated that it had great doubts about the project and thus greatly diminished the prospect that Indonesian gas would flow into California during the 1980s.

In essence, economic considerations coupled with interest-group lobbying altered the forecast for the development of a vigorous LNG import trade for the United States. The Point Conception project, which was designed to import Indonesian and Alaskan gas into California, illustrates how diverse interest groups can combine to halt huge developments. American Indians, archaeologists, local environmental groups, the U.S. Air Force, local ranchers, and the California Gas Producers Association all opposed it. The project, particularly after the delays, was suspect on straight economic grounds, but the environmentalist lobby successfully made safety into a major issue.[27] The environmental groups received crucial support from the domestic gas producers, which had launched more active exploration schedules in order to profit from rising prices and seemingly secure utility markets.

The United States has acted to ensure that Secretary Schlesinger's ranking of gas options came about. The domestic industry and the pipelines worked against excessive gas diversification. Mexico cut back the amount of gas it was willing to supply the United States. The soft market conditions have diminished the demand for Canadian gas.

Without the experience, expertise, and economies of scale generated by operating long-haul LNG projects from Algeria, Indonesia, and conceivably Nigeria, the prospects for financing and implementing short-haul projects from Trinidad, Ecuador, Colombia, or Argentina are diminished (except perhaps as a replacement for lost Algerian gas for shipment to Maryland or Georgia). In addition, given its high cost it is questionable whether the development of synthetic gas from coal will approach the more optimistic estimates of its potential in the 1980s without maintenance of government loans and subsidies.[28] David Stockman's attempt to remove most government synfuel support places increased responsibility for maintaining U.S. natural gas supplies on the domestic market (including the North Slope).

From 1979 to 1982 the United States experienced a gas glut. The high transport and processing costs involved with natural gas and the availability of fuel oil that could be substituted for gas in many instances meant that natural gas supplies exceeded demand. One reasonable guess is that when natural gas deregulation takes effect, gas at the wellhead will normally command approximately 65 to 75 percent, on a delivered parity price basis, of the price of Number 6 fuel oil.

When the gas glut disappears, however, the United States could face a serious gas production problem. Current government policies assume that sufficient gas exists and can be rapidly produced in the lower forty-eight states to meet needs in the foreseeable future. It is assumed that in an emergency gas could be made available from Alaska, Canada, and Mexico. However, it is not evident that the Reagan administration or any future U.S. administration will be able to rely on these sources to meet any shortfalls.

On the one hand, the thinking goes as follows. As gas prices increase with or without deregulation, exploration and production attention will be diverted from Alaska, from LNG, and from "deep" gas (which would lose its price advantage under deregulation) and back to the lower forty-eight states. One recent study claimed that although drilling in the United States is increasing, "90 percent of the gas well completions are occurring in areas that are thought to contain 30 percent of the gas." About two-thirds of potential U.S. gas is not adequately exploited, primarily because it is not economic at current prices.[29] Further, the president of the Gas Research Institute has suggested that although oil and gas are readily interchangeable for many uses and the worldwide resource base for conventional gas is about equal to the base for oil, "gas is produced at only about one-third to one-half of the rate of crude."[30] If the United States actually contains the forty-to-seventy-year supply of reserves he suggested, then the deregulation of gas prices will spur exploration in the lower forty-eight states, and the necessity of building the Alaskan gas pipeline or of developing alternative LNG sources will diminish.

Those opposing this scenario fear that it will not work out that way. They complain that relying on domestic gas resources that are notoriously difficult to predict, discover, and exploit foolishly puts all of the United States's eggs in a single basket. They would prefer to encourage the development of new natural gas sources in Alaska, Canada, Mexico, or wherever else they may be found and are willing to pay more for energy to ensure that it will be there in sufficient quantities when it is needed. They argue that it is not at all clear that gas production in the 1980s will climb at the rate predicted by the Reagan administration.[31] The United States is already the most explored piece of real estate in the world. By placing stress on North American production, the United States may condemn itself to medium-term shortages that will force belated, expensive scrambling for alternative resources.

Prospects for the Japanese Gas Trade in the 1980s

The United States is blessed with abundant hydrocarbon resources; Japan inherited no major domestic oil or gas deposits. In order to support an industrial society, Japan became a major importer of petroleum products and sought to expand its sphere of influence, in part to provide secure supplies of oil. In 1980, 73 percent of Japan's energy was derived from foreign oil imports, up from 60 percent in 1965. At the same time, Japanese energy produced from hydropower and domestic fossil fuels fell from 34 percent in 1965 to 8 percent in 1980.[32] Rather than grow still more dependent on imported oil, the Japanese government has announced its intention of diversifying the country's energy mix by vastly increasing natural gas and coal imports and rapidly expanding its nuclear power generating capacity. Exxon estimates that by the year 2000, 43 percent of Japan's energy will come from oil imports, 31 percent from gas and coal imports, 18 percent from nuclear power, and 8 percent from other domestic sources. As the dream of a gas pipeline from the Asian mainland remains quite distant, the gas trade of Japan during the 1980s means LNG. In consequence, Japan has become the world's leading LNG importer, taking 2.3 billion cubic feet per day in 1981, with expectations of doubling that intake by 1987.[33]

Japan began importing natural gas from Brunei in 1972 and from Abu Dhabi and Indonesia in 1977; it expects to start taking Malaysian gas shortly. Australian LNG imports are expected later in the 1980s, and Thai and Canadian gas could follow.[34] The United States can bet on indigenous gas and hope to persuade Canada and Mexico to provide more gas in an emergency; Japan has no such luxury. Japan needs the gas desperately and will pay top prices to secure it. LNG is not a marginal source of fuel for Japan. It does not substitute for town gas as a domestic and industrial peak shaver. Rather it is fast becoming a substitute for heating oil as a fuel for power stations.[35] Japan, alone among major gas users, has steady demand for gas throughout the year. Demand does not peak in winter. Because more LNG is substituted for higher-priced fuels in Japan than elsewhere, it is less of a sacrifice for the Japanese to pay higher prices. Over the long term Japan's top price is likely to serve as the effective cap price on world price bidding.

Although no nation wants to pay more than it must to secure gas, European and U.S. users realize that if necessary Japanese users will leapfrog prices paid by foreign competitors.[36] Japan's dearth of local gas or of alternative fuels means that it is unable to turn away from hardening markets.

The Japanese perceive the world gas market in terms unfamiliar to commentators on the U.S. gas debate. They do not view the specter of future price rises for LNG as a potential threat to the LNG business. Oil prices are seen as influencing gas markets, and particularly the LNG trade.[37] They are willing to link LNG prices to the cost of fuels they would have to purchase if LNG imports were cut off.

The Japanese view of the linkage between oil and gas prices was crystallized by the U.S.-Algerian negotiations over pricing. As the talks dragged on, they caused a hiatus in Japanese negotiations with Pertamina. When it became clear that no U.S.-Algerian accord would emerge, the Japanese felt free to forge their own accord. Almost immediately they signed an agreement relating LNG prices directly to one of the major Indonesian crudes and signed a contract to increase their LNG purchases from Badak, Indonesia, by almost 40 percent. After a brief disagreement, the new contract price was set at $5.87 per million Btus (f.o.b.). Originally, the Indonesians had demanded $6.35 per million Btus (f.o.b.), compared to the $5.52 the Japanese were then paying for delivered gas. Effectively, the price rose around $0.60 per million Btus (with transport costs included), and the link between gas prices and the price of Indonesian crude was securely established. One anomaly is that through the linking of LNG to the absolute cost of crude, the price to the Japanese for LNG actually fell somewhat during 1981.[38]

Although the Japanese were prepared to hold up their Indonesian agreement for the sake of U.S. goodwill and to help the United States obtain a good price from Algeria—a tactic used to a lesser extent by the French—their opposition to crude/gas pricing parity was much less substantial from the beginning. To irritated U.S. officials, the Japanese pointed out that the Department of Energy had apparently forgotten throughout the Algerian negotiations that Japan was paying well over $5 per million Btus for 135 million cubic feet of Alaskan gas per day. Put that way, Alaskan gas was closely tied to Indonesian crude anyway, so the rhetoric about OPEC crude/gas parity was the product of circumstances and sea distance, not principle. Belkacem Nabi, the Algerian energy minister, was actually campaigning for a price already paid firmly elsewhere. His misfortune was to have to deal with a country whose assessment of indigenous resources was complicated by immense legal and governmental intervention and by a marked prejudice against the pricing rationale put forward by OPEC nations. One noted gas transport expert put it succinctly, "The gas/crude parity threat is something believed in by only three different sets of people: OPEC headquarters, journalists, and the U.S. Department of Energy."[39]

The Japanese certainly do not believe in it. In fact, a marked skepticism about the diplomatic effectiveness of constantly condemning OPEC for its price "greed" is matched in Japan by an awareness of the totality of the energy market. Despite the obvious predominance of oil and the substantial numbers of very large crude carriers at anchor in Japanese waters as floating storage, Japan is a leader in energy diversification. The Japanese believe that by utilizing LNG and liquefied petroleum gas, as well as coal imports, they will replace expensive oil and also relieve pressures on oil prices. As recent events have demonstrated, a marked depression in the Western industrial countries can quite rapidly eliminate the additional premiums normally charged on and above OPEC reference prices and also force some producers of expensive crude, like the British National Oil Corporation, to lower prices.[40] (This sensitivity of prices to economic glut would be maximized if natural gas prices were linked to a basket composed mainly of heavier fuels. As the market slows, heavier fuels drop faster than others; therefore natural gas prices would also be pulled down.) The Japanese apparently feel that by diversifying their hydrocarbon imports they can damp and perhaps even reverse the trend toward rising crude prices. They simply do not believe that gas/crude price parity necessarily leads to high crude and gas prices.

The Japanese bargaining approach also is at odds with the strategy adopted by the United States. U.S. negotiators did not attempt to utilize the combined bargaining power of the more than 1.5 billion cubic feet per day that the Algerians would sacrifice in losing the United States as a customer.[41] Nor did the U.S. government help companies secure an alternative source of LNG as a bargaining lever or try to help U.S. corporations work out their policies for gas pricing and demand on the basis of national, as opposed to regional, priorities. Individual projects had to survive or die on their own merits.

The Japanese do things differently. Electrical power companies, as well as straightforward gas utilities, are involved in the bargaining.[42] Hence, the recent agreement with the Indonesians for Badak gas was signed by Chubu Electric Power, Kansai Electric Power, Osaka Gas, and Toho Gas. Nippon Steel even takes 87 million cubic feet per day from the Arun, Indonesia, field, but it is not a separate bargain. Apart from the Alaskan contract, only one contract is for less than 475 million cubic feet per day: one with Abu Dhabi, where development is continuing off Das Island. The mix of suppliers is also wide. In addition, the Bintulu plant in Sarawak, Malaysia, is scheduled to begin deliveries in

1982, and Tokyo Electric, Kansai Electric, Chubu Electric, Osaka Gas, and Toho Gas intend to begin in 1986 importing 852 million cubic feet per day from Withnell Bay in Australia. In effect, the *zaibatsu* principle of collective bargaining covers all the major buyers, who negotiate together with a wide variety of suppliers.

Another indicator of the seriousness with which the Japanese approach the LNG trade is their decision to use their shipyards to build LNG carriers in spite of the excess tonnage elsewhere in the world. The Japanese are starting to make it a condition of purchase of gas that it be carried under Japanese flag. The Badak agreement was accompanied by an order for three vessels to the Kawasaki and Mitsubishi yards, with the finance arranged by the Japanese Development Bank at an interest rate of 8 percent.[43] As with the General Dynamics vessels, the original design comes from Moss Rosenburg in Norway and is under license, but there the similarity ends. U.S.-built LNG carriers depend on the Construction Differential Subsidy program, which severely limits the flag's operational flexibility and the potential use of foreign repair yards. In contrast, Kawasaki's previously built LNG carriers were sold to non-Japanese owners who were attracted by their technological sophistication and low cost.[44]

In consequence, not only are the Japanese going into an area of shipping investment themselves, even though the El Paso contract termination left six vessels available for sale (and six others laid up), but by neat financial footwork they gained their expertise selling vessels that could remain laid up while they built their own. LNG shipping is thus no longer a preserve of Western European and U.S. companies on charter to the world's largest importer.

Overall, Japanese importation of LNG has not suffered from the problems besetting U.S. importation and has set the world price due to Japan's lack of alternative fuels. The Japanese are willing to pay top prices to ensure they get the gas they require. Environmentalists in Japan have tended to see the advantage of methane as a clean-burning fuel rather than fight on the issue of explosive danger. Perhaps the credibility of Japanese technicians is greater. (The master of one LNG carrier moving into Japan killed himself rather than face an inquiry into a collision.[45]) Although there have been difficulties in maintaining supply, most notably on Das Island, where only one storage tank is available, and because the vessels required for the Bintulu run were completed well before the plant, there has never been the doubt surrounding the Japanese intentions that has bedeviled U.S. executives working in the field. LNG has come to stay in Japan in spite of, and perhaps because of, the very small proportion (3 percent) of total energy currently provided by natural gas.

Prospects for the Western European Gas Trade in the 1980s

Western Europe occupies the middle ground between North America's relative self-sufficiency and Japan's dearth of energy resources. The commotion over Algerian and Libyan LNG, Soviet pipelines, and North Sea oil and gas makes it easy to forget that the European continent remains a major gas producer. Although external sources are needed, Table 2 indicates that the Netherlands, the United Kingdom, and Romania all produce more natural gas than Algeria or Libya. Norway, West Germany, Italy, and France are also major producers. Norway and the United Kingdom have actually added to their reserves substantially by bringing North Sea discoveries on line. Their contribution is significant because gas production is expected to decline in the Netherlands and West Germany in the late 1980s.

European policies have differed from those in the United States in part because European gas production achieved major dimensions only during the 1970s. In 1965 only 4 percent of European energy was provided by European gas. By 1980 indigenous gas provided 12 percent of Europe's energy and accounted for 14 percent of world gas consumption. Expectations are that European production will slip between now and the end of the century but that large quantities of imported gas and gasified coal will take up the slack.[46] The need for new sources will be intensified because the Netherlands, the region's main gas exporter, has expressed a desire to preserve more of its supplies for the internal market.

European gas politics may be viewed as combining elements of regional cooperation with national and sectoral competition. This dichotomy held force while Europe produced most of its own gas and is likely to continue as North African, West African, and Soviet imports increase in the future. There is also talk of Middle Eastern export projects, but their likelihood and timing are uncertain.

On the one hand, Western Europe can be viewed as an integrated gas grid. Gas is efficiently pipelined from one country to another as supply and demand require. West Germany serves as the "turntable" because the two major European pipelines connect there.[47] Supplies from the Netherlands augmented by North Sea gas are the main source of imports for most other Western European nations. Italy, Spain, and France are also ports of entry for Algerian and Libyan LNG. West Germany, Belgium, and the Netherlands are scheduled to begin importing Algerian LNG during the 1980s. Added gas imports to any single country will, because of the gas grid, help meet the entire region's energy needs.

On the other hand, each nation wants to establish its own secure

TABLE 2
Twenty-Five Leading Gas-Producing Nations in 1981[a]
(Billions of Cubic Feet)

1981 Rank	Country	1981	1980	1979	1977	1975	1973	1973 Rank
1	United States	19,596	20,268	19,999	20,338	20,465	22,854	1
2	Soviet Union	16,390	15,363	14,337	12,395	10,202	8,263	2
3	Netherlands	3,054	2,800	2,718	2,932	3,199	2,590	4
4	Canada	2,623	2,668	3,646	3,301	3,422	3,241	3
5	Mexico	1,486	1,184	975	745	772	686	9
6	Romania	1,440	1,185	1,210	1,006	935	1,303	7
7	United Kingdom	1,427	2,308	1,966	1,500	1,231	1,152	8
8	Algeria	1,149	517	302	284	20	20	
9	Indonesia	1,075	1,028	816	352	203	129	20
10	Norway	923	698	415	66	-	-	
11	Libya	674	133	162	489	134	43	
12	West Germany	636	739	826	908	690	590	10
13	Venezuela	602	518	406	393	205	1,741	5
14	Pakistan	600	600	180	91	155	128	21
15	Italy	500	525	534	449	533	487	11
16	China	459	484	512	413	300	230	15
17	Saudi Arabia	435	310	209	121	na	na	
18	Australia	377	275	254	237	183	149	18
19	Kuwait	340	291	206	186	175	51	29
20	Argentina	330	297	242	250	273	242	13
21	Brunei-Malaysia	303	318	303	187	19	-	
22	France	265	264	239	257	267	258	18
23	Qatar	205	38	27	70	-	7	
24	Abu Dhabi	204	116	40	137	na	na	
25	Trinidad	192	189	165	150	51	137	19
	Total World	57,816	56,270	54,844	52,510	46,959	48,074	

Sources: International Petroleum Encyclopedia, 1981, p. 274; 1982, p. 354.

a. Except for figures on the Soviet Union, Romania, and China; production figures for Communist countries are not disaggregated. Gas production of the remaining Communist nations totaled 921 bcf in 1981, 878 bcf in 1980, 1,181 bcf in 1979, 812 bcf in 1977, 522 bcf in 1975, and 631 bcf in 1973. Estimates for 1980 production by the Petroleum Economist, August 1981, p. 336 would place East Germany in slot number 16 for 1980 and Poland and Hungary at the bottom of this list of twenty-five producers. The most significant change in ranking during the past eight years was Iran's decline from the sixth largest producer of natural gas in 1973 with 1,689 bcf of production to a mere 52 bcf in 1981. The existence of massive Iranian natural gas reserves suggest that Iranian production should rebound once the political situation in that country stabilizes.

source of supply if possible. And national syndicates compete to lead in new gas developments in order to take the greatest share of available profits. Utilities and oil companies in each nation compete with each other and with foreign rivals to initiate gas purchases. Peter Cowhey has noted that:

> French and West German syndicates planned to cooperate in sharing supplies being sought from the Soviet Union, but they competed for leadership concerning the acquisition of gas. At the same time, a syndicate from the Continent and one from Britain were bidding to be the principal distributor of Norwegian gas to the rest of Europe. Moreover, France's LNG projects and Italy's new pipeline to North Africa are economic rivals. Thus, the logic of efficiency and insurance have propelled the creation of allocation rules for sharing gas supplies, but the purchase from foreign sources poses the classic problems of each utility wanting to gain first claim on perhaps limited supplies.[48]

European banks replicated the same pattern of cooperation and competition. To fund major gas developments, financiers from all the major participants were needed, but fierce competition for the role of lead manager was always present. (U.S. banks actively competed for the North Sea and LNG business but not in financing the Soviet–West German pipeline.)

If the Japanese management of the gas import problem is in marked contrast to the U.S. approach, the European experience lies somewhere between the two. As in the United States, the assessment of indigenous resources is extremely difficult, yet substantial quantities of gas exist. But, as in Japan, few analysts dispute the need for increasing the scope and diversity of natural gas imports. Europe will almost certainly need considerable quantities of methane from external sources by the end of the century if gas is to maintain its rough market share.[49] One oil company, Phillips, has estimated the gas shortfall in Europe at almost 2 Tcf per year by 1995 and 3.6 Tcf per year by 2000. This estimated shortfall represents almost 30 percent of total European gas demand.[50]

Europe seems resigned to importing large quantities of natural gas but hopes to develop a diversity of opportunities for imports sufficient that if one or another fails to come about, crisis will not follow automatically. Four major sources of gas (beyond domestic sources and synthetic gas from coal) are expected to be injected into the European energy grid. Gas could flow from the North Sea, the Soviet Union, North Africa, or at a later date, from West Africa. Starting closest to home, there are substantial gas deposits under the North Sea. But, North Sea gas-bearing geological structures have proved highly unpredictable and seem to be getting more so as the Norwegians move north of the 62nd parallel and the British search in deeper and deeper waters. Although the North Sea will undoubtedly yield much more gas, it is becoming ever more expensive to produce it, and this escalation of costs could act as a deterrent.[51] Moreover, available Norwegian gas is committed through the late 1980s and although the Norwegians could increase their production thereafter, it is not clear that they would be willing to disrupt their economy in order to do so. They do not want to become the accepted primary source of gas for Europe because that would limit their ability to change their policies. And, as British Petroleum has recently discovered, high investment in secure domestic sources may leave a corporation extremely exposed to external sources of cheap hydrocarbons, even if the price fluctuations are very brief.[52] In addition, it is only now becoming clear how North Sea gas from the northern fields will be disbursed.

The British government, through British Gas, proposed to lead a consortium to construct a U.K. gas-gathering pipeline connecting the Magnus and Fulmer fields to St. Fergus on the Scottish mainland. However, financial institutions hesitated to provide the bulk of the funds needed to complete the $5 billion project, in part because they were uncertain that there were enough reserves to justify the necessary investment and in part because the U.K. Treasury adamantly refused to allow the financing package to adversely affect the British national debt. By the spring of 1981 this project was faltering badly, and in September the government finally scrapped its proposed gas-gathering system. Private consortia acted immediately to initiate an even larger system of pipelines.[53]

In contrast, the Norwegians have moved ahead with their plan to build a $2.2 billion pipeline that will open up the northern North Sea fields to continental buyers. As the Norwegian government is integrally involved, financing should prove much simpler. Already, tentative agreement has been reached to sell gas to a seven-member continental importing consortium led by Ruhrgas of West Germany. If the Norwegian pipeline continues to move ahead, it is likely that the hands of continental importers will be strengthened in future negotiations.[54] The British position could become even more tenuous, but the continent's position will be much strengthened.

The second possible windfall source of gas for Western Europe would be provided by a 3,500-mile pipeline linking the Western Siberian gas fields to the West German pipeline system. The Soviet Union first suggested the possibility of such a project as part of a twenty-five-year economic cooperation agreement in 1978. Originally, the planned pipeline depended on the expansion of the Irano-Soviet deals and the doubling of the existing IGAT 1 line from the south. The Iranian revolution halted expansion plans. Other problems also delayed the signing of an agreement. Although Austria, Belgium, France, Italy, the Netherlands, Sweden, and Switzerland all joined West Germany in agreeing to participate in the project, the United States opposed its construction. Both the Carter and Reagan administrations, to the considerable irritation of the Europeans, urged that the money could be better spent in redoubling the exploration efforts of the British, Dutch, and Norwegians.[55] In addition, technical problems exist.[56]

But despite the geopolitical obstacles, the project proceeded and contracts were signed. The long dispute over financing terms was resolved. In the early summer of 1981 the Soviets sought to finance purchases of pipe and other equipment needed for construction at 7.8 percent interest rates. The German banks, already highly exposed to Soviet and Eastern European risks and pounded by rising interest rates and a declining mark, were unwilling to provide discretionary financing. After President Reagan failed to persuade Chancellor Schmidt to scrap the pipeline at the Ottawa Conference in July 1981, progress was made on financial negotiations. The Soviets announced that they would build the two sections of the double pipeline sequentially rather than simultaneously. This brought down their immediate financing requirements and allowed them to agree to a floating rather than a fixed rate on their loans.[57]

With the financing more or less settled, the Soviet Union was able to negotiate agreement protocols for the majority of the 40 billion cubic meters (roughly 4 billion cubic feet per day) of gas they planned to sell annually. In late October 1981 Italy agreed to a "correct" market price backed up by a guaranteed floor price. The escalation of price was based on a basket of competing oil products in which crude oil represented no more than 25 percent of the escalation formula. Six weeks later, the West Germans agreed to take just over one-quarter of the Soviet gas with the price set in marks. The base price was set at the equivalent of $4.65 per million Btus as of July 1, 1981. By 1987, three and a half years after the gas was scheduled to begin to flow, the guaranteed minimum price floor in the German contract would reach the mark equivalent of $5.40 per million Btus. Escalation of the price base would be indexed 20 percent to crude oil, 40 percent to gas oil, and 40 percent to low-sulfur fuel oil. Finally, on January 22, 1982, the French government signed a twenty-five-year contract for Soviet gas because the Soviets agreed to a lower base price (because of the greater distance from the gas fields) than the Germans would pay, because the contract would be drawn up in French francs (which would shelter the French from franc-dollar fluctuations), and because it bolstered the French bargaining position in dealing with the Algerians in negotiations that began the next day. Provisions for a guaranteed minimum (floor) price and price-escalation clauses are essentially the same as in the German contract.[58]

Apparently the Soviet Union gave in on a number of points, including its demand for a closer link with crude prices, in the face of stiff opposition, particularly from West Germany, where large declines in energy consumption diminished the immediate need for Soviet gas.[59] Admitting that the Soviet and West German economies are becoming ever more closely tied, Western European analysts see the Soviet gas pipeline as a method for diminishing their eventual dependence on the even more erratic behavior of the Algerians and Libyans. By bringing forward as many gas projects as possible, they spread their risks and ensure, to as great an extent as possible, that at least some gas will flow. Indeed, if a surplus of supply over demand continues or arises again, Western Europe may actually hold considerable leverage over a Soviet government increasingly dependent on gas receipts for hard-currency assets.

The Reagan administration, however, viewed the gas pipeline very differently. On June 18, 1982, President Reagan, citing Soviet disregard for Polish rights and sovereignty as his proximate cause, banned the export of U.S.-licensed products to support the Soviet pipeline projects. In the months that followed the decision, sanctions were toughened to the extent that the United States attempted to impose extraterritorial jurisdiction over European and Japanese companies providing support to the gas pipeline projects that was based on technology licensed from U.S. firms. The U.S. government argued that the pipeline should not be completed because it would leave many European countries overly dependent on Soviet gas and because it was unwise to bolster the Soviet economy and military through the infusion of so much hard currency. The Reagan administration also complained that it was foolish to subsidize the pipeline with cheap loans.

The impact of the sanctions was immediate but apparently counterproductive to the U.S. aims. Many in the administration privately opposed the policy, and the business community was almost unanimously negative. Every European country affected by the sanction decried the U.S. position and ordered its companies to fulfill their contractual commitments to the Soviets. Critics charged that the U.S. position was untenable and doomed to failure; the pipeline would be completed anyway. The Soviet Union, in fact, seems to have taken the U.S. position as a challenge. The pipeline was given the money and technicians it had sometimes been denied in the past, and work to develop needed technology within the Soviet Union was accelerated. The poor state of the Soviet economy also meant that the Soviets' demand for gas was sufficiently low that they could afford to divert gas that would otherwise have been used at home to meet their commitments to Europe and embarrass the Reagan administration. It now appears that the pipeline system will proceed despite U.S. opposition. The sanctions were lifted in 1982.

Even if the Soviet deal had crumbled, however, LNG or pipelined gas from North Africa provides an alternative source of imports. Currently LNG flows into France, Italy, Spain, and in marginal amounts, into the United Kingdom from Algeria and Libya. At the beginning of 1981 contracted amounts equaled 1.71 billion cubic feet per day, but deliveries fell considerably below this level. LNG involvement with Libya has proved difficult, although the Italians and Spanish were, at last report, paying only $3.40 per thousand Btus. Algeria, the larger supplier, is contracted for 1.365 billion cubic feet per day but has suffered from considerable technical problems as well as price disputes. In 1979 its Skikda liquefaction plant produced just under half the LNG that it had contracted to deliver to France.

The most important development for the future of Algerian LNG exports to Europe, however, is undoubtedly the Transmediterranean pipeline, which transfers methane from Algeria to Italy without resorting to liquefaction. In part because of the technical expertise of the remarkable pipelaying concern, Castoro Sei, this project progressed with a speed and efficiency that contrasts sharply with the problems of LNG plants. In consequence, the Algerian Department of Energy stated that Algeria would abandon planned increases in LNG production above present levels. Capital costs have been rising at 25 percent per year while LNG prices received by the Algerians have remained nearly static. The technical success of the $4 billion, 675-mile Transmediterranean pipeline has reawakened interest in the Segamo project to Spain. However, although the pipeline was successfully tested in the late summer of 1982, regular deliveries had not begun as of October 1982 because disputes on pricing remained. Nonetheless, the Algerians would still like to persuade two Northern European gas utilities, Ruhrgas-Salgitter and Gasunie, to accept pipelined gas.[60] Part of the motivation for the Italian gas line was the assumption that the Italian state utility could act as a middleman, but the Northern Europeans are worried about the size of the potential price markup.

The final area of intense European interest has been West Africa: mainly Nigeria, and more recently Cameroon. (Geography makes it more sensible to export Middle Eastern LNG to Japan than to Europe.) During 1980 Nigeria signed contracts to deliver 784 million cubic feet per day to a large consortium of Belgian, French, Italian, Dutch, Spanish, and West German buyers starting in 1984 or 1985.[61] Because Nigeria flares off around 1.9 billion cubic feet per day—Europe's projected 1995 gas shortfall—this seemed an excellent prospect. Unfortunately, development of the Bonny project was delayed and now probably killed for the 1980s first by the reluctance of the United States to come to firm arrangements to buy an amount equal to that purchased by Western

Europe and then by quarrels over the plant between Nigeria and two oil companies, Phillips Petroleum and British Petroleum. The United States failed to grant regulatory approval to four utilities to import 833 million cubic feet per day of Nigerian gas, thereby excluding the United States from the first round of the Bonny project. With an estimated cost of $12 billion for the Bonny liquefaction plant, Nigeria at first allocated only about $555 million for its contribution during the first five years and told Western oil companies involved that they could move forward as rapidly as they wished. However, under Nigerian law these companies could own a total of only 40 percent of the plant but were being asked to commit a far higher percentage of the investment. Phillips Petroleum and then British Petroleum withdrew from the project during 1981. In early 1982 the Nigerian government refused to accept proposals from the remaining Bonny operators: Shell, Elf Aquitaine, and Agip. Although President Shagari is still voicing some optimism for Bonny's future, the Nigerian government announced an indefinite halt to LNG development in February 1982 to allow Nigeria to completely reformulate its natural gas export policies. LNG is not expected to be exported from Nigeria earlier than 1989 or 1990. In contrast, an LNG liquefaction plant with the capacity to export 500–600 million cubic feet per day is moving forward at Kribi, Cameroon. The project is being developed by Cameroon's national oil company, Mobil, Elf Aquitaine, Compagnie Française des Pétroles (CFP), and U.S. Shell's Pecten in equal partnership.[62] Unfortunately, there is some doubt about the adequacy of reserves to justify the project.

Uncertainties as to the Algerian and Nigerian supplies have therefore limited European enthusiasm for building ports of discharge. The Belgian reception terminal at Zeebrugge is proceeding, after delays, with a 400,000-cubic-meter storage capacity that should be capable of accepting 212 billion cubic feet per year if the Algerians can and will produce it.[63] However, the start-up date for the contract has already been postponed by two years, to 1984, and if shipments are ever resumed to the U.S. East Coast, it is doubtful that the Algerians would be capable of satisfying the agreement. The continuation of construction at Eemshaven in the Netherlands and Wilhelmsjaven in West Germany is the main basis for Northern European opposition to Algerian pipeline construction.

One group of analysts contended that pipelined gas could replace two 125,000-cubic-meter LNG carriers by 1982, eight by 1983, and ten by 1985, if the Segamo line to Spain and a second Italian line were built. The newly completed Transmediterranean pipeline can take 437.9 billion cubic feet per year now but could be upgraded to take 636 billion cubic feet per year.[64] In effect, European LNG is under serious threat not as in the United States from alternative supplies, but because the same supplies are too close to justify liquefaction. Moreover, opposition to LNG in Europe, although less vocal and less sustained than in the United States, is nonetheless present. Canvey Island's LNG terminal, although relatively small, has long been a cause of attacks on the Department of Environment in the U.K. Criticisms have grown more pointed as British requirements decline. Zeebrugge has also been a source of controversy.[65]

Certainly, other projects are possible at the correct distance, particularly if, as now seems unlikely, the Soviet deal should fail. The Japanese are studying prospects for imports from Chile by 1986. Qatar, particularly in light of giant new gas finds is also seen as a probable source of Japanese and European gas by the late 1980s. Although the possibility of all possible LNG projects coming on stream on schedule is remote and in any case would provide more than enough gas to make up for even the most dire predicted shortfalls, these projects provide insurance for Europe's energy planners.

Summary and Conclusions

In summary, delays and increasing project costs in the Western Hemisphere have made the outlook for LNG more pessimistic. In the Pacific the outlook is much brighter, and the day of offshore liquefaction plants for smaller quantities of gas does not seem far off.[66] Either way, the political and financial problems seem considerably greater than the environmental barriers. The United States, because of the richness of its resources and the internal strength of domestic producers and environmental lobbyists, seems likely to remain the most insular, least innovative long-haul gas trader. Security of supply, more than availability of supplies, has determined its new directions. Japanese policy is more coherent. Natural gas imports allow for diversification of dependence. The Japanese will continue to work on an entirely independent capacity to develop LNG projects with as much diversity of source and of resources as is practical. The Europeans are caught in between. Barring unexpected large finds in the North Sea or continued drops in demand, they need to develop close and long-haul gas supplies. National and sectoral competition complements regional energy integration to produce the entrepreneurial gas traders. Each project must prove to be economically viable because there are more prospects than may be necessary to provide natural gas between now and the end of the century. The Europeans are likely to explore as many possibilities as present themselves with the full knowledge that some of them will probably fail to develop for political, economic, or technical reasons. They are likely to concede higher returns to producing countries to keep them interested, but if most projects actually are successful, the possibility of a soft European gas market could lead to keeping producer demands in line.

Corporations involved in the production, transmission, and distribution of natural gas need smooth linkages among themselves, but they also compete feverishly with each other to gain an advantage. Producers of cheaper reserves and those that exploit "deep" or more expensive deposits are often at odds on pricing. In the United States, interstate and intrastate pipelines actively compete for supplies at predictable prices. Pipelines also compete with tankers carrying LNG. Utilities compete for adequate supplies. And each group competes with every other. A second reason to expect that Japan would be at one end of the spectrum of gas importers and the United States at the other is to recall the relationships between business and governments. In Japan the government makes decisions in consultation with business, in cooperation with business, but ultimately on the basis of national interest. The market, even with substantial regulations, is far more dominant in the United States. Domestic producers and pipelines have, for the most part, been able to align themselves with other groups hesitant about LNG to reinforce the domestic bias of U.S. gas producers. Europe, again, is somewhere in between.

Yet, if the natural gas trade is to become an integrated world trade instead of a series of bilateral bargains during this century, then greater cooperation among governments and corporations will be necessary. For example, the United States might have been more successful in discouraging Europe from contracting to buy pipelined Soviet gas had it actively become involved in the Bonny, Nigeria, project and helped to prevent its deferral. If the United States had provided financial muscle, an assured market, and consistent support for West African LNG, European prospects for receiving gas from Nigeria and Cameroon in this decade would have been much improved and hastened. However, the short-term prospects are that the three separate markets will proceed with their natural gas import projects independently. World energy markets are becoming more complex as a result.

Notes

1. For a brief survey of the creation of a world gas market see Hanns W. Maull, *Natural Gas and Economic Security* (Paris: Atlantic Institute for International Affairs, 1981), pp. 16–18.

2. LNG carriers are generally tailored for specific trade routes and cannot be used on others unless expensive alterations are undertaken. This is partly due to the composition of the gas, but it also is linked to the physical structure

of the export and import facilities. For instance, Algerian gas is side-loaded, while LNG from Brunei bound for Japan is stern-loaded. New projects have consistently chosen to construct new carriers rather than chartering and revamping laid-up LNG carriers. However, careful planning and the development of smaller import terminals promise to increase flexibility within the LNG trade.

3. Albert Anguilo, "Liquefied Natural Gas Systems," in Norman A. White (ed.), *Financing the International Petroleum Industry* (London: Graham & Trotman Ltd., 1978), pp. 125–137.

4. Substantial differences exist within the natural gas industry on policy questions, particularly relating to domestic pricing. Most gas producers, except those specializing in "deep" gas or heavily committed to the proposed Alaskan gas pipeline, want high prices at the wellhead and favor immediate price deregulation. Interstate and intrastate pipelines are brokers between producers and users. They are usually more concerned about disruptions in demand than with the gas supply outlook. Because price increases could promote conservation, curtail gas shipments, and thereby devastate them, most pipelines oppose early deregulations of gas prices. On a deeper level, *interstate* pipelines generally offer cautious support for the current Natural Gas Policy Act of 1978 (NGPA-78) pricing schedules. Many *intrastate* pipelines, in contrast, depend on more expensive gas that they bought on long-term contracts before 1978. These firms support the NGPA-78 schedules more strongly because deregulation could make it difficult for them to purchase and supply gas competitively. Rapid price deregulation might allow for a reversal of the pre-1978 situation. Interstate lines, bolstered by their cheap, long-term contracts, could ensure supplies for their customers while consumers in Texas, Oklahoma, and Louisiana might have supply problems as intrastate pipelines faltered. Utilities, which are always concerned with gas availability and demand, are generally hesitant to see prices rise too quickly. They fear that higher prices would lead to greater conservation and leave them with surplus capacity to produce electricity, restrict their revenues, and force the already reeling industry into further adjustments. Even outside the industry major differences persist. For instance, conservationists and environmental groups conceive a world in which less natural gas will be necessary. Many such groups favor rapid price deregulation (accompanied by windfall-profit taxes) to encourage a more rapid arrival of their vision. In contrast, consumer groups and organized labor bitterly oppose tampering with the NGPA-78 guidelines, which would control most gas prices until January 1, 1985.

5. Exxon, "World Energy Outlook," Exxon Background Series, December 1980, p. 31.

6. See, for instance, Carroll Wilson (ed.), *Energy: Global Prospects 1985–2000,* Report of the Workshop on Alternative Energy Strategies (New York: McGraw-Hill, 1977), pp. 147–166; and Bankers Trust, *U.S. Energy and Capital: A Forecast 1980–1990* (New York: Bankers Trust, 1980).

7. A. A. Meyerhoff, *Proved and Ultimate Reserves of Natural Gas Liquids in the World* (Tulsa, Okla.: Meyerhoff & Cox, 1979). By contrast, Michael Halbouty, a senior Reagan energy adviser, estimated that just under 40 percent

of remaining U.S. petroleum reserves remain undiscovered. Michael Halbouty and John Moody, "World Ultimate Reserves of Crude Oil," cited in B. A. Rahmer, "New Assessment of Resources," *Petroleum Economist,* December 1980, p. 501.

8. For a summary introduction to synfuels see *The Role of Synthetic Fuels in the United States Energy Future* (Houston: Exxon, no date); "Blessing or Boondoggle? The $88 Billion Quest for Synthetic Fuels," *New York Times,* September 21, 1980; *The Pros and Cons of a Crash Program to Commercialize Synfuels,* Report prepared for the Subcommittee on Energy Development and Applications of the Committee on Science and Technology, U.S. House of Representatives, 96th Cong., 2nd sess., February 1980.

9. Congressional Quarterly, *Energy Policy,* 1st ed. (Washington, D.C.: Congressional Quarterly, Inc., April 1979), pp. 67–68.

10. Richard James, "Alaskan Gas Pipeline Promoters Ask: 'Buddy, Could You Spare $22 Billion?' " *Wall Street Journal,* July 2, 1981, p. 10. By April 1982 the projected costs of the Alaskan segment had escalated to $27 billion and the future of the project was in doubt. "Alaska's Gas Pipeline Faces a Deep Freeze," *Business Week,* May 3, 1982, p. 39.

11. Canadian gas producers in Alberta, in contrast, favored selling their gas to the United States because Ottawa insisted that inter-Canadian sales prices remain at artificially low levels. However the temporary settlement of the Alberta-Ottawa price squabble and the prospects for an indefinite delay in the Alaskan portion of the gas pipeline bode well for steady and perhaps even increased gas exports to the United States into the late 1980s. "Alberta and Ottawa Stop Firing," *Economist,* September 5, 1981, p. 64; *Petroleum Intelligence Weekly,* June 1, 1981, p. 9.

12. See "Canadian Energy Policy Slowing Action," *Oil & Gas Journal,* December 22, 1980, pp. 36–37; "Wildcat Canada Resigns from the World," *Economist,* November 1, 1980. However, although Canadian oil and gas exports to the United States could fall during the 1980s, Robert Bourassa, former prime minister of Quebec (1970–1976), believes that the James Bay hydroelectric facility could export up to 10,000 megawatts a year to New England when completed. Talk at the University of Southern California, Los Angeles, March 11, 1981.

13. Jose Puenta Leyva, "The Natural Gas Controversy," in Susan Kaufman Purcell (ed.), *Mexico-United States Relations,* Proceedings of the Academy of Political Science, vol. 34, no. 1 (New York: Academy of Political Science, 1981), pp. 158–167; "Mexico-U.S. Deal Expected Soon on Doubled Gas Supply," *Petroleum Intelligence Weekly,* January 11, 1982, p. 3.

14. Note that the LNG business is not confined to trade. The United States is dotted with more than seventy LNG peak-shaving facilities designed to liquefy and store natural gas in the summer for use as needed during the winter. These are particularly useful in the Northeast, where the inability to pump sufficient gas through the two pipelines feeding the region resulted in severe shortages during the winter of 1980–1981.

15. Lists are in *Pipeline & Gas Journal,* November 1980, pp. 21–25.

16. Annual reports, The Cabot Corporation.

17. Figures from J. G. Seay, P. J. Anderson, and E. J. Daniels, "LNG Base-load Projects Continue to Grow," *Oil & Gas Journal,* December 18, 1978, pp. 70–81.

18. Alexander Stuart, "El Paso in the Grip of the Frozen Fuel," *Fortune,* July 14, 1980, p. 71.

19. E. F. Shumaker, "Ship-to-Ship Transfer of LNG, the *El Paso Paul Kayser/ El Paso Sonatrach* Gas Transfer Operation," *Gastech Houston: Proceedings Gastech 79 LNG/LPG Conference* (Rickmansworth Herts.: Gastech Ltd., 1980), pp. 173–175.

20. "Qatar: Gas Reserves Pose Some Problems," *Financial Times,* February 22, 1979, p. 24; Lee N. Davis, *Frozen Fire* (San Francisco: Friends of the Earth, 1979), pp. 279–280.

21. According to Seay, Anderson, and Daniels, "LNG Base-load Projects," as of late 1978 two projects providing LNG to the United States were in the planning stages and thirteen more were being considered. If all these had actually been brought on-line, LNG would have provided about 5 Tcf per year, a quarter of U.S. natural gas usage in the early 1980s.

22. Fereidun Fesharaki alerted us to this argument.

23. Gas prices are generally quoted in dollars per million Btus. To obtain the equivalent price per thousand cubic feet, multiply by 0.914913.

24. The Distrigas and Lake Charles projects have continued to progress in large part because the Algerians are responsible for the delivery of the LNG to U.S. ports and do not pass ownership to the importers at the flange in Algeria as is the case with the El Paso projects. The Distrigas and Lake Charles projects link LNG prices to No. 2 and No. 6 heating oil in New York.

25. Alexander Stuart, "El Paso Comes in from the Cold," *Fortune,* March 23, 1981, pp. 55–56. For further information on the disarray in LNG markets in 1981 see Jeffrey Segal, "LNG Market: Pricing Structure in Disarray," *Petroleum Economist,* December 1981, pp. 517–520.

26. "Algeria Wins Record Price for Its LNG from Belgium, Including Link to Oil Cost," *Wall Street Journal,* April 9, 1981, p. 26; "Algeria Wins Chief Goals in Gas Deal with France," *Petroleum Intelligence Weekly,* February 8, 1982, p. 5; "Algerian LNG to Be Shipped to Panhandle," *Journal of Commerce,* August 10, 1982; "Algeria's Low Gas Price Looks High in U.S.," *Business Week,* August 23, 1982, p. 27. Consolidated withdrew on November 1, 1982.

27. Chris Cragg, "Liquefied Gas Report," *Seatrade,* November 1980, pp. 137, 149. Indeed, when LNG carriers have needed repairs, even if the problem was not connected to the LNG storage tanks, most ports have been reluctant to harbor damaged vessels. However, as of March 1982 the last of the environmental issues, the seismic question, was close to resolution.

28. See "Reagan to Settle Synthetic Fuels Dispute: Budget Director, Energy Chief at Odds on $3.5-Billion Projects," *Los Angeles Times,* July 23, 1981, Part I, p. 6. Also see Chapter 6 in this volume on types of government support that might stimulate synfuel production.

29. Robert Kalisch, "The Outlook for International Trade in Natural Gas,"

in Joy Dunkerly (ed.), *International Energy Strategies* (Cambridge, Mass.: Oelgeschlager, Gunn, & Hain, 1980), p. 401.

30. Henry R. Linden, "What Really Limits Gas Supply?" *Pipeline & Gas Journal,* May 1980, p. 17. About 50 percent of oil produced worldwide is being traded; only about 15 percent of natural gas is traded.

31. The Reagan administration is following policies of the sort advocated by Edmund Faltermeyer, "How to Stop Worrying About Natural Gas," *Fortune,* August 1977, pp. 156–170. The fate of other energy projects and sources may be indicated by Eliot Marshall, " 'Black Book' Threatens Synfuels Projects," *Science,* February 27, 1981, p. 100.

32. Exxon, "World Energy Outlook," December 1980, p. 35.

33. N. Proess, *LNG World Overview* (London: Gotaas-Larsen Shipping Corporation, January 1, 1981), is an indispensable collection of statistics on LNG price and quantity.

34. Seay, Anderson, and Daniels, "LNG Base-load Projects"; and "Firms Mull Thai Gas Liquefaction Export Project," *Oil & Gas Journal,* September 7, 1981.

35. M.W.H. Peebles, *The Evolution of the Gas Industry* (London: Macmillan, 1980), pp. 104–111.

36. In early 1982 the French price actually exceeded the Japanese price, but this was anomalous.

37. For some of the complexities see M.W.H. Peebles, "International Trade in Natural Gas with Particular Reference to LNG," London, Institute of Gas Engineers, 1981.

38. Henri Hyams, "Japan Wins Export Deal with Indonesia," *Seatrade,* April 1981, p. 57; Segal, "LNG Market," p. 520.

39. Private discussions with one of the authors.

40. Due to the oil surplus the British National Oil Company and Norwegian North Sea oil producers dropped their prices by $4.25 and $4.00 per barrel respectively in June 1981. It was the first ever decline in their prices. The market continued to soften in early 1982.

41. This is calculated as follows: 450 million cubic feet per day scheduled for delivery to Lake Charles, Louisiana, plus 120 million cubic feet per day being delivered to Distrigas near Boston, plus 1 billion cubic feet per day sold to El Paso for its two projects.

42. See Proess, *LNG World Overview,* for a list of the various Japanese consortia.

43. Note, for instance, that when three LNG carriers built in the Avondale yards in the United States failed to meet specifications, the only yard that anyone believed might be able to correct the difficulties was Mitsubishi's.

44. Henri Hyams, "Japan Wins Export Deal."

45. The master of the *LNG Taurus* shot himself when his vessel ran aground off Japan. The vessel was subsequently floated off without difficulty. "Grounded LNG Ship's Master Kills Himself," *Lloyd's List,* December 16, 1980.

46. Exxon, "World Energy Outlook," December 1980, pp. 32–33.

47. Peter F. Cowhey, *The Problems of Plenty: Energy Policy and International Politics* (Berkeley: University of California Press, forthcoming), Chapter 8.

48. Ibid.

49. "An $116 Billion Hostage to Fortune," *Financial Times,* December 16, 1980.

50. P. W. Tucker and C. Timms, *European Gas Prospects* (London: Phillips Petroleum, 1980). This estimate includes contracted Algerian, Libyan, and Soviet supplies as well as indigenous gas but may not take into account the recent massive Norwegian discoveries in the "golded block" or the alternative attractions of liquefied petroleum gas. Energy growth of 1.75 percent is assumed.

51. "Banks Want Backing on Pipeline Project," *Seatrade,* June 1981, pp. 57–59.

52. Before the North Sea reference price fell by $4.25 per barrel, British Petroleum was reportedly losing $6 million per week on downstream refining due to use of indigenous resources.

53. The U.K. gas-gathering system took three years to plan. During that time cost escalations raised the price from $11.1 billion to $12.7 billion and finally to $15 billion, while the line itself was shortened. When the British government withdrew from the project, private companies offered their own alternatives. Robert Steve, "U.K. North Sea Tips 1.8 Million b/d," *Offshore,* June 20, 1981, pp. 115–119; "North Sea Firms Not Sorry to See UK Gas Plan Killed," *Petroleum Intelligence Weekly,* September 21, 1981, p. 6; "N. Sea Oil Groups Plan Major Gas Pipeline Network," *Financial Times,* October 12, 1981, p. 1.

54. "A Gas-Export Plan for Western Europe," *World Business Weekly,* June 22, 1981, p. 16. Other consortium members include West Germany's Thyssengas, BEB (Shell and Esso), and BP Deutsche, Belgium's Distrigas, the Dutch Gasunie, and Gas de France.

55. "Progress Resumes on the Soviet Gas Pipeline to Western Eurpe," *World Business Weekly,* June 29, 1981, pp. 15–16.

56. Robert Campbell, "Soviet Technology Imports: The Gas Pipeline Case," Discussion Paper No. 91, California Seminar on International Security and Foreign Policy, Santa Monica, Calif., February 1981.

57. "Soviet Union Pipeline Suppliers Line Up for $8 Billion," *Business Week,* August 10, 1981, pp. 36–37.

58. "Italy to Purchase Natural Gas from the Soviets," *Wall Street Journal,* October 16, 1981, p. 31; "European Buyers Favoring Soviets' Gas Pricing 'Concept'," *Petroleum Intelligence Weekly,* October 26, 1981, p. 3; "Soviet-German Deal Sets Gas Price Floor at $5.40 in Marks," *Petroleum Intelligence Weekly,* December 7, 1981, p. 5; "France Gets Terms It Wanted for Soviet Gas Contract," *Petroleum Intelligence Weekly,* February 1, 1982, pp. 42–43.

59. "Bonn's Soviet Gas Deal: A Pipeline or a Pipe Dream?" *Business Week,* July 13, 1981, pp. 42–43.

60. "Gas Export Policy Gets Its Big Rethink," *Petroleum Economist,* August 1980, pp. 347–348.

61. "Nigerian Gas Negotiations Nearing Completion," *Seatrade,* April 1980, pp. 39–41; Jeffrey Segal, "LNG Market: Slower Growth for the 1980s," *Petroleum Economist,* December 1980, p. 515.

62. "Bonny Delayed by Lack of Funds," *Seatrade,* March 1981, p. 59; "Nigeria Defers LNG Indefinitely But Cameroon Persists," *Petroleum Intelligence Weekly,* February 8, 1982, p. 6.

63. "Zeebrugge's Expansion Plans Under Attack," *Seatrade,* February 1981, pp. 107–109.

64. *LNG Shipping in the Eighties* (London: H. P. Drewry Shipping Consultants, June 1980), p. 15.

65. U.K. Health and Safety Executive, *Canvey Island* (London: HMSO, 1978); "British Gas Caught in Planning Trap," *Seatrade,* April 1981, pp. 57–59.

66. Pertamina is now tendering for a floating liquefaction plant. "Liquefying Research Offshore Payoff," *Seatrade,* January 1981, p. 55.

3
The World Coal Trade in the 1980s: The Rebirth of a Market

Michael Gaffen

This chapter examines the factors shaping the future of the world coal trade. I postulate that the expansion of the world coal industry poses risks for both buyers and sellers due to the long lead times for development, coal's previously shrinking share of the world energy market, and the need for elaborate investments in new transportation infrastructure. Accordingly, new coal supplies will be developed only if strong and persistent signals from governments and customers encourage new investment.

Although neither corporations nor governments have been paragons of consistency concerning energy investments in recent years, as constraints on the use of oil and gas increase and delays and uncertainties cloud the future of nuclear power, coal can assume a growing role in the world energy market at very competitive prices. This reflects the fact that all major parties in the world energy market recognize that coal reserves constitute 80 percent of the world's reserves of all technically and economically recoverable fossil fuels; the United States's coal reserves alone contain the energy equivalent of oil reserves five times larger than those held by OPEC nations.

The composition of the world's energy supplies and consumption has changed significantly since the Arab oil embargo of 1973. In 1973 oil and gas together composed approximately two-thirds of the total world energy supply, and their share of the market was on an upswing. But developments in the Middle East throughout the 1970s caused the major energy-consuming nations to shift away from dependence on Middle Eastern supplies.

Besides rigorous conservation measures to curb the growth in demand for energy, especially oil, the chief alternatives to imported oil were natural gas, nuclear energy, renewable resources, and coal. The use of natural gas grew at a rate almost comparable to that of oil prior to 1972, but it has begun to slow down since then. Problems associated with the financing, marketing, and pricing of gas, especially gas traded on world markets, are likely to constrain the expansion of gas consumption.

Nuclear energy has made a substantial contribution to the supply of electricity in some industrialized countries. But it has suffered, especially since the late 1970s, from well-publicized environmental and siting setbacks. Since the mid-1970s, the choice of fuel for new power plants in major industrialized countries has been primarily coal or nuclear energy. Political uncertainties and a decline in public confidence in the safety of nuclear power have impaired rapid growth of nuclear energy. Thus, shortfalls in expected nuclear power development will provide an opportunity for steam coal to further penetrate the electric utility market.

Renewable energy sources, which include hydroelectric power, geothermal resources, and solar energy, collectively provided approximately 5 percent of world energy supplies in the fifteen years prior to the 1973 embargo. Their share of world energy supplies is expected to be approximately the same in the 1980s and 1990s. Additions to supplies to meet growing world energy needs from hydropower and geothermal resources will be limited to their geographic sites; the pace of solar energy's contribution will be restricted by the rate at which new technology becomes economic and penetrates various parts of the energy market.

Already, important changes have surfaced in the world coal trade in response to the energy crisis. Before 1973 international trade in coal was dominated by metallurgical coal (used primarily for producing coke in steel mills); the demand for steam coal imports (suitable for electricity generation or industrial boilers in factories) was insignificant. But by the end of the 1970s the use of steam coal had increased as major industrial nations began to substitute coal for oil and gas in electric power plants and industrial facilities. This has prompted a revival of the world trade in steam coal and has formed the basis for predicting a sharp increase in the total size of the international coal market.

This chapter examines the probability that reality will live up to the predictions of a boom in the world coal trade. Many coal studies emphasize the competition for markets between fuels or the environmental constraints hampering the use of coal, but I shall stress the problem of managing risk in a market that does not always fit the models of the economics textbooks. The future expansion of the market depends on finding flexible responses to these risks.

TABLE 1
World Coal Reserves (Billions of short tons)

Country	Billion Tons[a]
Australia	39.6
Canada	4.2
China	109.1
India	13.9
Poland	61.8
South Africa	43.9
United Kingdom	49.6
United States	284.2
Soviet Union	160.9
West Germany	34.6
Other Countries	58.2
Total World	860.0

Source: Report of the World Energy Conference on Energy Resources (London, 1980).

a. Coal equivalent, or technically and economically recoverable reserves. Includes anthracite and bituminous coal.

The argument of this chapter unfolds in four parts. The first part sketches out which nations plan to become significant importers of coal and which countries are likely to dominate the export side of the market. The second part focuses on the prospects of exports from the United States in order to show how the interrelated problems of transportation and contract guarantees influence the future. The third part then suggests how the companies operating on the coal market are changing and what types of new trading relationships must emerge in order to minimize risk. The fourth part summarizes the argument by distinguishing the major types of risks and their prospective solutions.

An Overview of the World Coal Market

Table 1 sets the stage by indicating the coal reserves held by the key nations. As the industrialized countries increasingly move to steam coal to fuel new electric power and industrial facilities, the world steam coal market could grow from the 1980 level of 85 million tons to 160 million tons by 1985. (Tons are short tons unless otherwise specified.) It could further increase to more than 500 million tons by the year

2000, as illustrated in Figure 1. Total world coal trade (primarily metallurgical coal) totaled 270 million tons in 1980. (See Figure 2.)

An assessment of the international energy market indicates that the major industrial coal-importing countries in Western Europe will be France, Italy, West Germany, Spain, Denmark, and the Netherlands. Projected steam coal imports for 1980 through 2000 are shown in Figure 3. The United Kingdom will probably remain self-sufficient in coal through the end of the century. The major coal importers in the Pacific Rim will be Japan, Korea, Taiwan, Hong Kong, and Singapore. The energy policies of the larger countries require a brief evaluation before the prospects for the coal trade are analyzed in detail.

France concentrated on an ambitious nuclear program in the 1970s but recently reversed its plans for a rapid phaseout of most domestic coal use. For example, France has encouraged the conversion of state-owned electric power plants to coal and has plans for several new coal-fired power plants. Nonetheless, French use of coal could remain stable unless governmental energy policy is changed. Coal consumption will amount to about 50 million tons annually through the end of the 1980s; but during this period coal imports will increase as domestic production continues to decline. France plans to import coal from non-European countries only after it exhausts domestic production and those supplies negotiated with other European countries. The French were the largest importers of U.S. steam coal in 1980 and have shown strong interest in increasing purchases of U.S. coal in the future.

West Germany has traditionally subsidized a large domestic coal industry. However, the government has approved proposals to promote increases in coal-fired electricity generation, including the granting of import licenses to allow electric utilities to import incremental coal requirements. Germany has also announced that it will not license new oil-fired plants and will phase out those now in service. Increased coal use in industrial plants and plans for coal gasification and liquefaction may account for an additional demand of 10 million tons annually by 1990. The government has liberalized import quotas on coal for electric power generation and industrial use, which will become progressively larger during the 1980s and 1990s.

By 1990 the government of Japan, which imports all its oil, expects to import significant levels of steam coal because of its ban on the construction of new oil-fired plants and its requirement for the conversion of oil-fired plants, when possible, to either coal or liquefied natural gas. Japan is already the largest coal importer in the world, with metallurgical coal making up the bulk of its imports. Government plans to produce synthetic oil from coal and the use of coal-oil mixtures also will require additional coal imports. In the near term, industrial applications (such

FIGURE 1

World Steam Coal Trade

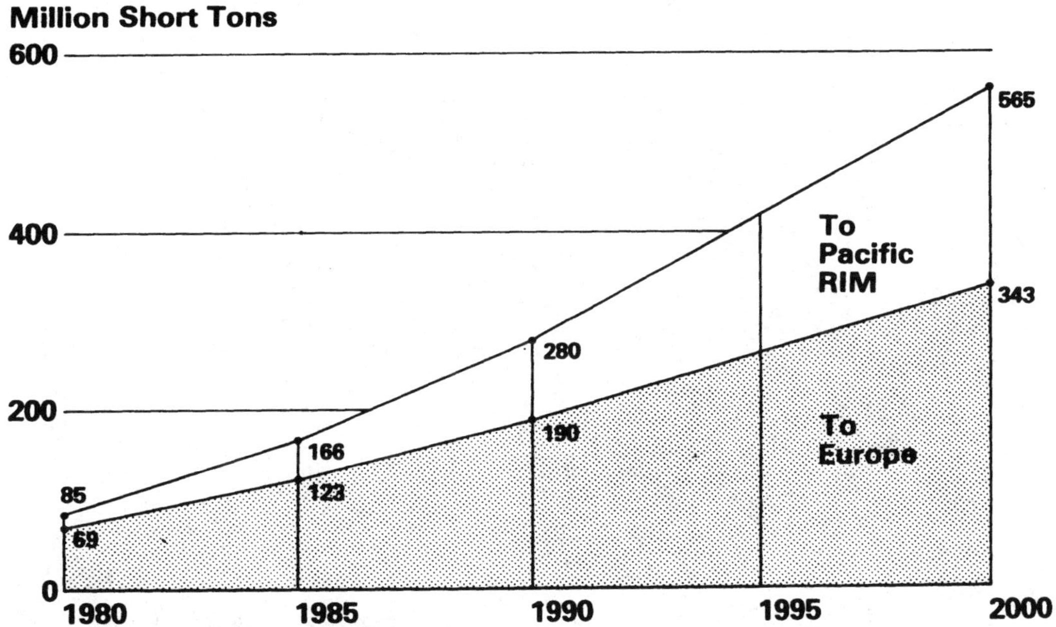

Source: U.S. Department of Energy, Interagency Coal Export Task Force, *Interim Report of the Interagency Coal Export Task Force* (Washington, D.C.: Government Printing Office, January 1981) (DOE/FE-0012).

FIGURE 2

World Coal Exports and Imports by Countries 1980

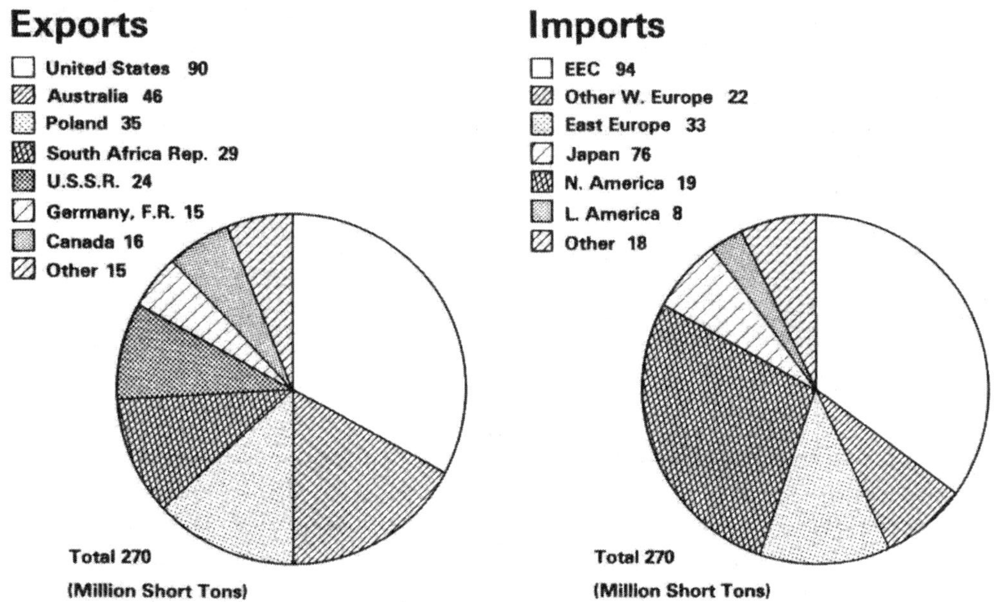

Source: U.S. Department of Energy, Interagency Coal Export Task Force, *Interim Report of the Interagency Coal Export Task Force* (Washington, D.C.: Government Printing Office, January 1981) (DOE/FE-0012).

FIGURE 3

World Steam Coal Imports

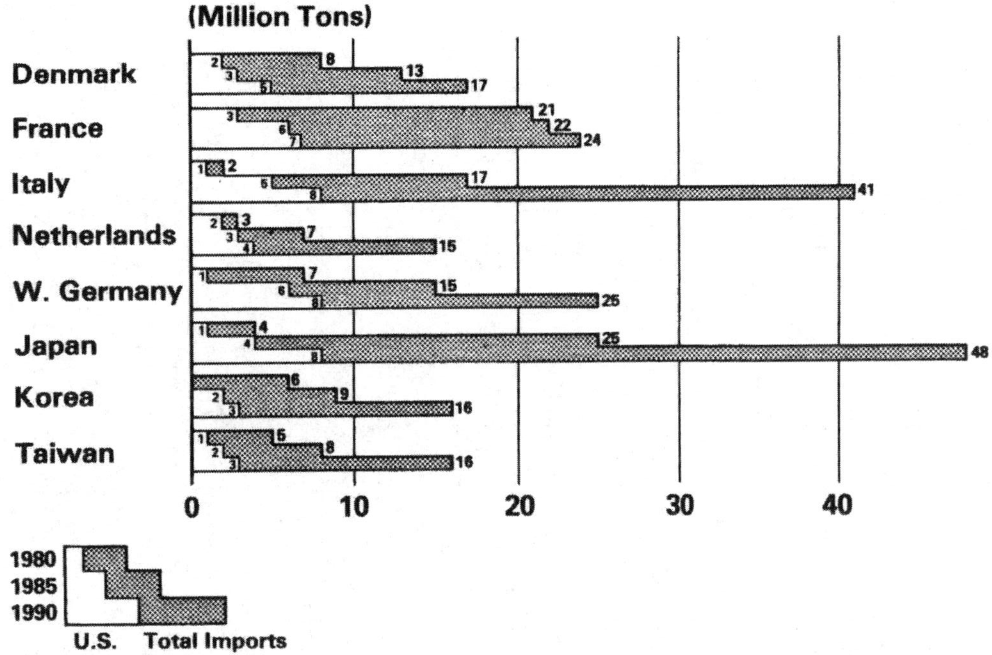

Source: U.S. Department of Energy, Interagency Coal Export Task Force, *Interim Report of the Interagency Coal Export Task Force* (Washington, D.C.: Government Printing Office, January 1981) (DOE/FE-0012).

as the conversion of cement plants, and of pulp and paper mills, from oil to coal) will also be important.

Japan's hope of limiting coal imports from any single exporting nation to one third of imports indicates that the Japanese business will be spread across several nations. But there may be a substantial lag in achieving the target for diversification. By 1990 about 40 percent of Japan's steam coal imports may come from Australia; the United States will hold roughly 20 percent of the market. Unless Japan is willing to rely on Australia for an even larger share of imports (an unlikely event given Japan's concern about Australian labor troubles), a further expansion of imports will accrue to the United States.

These examples of industrial countries demonstrate a valid basis for anticipating significant increases in foreign demand for coal. The United States has the largest accessible coal reserves of any country in the world and up to one-third of the world's economically and technically recoverable coal. However, competition with U.S. coal (primarily from South Africa, Poland, and Australia and, to a lesser extent, from China and Canada) may be formidable. (See Figure 4.)

South Africa is probably the only developed market economy fueled primarily by coal. In 1980 coal met almost 80 percent of its total primary energy needs. Eighty-five percent of its coal-mining operations are underground, but the share of surface mining has been increasing steadily as labor costs grow. SASOL, the world's only commercial coal liquefaction program, operates in South Africa.

South Africa has traditionally exported small quantities of coal. Until 1973, total annual exports were about 1.5 million tons, of which more than half was anthracite. By 1980, some 2.2 million tons of anthracite and 27 million tons of bituminous coal were exported, totaling 21 percent of the 112 million tons of total production.

This expansion of coal exports was made possible by the opening of a new coal terminal at Richards Bay—one of the world's most modern facilities, able to handle vessels with a capacity of 150,000 deadweight tons (dwt) at a loading rate of 6,500 dwt per hour. It is believed that large bulk carriers, up to 250,000 dwt-capacity vessels, could be serviced. Richards Bay is connected to the Transvaal coal-producing region by a railroad line built exclusively to service the port.

Despite favorable transportation factors, long-term government export policy is unclear. Given South Africa's national dependence on coal, future coal exports may be limited for energy security reasons. The government has not defined long-term strategy but has not erected any barriers to coal export trade.

Due to its geographic proximity to European clients and its low-cost coal, Poland could also challenge U.S. coal exports to Europe. Poland

FIGURE 4

World Steam Coal Exports

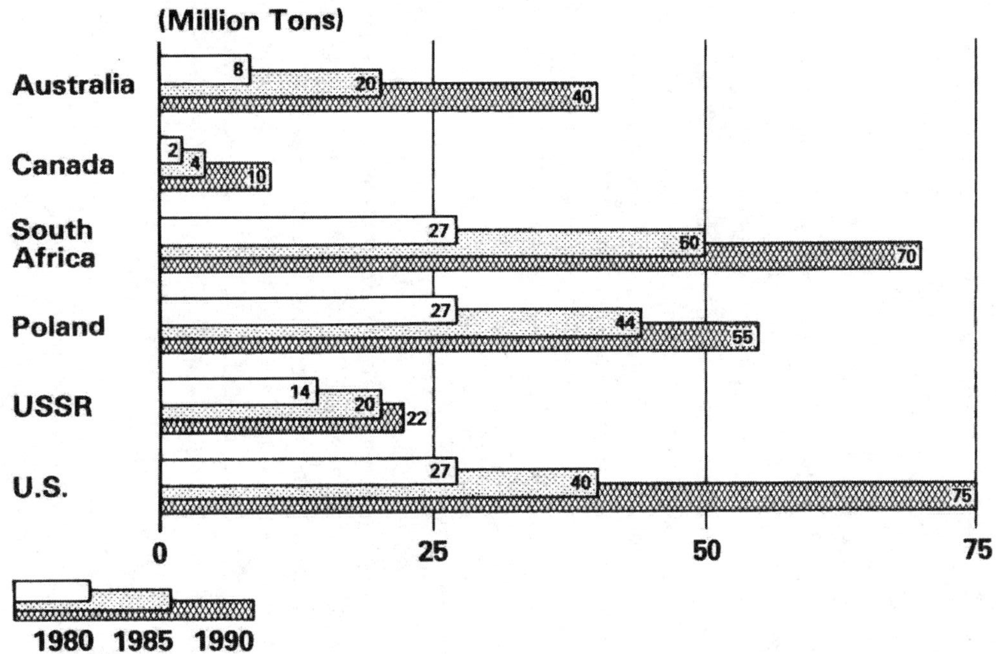

Source: U.S. Department of Energy, Interagency Coal Export Task Force, *Interim Report of the Interagency Coal Export Task Force* (Washington, D.C.: Government Printing Office, January 1981) (DOE/FE-0012).

possesses extensive, developed bituminous coal deposits in addition to lignite deposits that are not yet fully exploited. A major steam coal supplier to Western Europe, Poland exported about 20 percent of its production in 1979. Plans for expanded production of bituminous coal (both coking and steam), if realized, could support an export volume at the 1979 level until at least 1990. To finance the construction of additional production capacity and the necessary infrastructure, the Polish authorities have required financial participation by potential buyers. This would promote a shift toward longer-term contracts. However, due to the uncertain labor situation since mid-1979, many buyers doubt that Poland can be looked to for significant new volumes of coal exports. In addition, Poland may increasingly divert its coal to the energy-short Eastern European nations.

Two other countries often mentioned as potential exporters, China and Canada, are also unlikely to play a dominant role in the world market. China presently produces approximately 450 million tons of coal per year, almost all of which is consumed internally. However, with substantial investments (in a country hard pressed for capital), China could become a net exporter of coal during this century. Canada has substantial coal reserves and has just completed modern coal ports in Western Canada. Although Canada is expected to be an exporter of coal, especially to the Pacific Rim, its total volume of supply will not allow it to rival Australia or the United States. Moreover, it will continue to import some types of coal from the United States.

The principal competitor for the United States is Australia. The United States exported about 3 percent of its steam coal in 1980 (if shipments to Canada are included). In the same year, Australia supplied 85 percent of the imports of the Pacific Rim by exporting more than 50 percent of its steam coal production. Although more than 75 percent of its exports went to Japan, Australia has recently embarked on a policy aimed at diversifying its market, a tactic that current market conditions make feasible. Its export drive is assisted by the fact that Australia's coal has a low sulfur content, thus reducing the cost of pollution-control equipment for utilities.

Australian exporters do have some problems. The long distance separating Australia from Europe is an inherent economic disadvantage. As bunker fuel costs increased significantly after 1974, Australian coal exports to Europe suffered. Moreover, the railroad network must be revamped and expanded and the port infrastructure must be modified if greatly increased coal volumes are to be transported. Presently some 60 million tons per year of throughput capacity exists in Australian coal ports. The port in New South Wales (the only Australian region that exports steam coal) is inadequate for servicing ships of more than

50,000 dwt; but almost all Australian coking coal exports to Europe have been shipped from Hay Point in Queensland, a modern coal port and terminal that can handle 120,000-dwt ships.

In summary, through 1985 inadequate transportation and port capacity could threaten the competitive position of Australian steam coal in European markets. But Australia should complete its infrastructure expansion. In the late 1980s Australia then could support the growing demand for coal in the Pacific Rim, at least through 2000, retain its market share, and continue to supply low-sulfur, high-heating-value coal.

Given the strengths of the Australian industry, what are the prospects for the United States? In 1980 the United States had a cost disadvantage in the delivered price of steam coal to Europe and Japan. (See Figure 5.) Given the size of its reserves, however, the United States has an advantage in its ability to provide any reasonably expected volume of coal in the mid-term; other suppliers may be limited in terms of export levels. In 1980, it exported 92 million tons of coal, 40 percent higher than its 1979 level. In 1981 U.S. coal exports set another record, 112 million tons. By the year 2000 its share of the world market could be 40 percent. But this growth depends on the United States's developing its transportation and handling infrastructure in a manner geared to increase the efficiency of coal transportation and perhaps lower the per-ton delivered costs to the importers. These challenges are examined in the next section.

Domestic Factors Affecting U.S. Capacity to Meet Export Demand

It has become commonplace to doubt the ability of the United States to capitalize on its potential advantages in the world energy market. Certainly, many have argued that the United States is entirely too optimistic about its future role in the world coal market. They particularly point to the fact that U.S. coal exports are more expensive than those of its competitors. However, I am cautiously optimistic about U.S. prospects. In this section I first argue that the fundamentals influencing production costs favor the United States over the long term. The problems, I then suggest, pertain to the complexities of transportation. On this score there may be no single "right answer" for forecasting. The United States may have great success in upgrading some transportation capabilities and the mines they serve while it stumbles badly in regard to others.

If one compares the costs of new deep- and surface-mined coal in the United States with those of their competitive counterparts overseas,

FIGURE 5

Delivered Costs of Coal

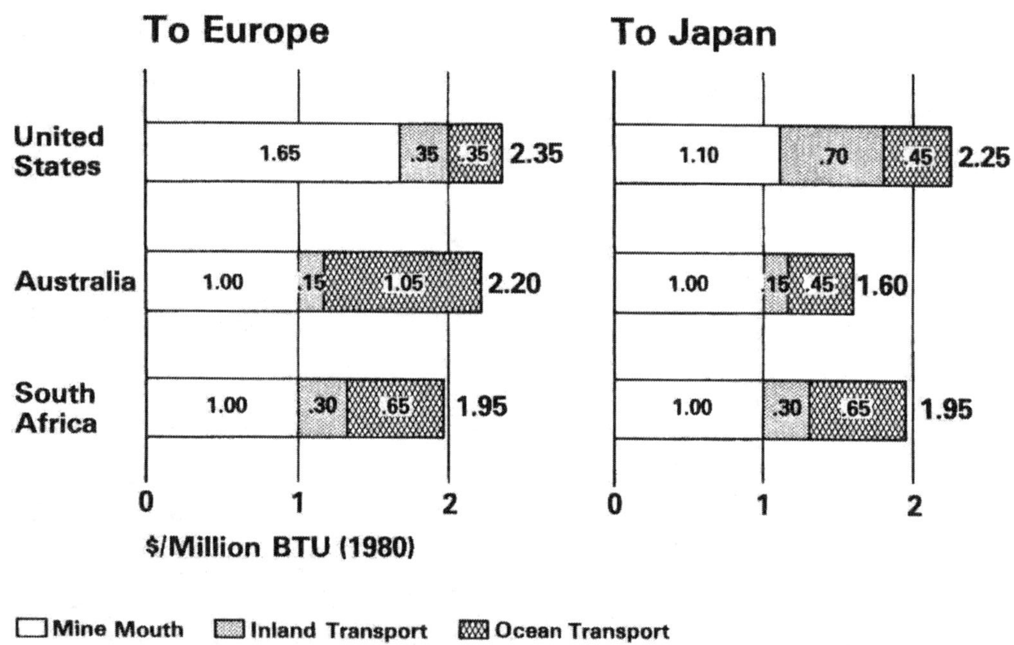

Source: U.S. Department of Energy, Interagency Coal Export Task Force, *Interim Report of the Interagency Coal Export Task Force* (Washington, D.C.: Government Printing Office, January 1981) (DOE/FE-0012).

the cost of mining coal does not vary significantly from country to country. U.S. mining costs are not sufficiently higher than those of its competitors to exclude the United States from any major market. Indeed, one could plausibly argue that it will have a marked advantage someday. The United States is more advanced, relative to other coal exporters, in the application of health, safety, and environmental regulations in the mining, storage, and shipment of coal. During the 1980s other coal-producing countries will probably duplicate U.S. regulations, thereby driving their mining costs up to a point equal to, or higher than, those in the United States. Nonetheless, the overseas delivered cost of U.S. coal in 1980 exceeded that of its competitors because of transportation costs.

Coal is a relatively low value bulk commodity with relatively high transportation costs. The major cost differences are related to distances traveled inland, together with cost related to transportation, port handling, and overseas shipping inefficiencies. Historically, total U.S. coal exports have not exceeded 10 percent of domestic consumption. Moreover, most of the U.S. infrastructure for transport, port facilities, and shipping has been designed for metallurgical coal, which historically has constituted the lion's share of U.S. coal exports; steam coal shipments overseas have been insignificant. This infrastructure cannot accommodate a significant expansion of U.S. steam coal exports without major improvement.

The principal complaints of foreign buyers with respect to U.S. coal costs center on three areas of transportation and handling. The first relates to the cost of overland transportation from the mine to the port. Critics contend that failure to use "unit trains" of about 100 cars to transport coal to the ports results in inefficiencies. However, the use of such trains is impractical in some cases, especially in the Appalachian region, because coal shipments must be assembled from a number of mines and because existing coal ports cannot unload and discharge a unit train quickly.

A second complaint concerns loading delays at U.S. coal ports, which resulted in high demurrage charges during late 1979 to early 1980, at their peak equal to the total transport cost to Europe, or about $15 per ton. The problem is that most eastern coal-shipping ports are designed primarily to handle metallurgical coal, which is traded in a large number of ranks and grades and is not therefore amenable to ground storage and bulk loading. Instead, it is stored in the same hopper cars used to transport it. Suitable ground storage space is often difficult to obtain in existing eastern ports. New facilities for steam coal trade are required, and a number are under development.

The third criticism pertains to transoceanic shipping costs. Current maximum port depths of 45 feet on the East Coast result in the need to use smaller coal carriers, thus foregoing the potential economies of scale available for 100,000-dwt or larger bulk carriers, which can now be accepted at a number of European ports. As a result, U.S. transportation costs per ton could be twice those of the larger coal ships utilized in the Australian or South African coal trade.

Although these criticisms of the aggregate U.S. transportation system are very serious, they actually miss many of the most important problems. The difficulties in transport are the result of variations in regional markets and infrastructure, including the following:

1. In the East, a principal problem is unavailability of ground storage space and bulk-handling facilities adapted for steam coal trade. Port depth constraints are an endemic problem due to the Continental Shelf.
2. In the Gulf states, ground storage is not a constraint, but it is necessary to expand barge-rail infrastructure to bring coal to the ports. Port depth may also be a problem.
3. In the West, there is a strong potential for coal exports. Port depth is not the principal problem; the inadequate infrastructure is. Additional rail links and facilities at the ports to handle and discharge unit trains would be required to avert this difficulty.

We have already examined a formidable list of difficulties relating to transport, but the factors relating to their solutions are even more complicated. They take us to the heart of the perennial questions in all international markets about the roles of the public and private sectors and the proper distribution of obligations between exporters and importers. In short they are the classic issues of "who pays, and when" and what guarantees are available to market participants. In regard to U.S. coal exports these issues have surfaced in the form of two debates. First, foreign buyers have insisted on new investments in transportation infrastructure as a condition for long-term contracts, but operators of coal ports have required long-term contracts as a condition for making significant capital investments. Methods to solve this "chicken before the egg" problem are under evaluation. Second, foreign buyers have expressed concern about the uncertainty of the future cost of rail transportation from the mines to the ports. Where transportation costs play so great a role, long-term contracts for coal haulage are crucial.

To understand how the broad issues of obligations and guarantees play themselves out in the case of the United States, we must once again plunge into the details of transportation choices. The discussion should demonstrate that it is necessary to read many tea leaves in order to predict the fate of the coal market.

Rail Transportation. The railroads will probably expand the physical line-haul capacity to accommodate projected increases in coal traffic. However, particularly in the West, where coal has not moved to northern Pacific ports in the past, the railroads may have to build or upgrade loading facilities and spurlines to the mines, construct sidings, expand yards, install heavier rail, and increase annual maintenance expenditures.

Generally, when a railroad has had good prospects of carrying additional coal traffic at adequate rates, it has been able to raise the necessary capital. The projected level of increases in coal traffic will occur over a period that should give the railroads sufficient time to adequately finance the investments. The problems usually occur in staging the investments or in adjusting operating practices to handle the traffic expeditiously.

Highway Transportation. In some eastern coal fields transporting coal involves truck haulage from the mines to rail lines. Investments in this type of equipment are not a problem; industry has ample capability to finance and build trucks. The problem lies in the highway infrastructure, which is already deteriorating in certain areas, with deferred maintenance running into the billions of dollars. Given the current condition of the roads and the very large increases in coal production necessary for domestic purposes, the upkeep of coal roads could become a barrier to coal exports in some regions.

Coal Slurry Pipeline Transportation. Almost five million tons per year of coal are currently being moved 273 miles as slurry in the Black Mesa pipeline from Kayenta, Arizona, to southern Nevada. After more than ten years of successful experience, the technology can be considered adequately proven.

At least ten other coal slurry pipelines are under consideration. Six would originate in the West; the others would originate in central Appalachia, eastern Kentucky, or Virginia. At least four of the pipelines could be built by the end of the 1980s if the impediments are mitigated. Only one western company and one eastern pipeline have located a firm water supply; the others are in various stages of negotiation for water rights.

The U.S. Maritime Administration and the Boeing company investigated the feasibility of exporting slurried western steam coal. As a general proposition, the study found the slurry system to be economically, technically, and institutionally feasible. Whether a specific coal slurry project turns out to be a gain in economic efficiency will depend on the characteristics of a specific site, the condition and suitability of rail facilities that are already in place, and the slurry/ocean transport system.

Moving coal to the West Coast in slurry pipelines could prove an efficient way of serving the Pacific market.

Waterway Transportation. No obvious constraints exist for the movement of western coal by water, which is transported first by rail to the middle Mississippi and then by barge to the Gulf. However, some parts of the waterways serving West Virginia, Kentucky, and Tennessee have current or potential capacity constraints. The Columbia–Snake River system in the Pacific Northwest has a potential for moving coal collected from western fields, but if it is used, the Bonneville Lock and Dam may need upgrading.

Other locks and dams that are potential bottlenecks to increased coal traffic could be improved. Fortunately, the barge industry appears capable of handling projected increases in coal shipments.

Port Constraints. The current channel depths at U.S. harbors limit the size of ships using the ports. In addition, coal transported from Atlantic and Gulf Coast ports to the Far East must pass by ship through the Panama Canal. The dimensions of the canal limit the ship size to 60,000–70,000 dwt. This constraint has spawned the so-called Panamax-class ship to maximize loads carried through the canal; these ships will dominate the shipping of eastern coal to the Far East.

Market Characteristics of the International Steam Coal Trade

Even if transportation problems are soluble and the enthusiasm for coal supplies continues, what will be the characteristics of the international coal market? So far, my analysis has focused on countries that will be the centers of supply and demand. But I have not analyzed the commercial units that will actually do the production and buying, nor have I explored the special characteristics of market relationships in the coal trade. This section explores the future of these units and changes in exchange relationships in order to set the stage for a final overview of the commercial risks that threaten the expansion of the market.

The participants in the international coal trade are already large and they are getting larger. This applies to all segments of the market: sellers, buyers, and traders. Why is this occurring and what implications does it have? I begin by looking at the change in the nature of the system of trading and then look at how this change interacts with other forces influencing the size of the firms.

Until recently, the bulk of the coal exported to Europe went through U.S. intermediaries. Producers sold to an independent set of professional trading companies, which, in turn, sold the coal to the large European electric utilities. Frequently, the trading companies also owned some coal mines.

The new trend in the world trade favors direct sales agreements between large producers and large consumers. One reason for this switch toward direct sales by producers is a matter of corporate tradition. As the large international oil companies play a more important part in the coal trade, they prefer to utilize their internal marketing organizations. (Similarly, partial exceptions to the trend, such as the Polish marketing monopoly, Weglokoks, are also a result of broader economic traditions.) But the real explanation of the new philosophy adopted by both buyers and sellers lies in the change of economic incentives brought about by increased trading volume. Let us first examine the incentives for producers.

Despite the prominence of large operators, the structure of the market for coal production is highly competitive. Increasing the size of the units will not lead to an oligopoly. The most likely scenario is an expanded steam coal trade conducted by a number of major producers. This will develop as large producers in the United States, and other coal areas not currently exporting, enter the coal trade. The determining factors on the selling side are structural and technical: Substantial increases in steam coal production for export will come from the large-scale mining developments and will be marketed directly by the producers. This prospect will apply particularly to the United States, where the traditional coal-exporting areas in the Appalachian region will initiate the expansion; but when delivered prices and transport costs permit, substantial export growth will come from the western states, where reserves are owned or leased by large corporations and are developed by capital-intensive strip-mining operations of high productivity.

The steep costs of expanding capacity to supply export coal will accelerate the movement of direct sales to foreign customers by the producers. In particular, vertical integration in coal export trading eliminates intermediaries and absorbs their marginal rent. It also permits closer control over the movement of coal and improves the producer's information about market conditions (a gain both for the sales division and for those planning production).

The principal importers of coal are large electric utilities. In order to improve information and bargaining power through expanded purchases, some of the electric companies are moving to collective purchasing of coal. Even more interesting, many large consumers of coal are actively participating in mining operations. Such participation provides the consumer with much better current cost and market information, even if it provides only a small proportion of the company's total coal supply.

Despite the trend toward direct sales, the brokers and traders will not disappear; and they will probably handle larger volumes of coal, although their relative importance will diminish. They will retain some of the electric power market because of their role as sources of market information and in diversifying the sources of supplies for individual consumers. For reasons of security of supplies, electric utilities consider diversity in source important. Brokers will also supply coal to a growing market in the industrial sector. This market presents problems of efficient supply that may have to be met by the development of new delivery systems and maintenance of increased stockpiles. Because of the greater risks of higher-volume trading, the demands for improved delivery systems, and economies of scale, the future will favor the development of larger brokers and traders, particularly those with access to capital outside the traditional sources.

The growth of larger traders and brokers often is a prelude to the development of a well-organized spot market for a commodity. However, a significant spot market is unlikely to develop in the case of coal because of the costs of handling, transporting, and storing coal. But spot availabilities will grow from irregular and exogenous causes and periodically from excess mine capacity during depressed market phases. The trend toward larger traded volumes may produce greater flexibility in switching shipments between individual buyers. However, coal is not a fungible commodity, and consumers will require flexible burning equipment.

The absence of a spot market is only one characteristic of the coal trade. Two others are the emphasis on personal contacts and the current paucity of long-term contracts. The international coal market at present functions through a series of overlapping personal contacts among producers, traders, and consumers. By conveying information on capabilities and longer-term requirements, these contacts maintain confidence between operators in a market in which secure and reliable trade flows are important to both sides. (For a lengthier discussion of the implications of markets with highly personalized transaction, see Chapter 8.)

A basic market function is to convey information on present and potential coal demand, supply, and relative prices. The market is moving toward long-term contracts beween sellers and buyers; this situation will permit improved flows of information. Information on the European steam coal–consuming market is not comparable with what is available for the utilities' steam coal market in the United States and the coking coal market in Japan.

Despite the obvious difficulties presented by numerous national markets with divergent domestic attitudes, policies, and problems, the collection and publication of the major elements in all large coal import contracts would assist in developing an orderly market. Improved information would increase the knowledge of current prices and trading conditions and provide a background in which negotiations could be conducted with greater confidence and more uniform information to assist both sides of the market.

Risks in the Coal Trade

The analysis has established that important changes must occur in the organization of the coal trade in order to deal with the risks posed by long lead times in development, erratic (albeit growing) demand, poor market information, strikes, and transportation bottlenecks. All these items appeared to some degree early in the explosive growth of the world oil trade, but we can more fully appreciate their significance for coal by comparing the present schedule of prospective exporting nations (such as the United States and Australia) with those that dominate the petroleum trade.

Unlike Mexico, Indonesia, or the Middle East nations, the industrial coal-exporting nations will not rely primarily on coal exports for their prosperity. This difference has profound implications for buyers. Countries that either consume a large share of their own output and/or do not heavily depend on the commodity's export for their prosperity are less reliable as suppliers. In essence, they find it more advantageous to disrupt exports to fill their own needs, or they may not have enough incentive to make the sacrifices (such as environmental disruptions) necessary to undertake promised expansions of production and transportation capacities. Thus, all the major types of risks that this section outlines are more acute because most of the major exporters are industrial countries.

Leaving historical comparisons aside, it is possible to summarize the risks involved in the international coal trade in terms of three classes: quantity risks, price risks, and transportation risks. The latter two are particular problems for buyers and sellers participating in the long-term contracts that will eventually dominate the coal trade.

Quantity risks fall into two categories. The first concerns the seller of coal, who faces uncertainties as to whether the buyer will take deliveries at contracted volumes. The second concerns the buyer: Such circumstances as inclement weather, strikes, or contract cancellation by the seller may interrupt expected supplies. For both parties long-term supply contracts are a means of reducing quantity risk, and for the seller "take-or-pay" contracts (under which the buyer agrees to buy the coal or pay a penalty), common in the United States but not yet common in international trade, could provide improved security. Consumers, especially electric power companies, for whom security of supplies is important, meet the risk by various means, including the maintenance of large stocks, the diversification of supply sources, and the participation in mining ventures in producing countries. Uncertainty over the future growth of demand for electricity creates a different type of quantity risk for electric power companies. This is partly moderated by the dependence of projected coal requirements on policies of substituting coal for other primary fuels, particularly oil and gas.

Price risks are of two main kinds: (1) inflation risks from worldwide inflation; and (2) market risks created by changes in the relative price of coal resulting from shifts in the market balance of supply and demand. In medium- and long-term contracts, both risks are handled by a periodic (annual or quarterly) review of the contract price. Otherwise, the principal instrument is the use of base-price escalation clauses in contracts. Escalation clauses deal with inflation risks by providing for increases in the base price in line with increases in specified items of the producers' or sellers' costs, as they occur. Market risks are dealt with by the periodic renegotiation of base price to take account of changes in market conditions. This renegotiation period could become shorter during times of sharp market change.

If price renegotiation or review becomes more frequent, the definition of a "medium-term" or "long-term" contract is important. Obviously, such contracts no longer exist if we define a contract's duration as the length of time that a quoted price remains fixed. However, this approach to defining a contract's life span is overly restrictive because it ignores the sophisticated understanding of the contractual relationship on the part of buyers and sellers. Even with price revisions, the contracting parties understand that a medium- or long-term contract obligates both sides implicitly to arrive at orderly adjustments on the basis of enlightened self-interest. Clear evidence of this expectation is the significance attached by participants to such contracts, as shown by their arduous work to conclude them. Moreover, once concluded, very few contracts are canceled. Nonetheless, some residual uncertainty over the terms of contracts will remain and in some circumstances may impede mine development by deterring potential sources of outside finance.

Currency risks arise in international coal trading, involving both sellers and buyers. The U.S. dollar is widely used as a contract-pricing currency, but contracts in the currencies of other exporting countries are not uncommon. In importing countries the risks created, in a world of fluctuating exchange rates, are generally passed through to the consumer. When commitments are short, as with contracts allowing annual price reviews, both traders and consumers may hedge the risk in forward exchange markets. Exporters carry some currency risk when they contract to supply at U.S. dollar prices coal that is produced outside the United States. Some of these contracts contain escalators that apply an adjustment in exchange rates to the proportion of total price accounted for by local currency costs.

Finally, transportation risks, including risks of heavy demurrage charges, are a potentially serious problem, exemplified by the recent severe congestion in U.S. ports and by less serious conditions in Australian and some European ports. Traders, who operate as principals and arrange shipping, have carried these risks. The costs will be passed directly to consumers. The electric power companies are accepting the incremental costs, although with varying reluctance because of potential constraints on their ability to recover costs by raising prices. Where consumers contract directly the transport risk falls entirely on them. Ultimately the real costs of port delays will pass to the end-consumers. The solution lies with improved transportation and terminal infrastructure; but those in exporting countries are likely to refuse to absorb any part of the incremental costs now being incurred. Improved and expanded infrastructure, particularly ports, will ultimately benefit all parties concerned with expanded coal trade.

Conclusion

The economic advantage of steam coal will increase from now until 2000 as the world faces higher prices, plus insecure and declining supplies of alternative fossil fuels on the world energy market. As transportation and port infrastructural problems are mitigated on the coal-consuming and -producing sides, coal's economic advantage will become more pronounced. It is expected that the major industrialized countries will increasingly substitute steam coal for oil and gas in the electric utility and industrial sectors, accelerating a trend that was initiated in the late 1970s.

The international coal trade is rapidly expanding in response to increased demand for steam coal. This highly competitive market will involve a more significant role for larger commercial producers and consumers. These commercial entities have the financial resources to undertake long-term coal agreements that entail considerable investments in infrastructure and a substantial long-term market commitment.

Collectively, these world market trends will stimulate the international steam coal market to function more efficiently and, as a result, yield benefits of stable, reliable, and lower-cost energy supplies. From the present to 2000 and beyond, there are strong positive prospects for an improved and expanded international coal trade that will benefit both producers and consumers.

References

Gordon, Richard L. *An Economic Analysis of World Energy Problems.* Cambridge, Mass.: M.I.T. Press, 1981.

Greene, Robert P., and Gallagher, Michael J. (eds.). *Future Coal Prospects: Country and Regional Assessments. World Coal Study.* Cambridge, Mass.: Ballinger Publishing Company, 1980.

International Energy Agency. *Steam Coal, Prospects to 2000.* Paris: OECD, 1978.

International Energy Agency. *Coal Prospects and Policies in IEA Countries—1981 Review.* Paris: OECD, 1982.

U.S. Department of Energy, Interagency Coal Export Task Force. *Interim Report of the Interagency Coal Export Task Force.* Washington, D.C.: Government Printing Office, January 1981 (DOE/FE-0012).

Wilson, Carroll L. *Coal—Bridge to the Future. Report of the World Coal Study.* Cambridge, Mass.: Ballinger Publishing Company, 1980.

Part 2

Government Regulation and Intervention

4
Policy and Politics of North Sea Oil and Gas Development

Merrie Klapp

Why did North Sea oil and gas policy evolve so that markets once dominated by multinational oil companies became sensitive to the influence of both governments and national industry groups? Some authors claim that market dynamics forced multinational oil companies to loosen their grasp. I argue that politics, even more than markets, molded North Sea policies. National shipping and fishing industries, which are clearly affected by any North Sea policy, show the power that other sectors can have in casting national energy policy. This chapter analyzes the interplay of sectors, markets, and regulations that set the structure of investment, production, and industrial organization for North Sea oil and gas in Norway and Britain. Alternative policy scenarios for the 1980s are then considered.[1] In particular, this chapter shows how, in order to supplement existing oil and gas returns, governments entered oil markets by using their regulatory power to gain contracts for state companies. While multinational oil companies accommodated production by state oil companies, national industry groups used their political influence with governments to gain benefits not obtained through the market.

Evolution of Government Policy for North Sea Exploitation

Peter Odell has argued that market price and supply fluctuations set the stage for both international oil company and government policies

The author is grateful to Ernst Haas, Melvin Webber, and Michael Teitz for their constructive criticism of earlier research that led to this chapter.

in the North Sea. He argued that during the 1960s smaller U.S. and European oil companies offered supplies at lower prices and thus forced major multinational oil companies to lower prices in Western Europe as well. This competition enabled Western European countries, except for Britain, to increase national refining capacity with cheaper crude. (International oil company penetration of 90 percent of the British domestic market kept prices in that country at international levels.) The lowered prices of imported oil also reduced the interest of oil companies in alternative oil supplies from the North Sea. North Sea governments became convinced that this lack of interest in rapid extraction signified a scarcity of supplies rather than decreased marketability and stressed conservation rather than rapid development.[2]

Looking beyond oil market fluctuations, Oystein Noreng has maintained that domestic political pressures influenced the course of government policies in Norway and Britain by pitting public against private control. Government bargaining with private companies became increasingly complex and potentially inefficient as government policymakers imposed new regulations in response to growing public demand for public controls. However, other than a cursory recognition of political issues, such as environmental damage and spin-offs of shares of the oil industry to domestic groups, Noreng left the impact of politics on government economic decision making as a black box. He neglected to analyze the domestic conflicts and trade-offs that carved up the economic rent and control of operations among foreign oil companies, governments, and domestic groups.[3]

In contrast to Odell, but taking Noreng's analysis one step further, I will show that the political trade-offs among companies, governments, and domestic groups helped break the pace and change the gait of government efforts to develop oil rapidly. At the start, both the Norwegian and British governments were interested in exploiting North Sea resources in order to reap immediate benefits in terms of increased gross national product (GNP), added tax revenue, and improved balance of payments. Political conflicts, however, arose over shares for the state oil monopoly, shares for domestic industrial groups, and party policies regarding the exploitation of North Sea oil and gas. Fearful of losing ground economically, domestic industry groups checked *both* interventionist government oil and gas strategies and private and state oil company offshore developments by launching electoral or financial threats to government stability. The governments responded by slowing oil development and conceding shares of oil industry operations or revenues (in the form of compensation) to politically volatile groups.

To understand the evolution of North Sea oil and gas policy we need to examine the interplay of markets and regulations affecting government and corporate policies. In essence, both Norwegian and British governments initially followed a regulatory policy permitting multinational oil companies to explore and exploit North Sea energy freely and at their own pace. The profitability, expertise, and experience of these companies promised an efficient use of offshore resources. And indeed, the oil companies did try to expand rapidly in order to maximize their returns on investment. So, despite legal control and authority to develop the oil and gas themselves, governments chose to employ a market allocation of those development rights based on profitability and efficiency. Because neither Britain nor Norway had domestic oil companies that could compete with the profitability of the major multinationals,[4] governments leased to the latter and simply collected taxes on their production.

Gas exploitation, however, took a different path from that of oil. In both countries national gas systems were managed by public utilities; they were not part of the international oil system organized by the multinationals.[5] Government agencies maintained close supervision of marketing and set price controls. To avoid this interference, the multinational companies favored oil over gas exploitation, as this allowed them nearly exclusive control over forward-linked operations.

However, by the early 1970s governments began seeking higher returns from offshore oil operations when higher oil prices increased corporate profits. But oil revenues from taxes and royalties were not sufficient to offset balance of payments deficits, nor could they cure unemployment or inflation related to rising oil prices. Labor governments in both countries saw increased central control and direct involvement in oil as well as gas development as a potential solution.

Governments hoped to supplement tax revenues with profits earned by producing oil themselves through state companies. After claiming a national share in offshore oil production, both governments tried to exclude or deter the formation of other national companies (other than those state companies already established for gas). The governments' dual role as market allocator and bidder for oil leases became the hinge for national state monopolies. Multinational oil companies accommodated this policy shift by agreeing to share control of oil production with state oil companies. They wanted, however, to retain control over oil exports, transportation, and international distribution because these activities were the key to retaining their overall profitability based on returns to scale, transfer-pricing, and optimization of vertically integrated operations.[6]

At the same time, private Norwegian and British companies in other maritime industries began eyeing offshore oil operations. Their success in entering the oil industry depended on economic and political considerations. Where domestic companies economically dominated their domestic industries, as in Norwegian shipping, these companies were able to win entry into the offshore industry. But where multinational oil companies already had a substantial presence in the industrial sector, as the oil companies had in British shipping, domestic shipping companies refrained from entry for fear of retaliation. For example, the tanker fleets of oil companies might not charter tankers from traditional British shipowners if the shipowners tried to compete for offshore oil production.

Political conditions also affected the ability of domestic groups to influence government policies about offshore activities. First, both Norway and Britain's political systems were organized so that parliamentary majorities pivoted on marginal group votes. Second, domestic groups such as shipping or fishing controlled key votes or parliamentary seats, although the specific groups differed in the two countries. Because governments monopolized the national share of oil markets by 1975, this leverage gave domestic groups political access to offshore industry. Shipping, fishing, and labor union interests in both countries could now reap benefits not obtained earlier through the market, either because government monopolies were just being established in oil activities or because domestic industries were not competitive for items such as offshore service contracts. By 1978 government policy in both nations had shifted to accommodate domestic political groups by (1) giving shipping companies and unions a share in oil development, (2) temporarily halting the expansion of oil production, and/or (3) offering compensation to fishermen.

By 1980 the focus had shifted back to gas. Despite increased oil production, governments were still dependent on oil imports. As governments tried to reduce their oil dependence, gas resurfaced as a viable energy prospect. Existing government control of gas prices and attempts to reach parity with oil prices again became foci of conflict between governments and multinational oil companies.

Norwegian Oil and Gas Policies

Following the division of the North Sea into Norwegian and British sectors in 1965,[7] the Norwegian government launched into oil and gas development. Hopes were high that these energy resources would contribute more to national economic growth within the next fifteen to twenty years than other offshore domestic industries, such as shipping or fishing. Between 1965 and 1969, forty-five blocks were licensed to oil companies offshore for exploration.[8]

Like other governments, the Norwegian government wanted to benefit from the efficiency of foreign multinational oil companies by giving them primary responsibility for exploitation of oil and gas. Besides, except for the partly state-owned Norwegian chemical company, Norsk Hydro, Norway lacked a national oil industry. So between 1966 and 1977 Phillips Petroleum, Exxon, Mobil, and Petronord (comprising Total, Elf, Entreprise de Recherches et d'Activités Pétroliéres [ERAP], and Aquitaine, as well as Norsk Hydro) started working in Norway.[9] They funneled the new North Sea supplies into their existing global oil transportation, refining, and marketing networks.

The Norwegian government followed a policy of minimal interference with multinational control over offshore oil markets. Apart from placing broad limits on oil production, it merely collected taxes. In the case of gas, it wanted to ensure control over export destinations while creating incentives for domestic as well as international firms to produce natural gas for export markets. Whereas royalties on oil production were eventually set according to a sliding scale from 8–16 percent, on gas production they were a flat rate of 12 percent of value. The Norwegian government, unlike its British counterpart, agreed to a "market" price formula for gas, giving the oil companies an incentive for producing from Ekofisk. The state's role in gas up to 1973 was through its 51 percent controlling interest in Norsk Hydro.[10] This company got 5 percent of the Norwegian share of more than half the joint Norwegian-British Frigg gas field. In 1974 the Norwegian government agreed to sell most of its share of the gas from Frigg to the British Gas Corporation. This funneled gas supplies of the partly government-owned Norsk Hydro and international oil companies into a British government gas monopoly. However, Norsk Hydro's role was downplayed once the Norwegian government assessed its share of incoming revenues and sought other channels of state involvement offshore.

By the early 1970s it was clear that the major benefits from oil and gas development were not accruing to Norway. Owing to various development cost deductions and reductions in tax yield from capital allowances, revenues from taxes and royalties provided the government with only a 20 percent share of total returns from oil production—a much smaller share than that received by OPEC governments. In 1972, although total gross product from production was $31.3 million, the central government's net income was only $6.3 million.[11] In 1971 Norwegian production of crude oil from the seventeen operating wells was about 6,000 barrels per day, only 1.5 percent of Western European output and an insignificant share of world production. Virtually all the Norwegian oil was exported, while Norway's imports neared 200,000 barrels per day.[12] In sum, the government wanted a larger share of revenues, and it wanted to halt the country's growing deficit in oil trade by producing more itself and keeping more for domestic use.

Faced with these macroeconomic concerns, government policy began to shift from a "hands-off" to a "hands-on" oil market approach. Anxious to stake out a claim to the industrial benefits offshore, the Norwegian government formed the completely state-owned oil company, Statoil, in 1972. Rather than work through private Norwegian companies, state production would provide the government with an income to supplement that from fees, royalties, and taxes. This also gave the state an opportunity to supply domestic oil needs directly as well as to buy oil from foreign companies. Besides, it wanted an "opportunity of influencing the decisions made by the individual licensees. The Government will thus be better able to guide and control activities to the extent desirable and necessary to ensure that continental shelf resources benefit the Norwegian community as a whole."[13] Practically speaking, this meant that the government could increase its control over the link between national production and offshore services.

Rather than threaten foreign companies by retracting oil licenses, thus losing their risk capital and know-how, the Norwegian government established cooperative production arrangements with them. Statoil participation was simply substituted for government participation after 1973. By 1975 Statoil controlled 50 percent of several blocks (with an option to take 75 percent in all blocks conceded afterwards).[14] Statoil agreed to distribute its supplies within the domestic market, allowing the oil companies to continue controlling oil exports.

Besides participating in oil production, the government also proposed to the Norwegian Parliament that Statoil earn additional profits and coordinate Norwegian oil industry development by integrating vertically while continuing to cooperate with private business interests. This would give it a central role in guiding the growth of related industries.

> Such a company will also give the Government a better opportunity to take advantage of the rights acquired under the contracts relating to Government's participation as a basis for engaging in transport, refining and marketing. The company's other objective will be to coordinate the Government's interests with the interests of private businesses within the petroleum sector through various types of cooperation agreements. The company would thereby play a major part in realizing the Government's policy of establishing an integrated Norwegian petroleum community.[15]

Statoil moved rapidly into the gas scene in 1973 by securing a 50 percent share in the pipeline company for the Ekofisk field and committing half Statoil's equity to the company.[16] The state oil company also had prospects for shipping and other transportation investments.

Despite formal recognition of private Norwegian oil companies, the Labor government worked to increase Statoil's monopoly over national participation in offshore production operations. Statoil was the "Labor party's baby," and the government used it to assert economic control of domestic oil production and keep Conservative party economic interests at bay politically. Up to 1973 the Ministry of Industry claimed that no Norwegian company or group of companies had sufficient financial strength and experience to be the operator for a block.[17]

The Labor government had several reasons for using its control over licensing to favor a Statoil monopoly over the government's 50 percent share of production. Limiting other Norwegian oil company contracts offshore would keep domestic private-sector interests from gaining a strong market position in national oil. The Labor government's economic and political power would thus be secured as oil continued to develop as the single most important sector in the national economy. Besides providing oil funds for government programs, oil revenues could give the government a new source of income and foreign exchange in the future. This would enable it to stop depending on the private sector's critical foreign exchange role in balancing international payments. In this way, the Labor government could diminish the strength of the private sector in the national economy by turning a public company into the nation's strongest firm. Furthermore, a Statoil monopoly over the share of oil to be produced by domestic industry would provide a basis later for extending the state company's control through investments in national refining, transportation, or marketing activities.

Aware of such possibilities, Norwegian industrialists focused on the economic and political importance of gaining their own share in North Sea oil profits. While the semiprivate Norsk Hydro continued to work within the Petronord group in producing gas from the Frigg field, other private Norwegian interests, including shipping, pooled capital to invest in oil and challenge the government policy. Norwegian shipping companies in particular saw entry into oil production as a way to maintain their relative strength vis-à-vis government oil. Offshore oil investments would also give shipping companies vertically linked oil production and transportation operations.

The shipping industry had important factors working in its favor in its struggle to enter the oil industry. To begin with, shipping had long been one of the country's most important and profitable foreign exchange earners. It was also a Norwegian-owned industry: Only about one-quarter of the fleet was foreign owned. This gave it a legitimate domestic identity. Moreover, shipowners had already expanded into oil-related operations. Tanker investments during the 1960s had made one-third of the Norwegian fleet oil tankers by 1970. The soaring profits from these tankers between 1970 and 1971, owing to shortages on the world tanker market, provided Norwegian shipowners with capital to reinvest.[18] As a result of these factors, fifty shipping companies and forty companies from other industries joined to form their own oil company, Saga Petroleum, in 1972.

Despite Saga's determined bid, the government's preferential treatment of Statoil limited Saga's participation in Norwegian licenses to only 8 percent of one block and 2 percent of two others by 1973. In comparison, Statoil received 50 percent of the Statfjord field.[19] Moreover, Statoil provoked shipowners by advancing concrete proposals to invest in shipping and other domestic industry operations linked to oil production. These different policies incited private industry to mobilize opposition in Parliament. Using their influence through the Conservative and Liberal parties, shipowners created an impasse for Statoil. Parliament controlled the state oil company's budget and in 1976 cut Statoil's request for share capital to finance its Statfjord development by 14 percent.[20]

By mobilizing this parliamentary threat to Statoil's funds, Norwegian shipping interests forced the government to compromise on state investments in oil-related markets, offshore and onshore. The government conceded that private shipping interests would control domestic subcontracting operations, such as supply boats and drilling rigs related to oil production, but insisted that Statoil retain its monopoly over the government share of production.[21] This trade-off was made informally between government oil interests working through the Ministry of Industry and Statoil, and Conservative party shipping interests in Saga. Previously, Exxon, Phillips, and other operators had subcontracted this work to other foreign companies. However, because Statoil participation offshore was up to 50 percent in many fields by 1975, the company could influence a corresponding share of subcontracting decisions. In addition, the government created continental shelf regulations that forced multinational oil companies to employ Norwegian subcontractors as long as they were competitive.[22] So, although Norwegian shipping did not gain a larger share of oil production, it won a share of subcontracting. The Norwegian portion of offshore subcontracts for offshore drilling and supply boat work increased steadily from 29 percent in 1975, to 41 percent in 1976, and then to 60 percent by 1978. Combining drilling rig and supply boat investments, the total value of the Norwegian offshore fleet owned by shipping companies in the late 1970s was about $2 billion.[23] The government also assured Norwegian shipowners that state companies would not invest in shipping-related operations, thereby preserving Norwegian shipping's share of any future shipments of Norwegian oil in national flag tankers. Of course, this agreement said nothing about oil pipeline transport, in which the government later did become actively involved, to the detriment of a tanker transportation alternative.

Although the government succeeded in retaining the Norwegian share of oil production for Statoil until 1978, that share was small in actual oil supplies. In 1976 Statoil controlled 50 percent of ten out of the eighteen blocks licensed after 1971. The company's production, however, was only about 3,500 barrels per day for domestic use, compared to the 272,000 barrels per day produced by foreign multinational oil companies in 1976. According to the net profit and carried interest production agreements with Statoil, foreign oil companies continued to control almost all Norwegian crude used for export to other countries. By 1979 total Norwegian crude oil production was 407,840 barrels per day.[24]

But by the late 1970s Norwegian policies had shifted again in response to international efforts to break the dependence of OECD countries on OPEC oil and find substitute energy sources. The Norwegian government began favoring domestic participation in production offshore, rather than just control over marketing. By 1980 a conflict had arisen between the Norwegian and U.S. governments as Norway pressed for parity between gas and oil prices. Norway argued that parity was necessary for Norwegian companies to enter the market and exploit gas resources profitably, while the United States argued that parity was neither necessary nor wise.[25] Less worried about parity, the multinational oil companies opposed conceding a larger share of national production to domestic interests. By 1981, the trend seemed to be toward nonparity prices but assured supply. Norwegian gas prices were nearing world market prices (on a delivered basis) for gas entering the new Norwegian North Sea gas-gathering system.[26]

Even though the Conservatives took control of the Norwegian government in 1981, there was little real change in Norway's oil and gas policy. Strong political opposition from Norwegian trade unions thwarted initial efforts to spin off Statoil's equity shares of operations to the private sector. The unions wanted to preserve public control of oil, and thereby their own political influence within that industry. As a result, the Conservatives were successful only at increasing private interest shares by expanding Saga and Norsk Hydro's participation relative to Statoil's and by making possible the participation of new Norwegian companies in new northern fields. Even U.S. government pressures on Norway to increase gas production targets within this decade in order to deflect purchases of Soviet gas had little impact on the Conservative government's production policy or on its efforts to achieve parity of oil and gas prices. The government did, however, favor continental buyers over British Gas, although British Gas claims that it offered a better deal.[27]

Norwegian policy also changed during the mid-1970s because other domestic industries were unable to compete with oil in offshore markets for space. By 1970, 40 percent of the Norwegian fish catch was coming from the North Sea. However, about 50 percent of the Norwegian sector south of the 62nd parallel was in various stages of oil and gas exploitation. Fishing suffered from operational interference: Nets were damaged and navigation was impeded by oil activities. The Directorate of Fisheries in Bergen estimated that access had been reduced between 15 and 85 percent in various major fishing grounds. Independently, government and fishing industry sources estimated fishing vessel losses of between 30 and 40 percent in catches of certain stocks during 1975–1977.[28]

By 1975–1976, southern fishermen had responded by organizing politically. To reduce their opposition to oil development, the government began granting compensation for gear damages through the Directorate of Fisheries. The total amount granted up to August 1977 was 9,133,563 Norwegian kroner ($1,665,049).[29] Compensation was not given for loss of space because fishing is legally a public right, not subject to private claims of property offshore.

North of the 62nd parallel, however, the Norwegian fishing industry and environmentalists temporarily halted the development of oil. In 1971 the government established that parallel as the northernmost limit for oil licensing because Norway, Britain, and the USSR disagreed on how to divide the continental shelf above that line. However, as spatial conflict between fishing and oil activities increased south of the 62nd parallel, fishing interests north of that line joined environmentalists and liberals lobbying in Parliament to prevent future northern oil operations. Supported by the Agrarian, Christian, Liberal, and Socialist parties, this "Green Opposition" called attention to oil spills, damage to the fishing industry, and changes in the economy and lifestyles in the region. In contrast, oilmen, backed by the Conservative party and a coalition of the construction, shipbuilding, and shipping industries, plus southern labor union groups, pressed for northern licensing. They argued that more drilling would increase the rate of oil production and economic growth, provide jobs, and increase government revenues.

The 62nd parallel became the battle line and Parliament, the battleground. Political debates raged over the data to start northern drilling. Northern Norwegian fishing had pivotal political clout because two seats critical to the Labor party's parliamentary majority were controlled by fishing communities. These fishing interests threatened to shift the Socialist votes of northern fishermen if the Labor government, which was supported by the Socialists in parliament, allowed drilling north of the 62nd parallel. Instead, in 1977 the Labor organizations of two northern fishing countries, Troms and Finnmark, decided to favor northern drilling because oil companies promised oil-related support and service industry development onshore. This shift of parliamentary support unbalanced the northern stronghold. Political debate diminished, and the government's environmental position eased. Parliamentary discussions focused on the operational issues of safe drilling procedures. By early 1978 opinion in Parliament had grown favorable to northern drilling starting in 1982.[30]

Three factors, however, continued to favor fishing and environmentalist interests. Oil spills and platform destruction in rough North Sea weather delayed northern drilling plans for environmental reasons. In addition, higher oil prices made previously uncommercial southern fields look very profitable, relaxing the pressure to develop northern ones.[31] Finally, northern capelin fishing continued to be very profitable, accounting for one-quarter of the total value of the Norwegian catch of 2,600 million Norwegian kroner ($457 million) in 1976.[32] So, while the government pursued a compensation policy toward southern fishermen, northern fishing temporarily generated a political threat to the Labor government that altered its oil policies.[33] Nonetheless, some drilling in northern waters was under way by early 1981.

British Oil and Gas Policies

The British government's goals for oil policy were similar to those in Norway at the start, but the two countries' domestic industries played different roles in bending policy outcomes toward their own interests. By the mid-1960s the British government was eager to develop a profit from its offshore oil and gas resources. It saw domestic oil production as a way to offset high oil imports and improve Britain's overall trade deficit (almost $1.8 billion in 1970). The government allowed multinational oil companies to develop oil but retained control of gas production itself. Gas supplies and prices were managed by the British Gas Council, the public utility operating the national gas system. Later, the Labour government, under domestic political pressure to tighten control over gas development, set up restrictions on gas exports. In 1968 and 1971, oil companies signed contracts for exclusive delivery of gas from southern fields in the British sector to the British Gas Council, making a government-owned enterprise the monopoly buyer for all British gas.[34]

With gas supplies firmly under government control, the Ministry of Power began haggling with oil companies over gas prices. It wanted a low buying price based on a "cost plus profit" formula rather than the "market price" used in Norway. The former favored a "reasonable" (rather than the maximum) rate of return on oil company investments. The Gas Council needed a low buying price to ensure the rapid increase in sales required to fill domestic gas capacity and offset the depreciation of its technology and capital expenditure. Besides, the government's idea was to use low prices as a way of siphoning off any "excess" gas profits from the oil companies to the government. Oil companies were clearly opposed because they wanted to maximize profits. They also argued that the "cost plus profit" formula did not take all costs into account, such as expenditures on unsuccessful wells. Besides, these companies wanted to keep prices high so that government gas marketing would be only marginally competitive with their oil-marketing systems. Gas contracts negotiated between 1968 and 1974 continued to give the Gas Council monopoly purchasing power. Whereas the 1968 contracts were closer to "market" prices, later ones reflected "European market" prices, less transport cost differentials, thereby favoring the British Gas Council by passing costs on to continental buyers.[35]

The tug-of-war over control of gas led oil companies to hold back production investment to levels that could be absorbed without expanding the government-run gas systems supplying Western Europe. Instead, they focused on oil where markets were free of government interference—distribution networks were international rather than nationally controlled.[36] The oil companies did not begin producing oil in the British sector until 1971, after initial discoveries in the late 1960s. The Conservatives, who had just ousted Labour, gave companies a freer hand offshore. Tory policy was to maximize national income through taxes and royalties rather than by producing oil directly. Delighted to spread the capital and technology risks of oil exploitation to others, the government leased offshore blocks to both national and foreign-based multinational oil companies. Until 1970 foreign companies received licenses for 62.5 percent of the area opened for bids. BP, Shell, Exxon, and Occidental were the major companies granted blocks.[37]

However, by the time Labour came back to power in 1974, Britain was experiencing the highest inflation rate, largest balance of payments deficit, and fastest-rising unemployment rate since World War II. In response, Labour adopted a new industrial policy designed to use government management and financial incentives to generate a surge of new industrial investment and restructure the basic organization of British industry, including oil.[38] The Labour government believed reorganization of the North Sea oil industry could reduce inflation and decrease the trade deficit. In 1974 it called for a "fairer share" policy that would increase government revenues by stricter taxation of the oil companies and state participation in offshore operations through the creation of a state-owned oil company. In 1975 the petroleum revenue tax (PRT) was placed on all profits, preventing companies from offsetting expenditure against dues across fields. The new state oil company was also given the option to take 51 percent of all future offshore licenses, as well as to renegotiate past licenses. Controls were also authorized on offshore production levels and royalty payments.[39]

In 1976 the government established the British National Oil Corporation (BNOC). By acquiring the offshore oil and gas interests of the National Coal Board and the Burmah Oil Company, BNOC gained an interest or operating responsibility in sixteen offshore fields. By January 1978, the Department of Energy and BNOC had signed forty-two agreements with oil companies, giving BNOC majority participation in fields licensed earlier. Although BNOC could, in most cases, take up to 51 percent of the oil produced, the international oil companies could purchase it all back.[40]

But while offshore oil production by BNOC and multinational oil companies in 1977 reached 770,000 barrels per day, British government returns from the PRT, other oil taxes, and royalties remained low. This was because oil companies were allowed to deduct capital and other allowances before any taxes were levied on their production profits. As a result, the government received only about £228 million ($456 million) in royalties and taxes from production in 1977, compared to the £909 million ($2,018 million) projected by MacKay and MacKay in 1975.[41]

Other British industries feared the expanding Labour government involvement in offshore markets. Traditional British shipowners, staunch supporters of noninterventionist conservative policies, wanted to prevent government from interfering in shipping. Government oil operations might lead to such interference or to competitive state investment in oil-related shipping markets.

Traditional shipowners worried also about the dual role of international oil companies as owners and consumers of British shipping services. After World War II, multinational oil companies developed a dominant position in national shipping, both financially and in tanker capacity. By 1968 five out of the top eight British shipping companies were oil companies. Of those, BP, Shell, and Exxon owned about two-thirds of the U.K.-registered tanker fleet, equivalent to two-fifths of total British tonnage between 1968 and 1973.[42] This vertical integration into British shipping gave international oil companies clout over traditional British shipowners by being both their major consumers and competitors for tanker services. Besides, traditional shipowners could not gain a foothold in the oil business because they depended on the oil companies' fluctuating and extremely competitive chartering and could not obtain long-term (more than five years) charters with provisions against rising costs.[43] Moreover, the oil companies' substantial share of British shipping gave them political influence in British shipping committees. As a result, British shipowners, unlike the Norwegians, did not venture into offshore oil production or subcontracting activities.

While shipping and other domestic industries stayed away, labor unions pressured the Labour government to involve British industry offshore. As Britain's economic slump worsened during the mid-1970s, unions and key national industries, such as construction, demanded that the government provide new employment opportunities. Vulnerable to pressures from these constituencies, the Labour government began applying minor pressure on the oil companies to use British companies for some subcontracting work. In 1975 the Secretary of State for Energy and United Kingdom Offshore Operators' Association (UKOOA), the representative organization for the forty-two oil company operators, agreed on a Memorandum of Understanding and a Code of Practice. These "ensured that British industry is given a full and fair opportunity to compete for business in the U.K. offshore market." British industry was to provide a "major and progressively increasing share of the goods and services required for the development of our continental shelf."[44] The Offshore Supplies Office (OSO) was set up by the Department of Energy to implement this policy.

Implementing the policy through the OSO rather than BNOC signaled the government's low priority on stimulating private industry offshore. The Labour government was more concerned about its own oil-production activities and had little reason to assist Conservative shipping except in response to union pressure for offshore employment. The government had already spent its political capital with the multinational oil companies while negotiating BNOC participation offshore.[45] Although the OSO provided some incentives for traditional British shipowners to invest in drilling rigs and supply boats, BNOC made almost no effort to contract their offshore or tanker services. Thus, government's limited political resources and the mutual lack of interest in cooperation between Labour oil and Conservative shipping constrained the integration of shipping with offshore oil.

Policies regarding BNOC changed when the Conservatives returned to power in 1979. Tory monetarist approaches to economic growth emphasized private investment rather than government intervention. The Conservatives spun off some of BNOC's activities into the private sector but could not afford to dismantle the company entirely because its revenues were too critical to the British economy. Even with a new

20 percent supplemental tax in 1981, tax and royalty revenues alone were still insufficient for government needs.[46] So the government backed off from selling $900 million worth of BNOC oil and gas interests but demanded that the company raise about $2.2 billion by 1980 through a forward sale of oil. This and another sale of some of the government's BP assets were aimed at reducing the company's public-sector borrowing requirement.

By 1980, the Department of Energy was also pumping $1.2 billion in private capital into BNOC through oil bond sales, introducing risk capital into certain operations, and breaking up its trading and production operations. BNOC retained its ability to buy up to 51 percent of crude production for national security reasons. The agency also revoked the monopoly privileges of state oil and gas companies. Although BNOC retained its 51 percent control of oil production, it reduced its equity share to 49 percent in new licensing rounds.[47] These structural changes aimed to convert the oil company into a mixed (rather than purely state owned) and single-operation (rather than vertically integrated) oil firm. In parallel, the Department of Energy partly eroded the British Gas Corporation's (BGC—previously the British Gas Council) monopoly over gas distribution by allowing oil companies and industrial consumers to negotiate deals independently.[48]

Between 1980 and 1982 other significant events eroded the power of BGC. The state company was unsuccessful both in becoming the developer of the gas-gathering system for U.K. offshore fields and in having Britain become the exclusive landing site for Norwegian-produced gas. The Treasury balked at guaranteeing the loans necessary to build the gathering system, and Norway chose to deliver its gas to West Germany. Moreover, most of the multinational oil companies refused to put up capital for a pipeline system as long as BGC remained the monopoly buyer. As a result, the British government decided to allow Shell and Exxon to lead the construction of a new tripartite gas-gathering project. In return for this investment, the multinational companies will have the freedom to sell gas on the open market.[49]

In summary, as of early 1982 private companies had regained some of their dominance in offshore markets and the government had retreated from a more entrepreneurial to a more regulatory role in implementing its oil and gas policy. Nonetheless, state companies still controlled significant shares of the oil and gas industry.

As in Norway, domestic industries facing financial or operational constraints on offshore investment had to adopt British-sector North Sea oil and gas policies to survive. Particularly after 1974, Scottish fishermen were displaced by oil activities. Between 1970 and 1974, 247 wells were drilled offshore, mostly within 200 kilometers of the Scottish or Shetland Islands coasts. Where the two industries' operations co-existed, oil installations and debris on the sea bottom damaged fishing gear, while 500-meter oil-safety zones increased hazards to navigation. Oil pollution was also a concern. Fishing industry representatives claimed reductions in operating space of up to 20 percent and estimated that between 1977 and 1978 the average loss of access would be another 25–30 percent. The economic losses were small by oil industry standards, but the potential loss of access was significant enough to worry fishing industry leaders about the future viability of North Sea fishing.[50]

Before 1974 opposition to oil by fishing interests was minor and had little effect on the Conservative government's policies. Government officials were estimating that revenues from oil production would be about seventy times those from fishing and therefore wanted to keep conflicts with fishing from impeding oil development. In 1974 the Department of Energy set up the Fisheries and Offshore Oil Consultative Group (FOOCG) as a forum for fishing, oil, and government representatives to work out the political aspects of the displacement of fishing offshore by oil.[51]

When Labour returned to power in 1974, however, fishing's electoral support became a source of industry leverage. Similar to the Norwegian situation, the British Labour government's parliamentary majority was small, so the possibility that fishermen might shift their partisan support became politically salient. Of the twenty-two parliamentary seats associated with fishing constituencies in 1978, nine were held with majorities of less than 6 percent. Labour risked losing seven of them.[52] In addition, the Labour party was concerned about the rise of the Scottish nationalist movement since 1975. One of the Scottish Nationalist party's aims was to gain increasing control over Scottish votes and resources for the Scottish regional government in Edinburgh. Many Scottish fishing communities had Labour representatives; the loss of those seats to the SNP could weaken Labour party control of Parliament. Accordingly, the potential partisan shift of fishing communities from Labour to other parties increased the industry's influence over Labour government policies.

By 1976 Scottish and English fleets also began organizing against the impending threat from oil and EEC fishery policies. The "political reality" was that the government was trading off British fishing for oil and EEC concessions linked to foreign fishing in British waters. A strong fishing lobby in Parliament could pressure government regarding the encroachment of these two offshore uses. The political "reorganization" that occurred followed regional lines and reflected divisions between the corporate and share-ownership segments of the fishing industry. In

August 1976, the company-owned English distant-water and Aberdeen fleets joined to form one unified federation, the British Fishing Federation (BFF), representing corporate fishing interests in Britain. Concurrently, Scottish inshore fishermen consolidated politically into the Scottish Fishermen's Federation (SFF) in order to strengthen Scottish share-owned industry influence.[53]

Yet despite its increasing political power, fishing was not critical to Labour government rule. Labour's majority in Parliament did not depend upon a small number of fishing votes, as it had in Norway. Thus fishing was unable to stop oil but did succeed in increasing compensation for oil damages and other fishing losses. In 1976 UKOOA set up a Compensation Fund for fishing gear damages, and FOOCG, as its administrating body, had paid out £106,636 ($213,227) by 1978.[54] The oil industry made sure that no legal responsibility was linked to payments of compensation. Fishermen also had to prove damages and provide evidence identifying companies responsible for the damage, which resulted in fewer claims and thus less help to working fishermen than in Norway. However, high prices, owing to scarce fish supplies nationally in 1975–1977, allowed British fishermen to offset temporarily the effect of low compensation.

Common Policy Outcomes in Norway and Britain

What conclusions can we draw by comparing the impact of British and Norwegian domestic industry politics on government regulation or production in offshore markets? In short, although domestic politics differed, policy outcomes were very similar. Between 1965 and the early 1970s, both Norwegian and British governments intervened in gas market pricing and distribution but left oil markets to multinational oil companies, just collecting taxes and royalties on their production. Soon after, economic distress and revenue shortfalls led Labor governments in both countries to seek more active state roles, generating oil profits and managing national oil supplies. State oil companies entered oil production markets in 1972 (Statoil) and 1974 (BNOC).

Different intersectoral ownership structures and contrasting domestic political situations produced variations in Norway and Britain's North Sea oil policies. In Norway, independent shipping companies had sufficient industrial strength to cross-invest into oil production and subcontracting. In order to gain compensation and access to market contracts or to halt oil, however, both shipping and fishing interests mobilized threats against government through Parliament. Trade unions pressured the government for offshore employment. In contrast, in Britain international oil companies dominated national shipping and were able to deter traditional shippers from entering oil production. So while British labor unions demanded offshore employment, shipping resisted government interference. Fishing interests lacked enough strength in Parliament to force major government or oil company concessions.

Despite these differences in industry structure and politics, very similar policies emerged for oil, gas, and related industry in the North Sea by the end of the 1970s. State oil companies and multinational oil companies controlled oil and gas production, but gas distribution was still primarily government controlled. In both countries governments procured offshore contracts for shipping through informal preferences regarding oil and gas subcontracting work, although the effort was far greater in Norway (reflecting shipping's greater leverage). In Norway, preferences were channeled through Statoil's share offshore, while in Britain the government's Offshore Supplies Office encouraged foreign operators to use some British companies offshore, mostly in response to labor union demands. Domestic industries that could not integrate with the oil industry were displaced. Both governments initiated compensation policies for fishing, although in Norway a northern fishing coalition temporarily halted government northern drilling plans anyway.

Why did common policy outcomes result if domestic politics differed? One obvious answer is that similar government and multinational oil company policies overwhelmed the divergent impacts of domestic industries. Both governments aimed to control gas pricing and distribution and to reserve the national share of oil production for state oil companies. In both countries, multinational oil companies responded to government intervention by retaining control over exports but conceding shares of production to state oil companies and, later, shares of subcontracting to domestic companies. Thus, different coalitions of domestic political influence in the two countries had more impact in determining amounts rather than kinds of concessions regarding production and subcontracting.

Norway and Britain's similar North Sea policy outcomes were reflected in the structure of sectoral investment, production, and industrial organization. Investment gains by state oil companies in oil production were limited by the fact that export-related downstream investments remained primarily in multinational oil company hands. In both countries, participation by the state oil company was 50–51 percent in production, but the amount of oil actually marketed was small compared to that marketed by the multinationals. Moreover, by 1982, both the British and Norwegian governments were trying to privatize BNOC's and Statoil's equity according to conservative economic strategies (the Norwegians with less success). Shipping investments in national industry offshore were also limited almost exclusively to subcontracting. These represented about 60 percent of supply boat work in the British sector. Only Norway's northern fishing industry was able to temporarily halt oil-sector investments and production plans. This resulted in high northern fishing production but delayed northern oil production. Conversely, where oil production reduced fishing production in both countries, governments paid some compensation with oil funds.

The evolution of some shared, rather than exclusive, markets altered offshore industry organization. In oil, state companies and national industry groups gained control in specific markets (production or subcontracting) but never linked investments. Control of such vertically integrated operations in production, transportation, and subcontracting remained in the hands of multinational oil companies. The control of gas was divided between national operations integrated by governments and international operations integrated by multinational oil companies. Fishing and oil shared industrial space in Britain and southern Norway, but up to 1980 fishing retained exclusive control in northern Norway.

Alternative Future Policy Scenarios

As world energy markets become more complex, international divisions of labor among foreign and national companies will tend to become more intricate and interdependent. Countries with national oil companies to represent them in joint investments or marketing will probably find it easier to achieve their oil-market agendas than those without. In order to secure opportunities in these new market arrangements, domestic industry and labor groups most probably will pressure governments to expand national capacity.

What is in store for Norway and Britain in the 1980s? We can isolate major factors that should affect the evolution of future North Sea policy. These include (1) changes in technology, capital availability, and industrial organization within the international oil industry; (2) national political shifts, such as union or other domestic opposition to energy development, affecting partisan control of government and its priorities in decision making; and (3) government and oil-company strategies to sustain revenue flows from oil and gas by conserving reserves.

First, multinational oil companies will probably continue to have the upper hand in coordinating exploration and production with international transportation and marketing operations for oil and gas because of their traditional advantages concerning returns to scale, diversity of supply, and market dominance. Therefore, the Norwegian and British governments will continue to frame oil and gas policies so that bargaining with multinational oil companies can successfully build domestic capacity as well as help achieve other national goals. This bargaining will be sensitive to fluctuations in world oil prices. If prices remain high, new North Sea fields as well as a large number of drilling opportunities around the world will continue to be commercially attractive. Multinational companies can use alternative global investments to drive harder bargains with national governments. However, the oil companies want neither to risk losing their existing fixed capital investments in Norway and Britain nor to shoulder new political risks that may be higher for investments elsewhere.

Conversely, governments can gain bargaining concessions from multinational oil companies by threatening their opportunities to develop new fields through allocating licenses to state companies or new foreign oil companies. If the two governments claim a bigger share of total revenues, foreign oil companies will undoubtedly try to retain their own profit shares by pressuring for raised production levels or expanded cost deductions.[55] Tougher bargains on both sides are likely to be driven while prices are high, favoring new investments and thus new opportunities to expand market shares. However, if prices continue to plummet over the next few years, higher-cost new and marginal fields everywhere will become unprofitable. While prices are low, both multinational oil companies and governments will probably simply try to retain their current production and relative shares. It is much more difficult to get a bigger piece of a pie that is diminishing than of one that is expanding.

International linkages among major oil companies, insurance companies, and banks could further alter the organization of international energy development. For instance, a shift in bank financing favoring independent or state oil companies would conflict with the interest of major oil companies, as it did in Indonesia during the early 1970s.[56] Such financing would mean that governments could produce more themselves without requiring the capital provided by multinational oil companies. However, governments would still be dependent upon these companies for access to the export markets the latter control. In addition, Norway and Britain could charge well-financed newcomers (independents) a premium for replacing the established multinational oil companies, or they could demand a higher percentage of profits, sales, or crude from the majors for retaining their contracts. But this approach risks the possibility that international bankers and others would shun North Sea investments because of the political uncertainties about state participation, production controls, or taxes.[57]

A second factor, national politics, is also likely to affect the evolution of North Sea policy. Whether domestic opposition to state policies actually changes the structure of the oil industry or simply alters amounts, rather than kinds, of participation by domestic actors is less clear. Certainly the 1979 shift to a Conservative government in Britain is important to the extent that government policy encourages private owners to buy up BNOC shares or entire operations. In contrast, strong labor union lobbies in Norway may continue to impede the new Conservative government's efforts to pursue similar state company divestment policies in that country. Thus, national politics may force even Conservative governments to engage in interventionist policies that deter further investments by multinational oil companies unless satisfactory profit arrangements can be made. Whether governments are forced to retain or, instead, are able to pursue joint venture or shared market arrangements with private domestic or foreign oil company interests will be critical. Conservative opposition will demand concessions for the private sector, while labor party and trade union groups continue pressing for a buildup of the national presence in industrial development. The fishing industry will also increase its parliamentary efforts to gain concessions from energy development. However, if the impacts of energy scarcity become too severe, fishing's strategies may have to shift entirely toward accommodation involving complex packages of compensatory benefits.

Third, as governments try to sustain national oil reserves through conservation policies that reduce production, they will also have to negotiate trade-offs of revenue shares with oil companies. Assuming increasing oil prices, governments can maintain revenues from oil even if they reduce production levels, thus giving them steady income sources beyond the twenty-year projections for most fields. The same strategy can benefit Statoil and BNOC as well as the multinational oil companies. However, governments will have to ensure sufficient supplies to the multinationals to serve their markets and ensure satisfactory profit margins on their investments. If governments cut back national production levels while taking an increasing share of total revenues, oil companies will certainly resist, even though high prices may offset any real losses.

What scenarios can we draw for the 1980s? The combination of these international shifts, domestic politics, and conservation strategies means theoretically that the economic utilization of resources will not be optimized in the short run. In neither Norway nor Britain is the most profitable use of resources likely to be the sole factor determining outcomes. Conservation of oil and gas reserves and income is a long-term economic strategy for both governments and oil companies and thus does not necessarily maximize short-term profitability. Besides, the bargaining over production levels, divisions of revenues, and shares of contracts between multinationals and governments, and the domestic politics fragmenting those negotiations, are *equity,* not efficiency, factors affecting outcomes. This politics of "fair shares" will continue to enter decisions about the industry's operations and about the balance between multinational, private domestic, and state-owned firms. Thus, both long-term economic strategies and equity politics will sway short-term optimizing decisions and thus the organization of efficiency over the long run.

Extrapolating from the interventionist strategy of the pre-1981 Norwegian Labor government and the restrained policy of the British Conservative government produces two quite different scenarios. In both countries government policies produce "inefficient" results (as judged by static microeconomic analysis), even though the Norwegian government wanted to make the state a leader in molding the national economy; the British government seems bent upon pruning the state's mission, particularly in the oil sector. Domestic politics make it difficult for either approach to succeed, regardless of the merits of either government's efforts. However, domestic groups such as fishing and shipping interests and trade unions may continue to have pivotal influence over Norwegian government oil policies, while those opposition groups in Britain continue to have less influence. As a result, different groups will benefit or at least benefit relatively more. The interventionist strategy of the pre-1981 Norwegian government would have tended to distribute opportunities to those groups wielding power over government decision making (domestic industry groups, labor unions, environmentalists) as well as to state organizations representing government purposes (Statoil). In contrast, the British government's strategy will tend to favor groups based on their economic efficiency (multinational oil companies) and the income they provide for governments (BNOC, British Gas), because opposition groups lack the clout to alter government policies in their favor. The Conservatives, however, may continue to offer concessions to private industry and labor groups simply to quell any emergent critical opposition.[58]

In pursuing its conservation strategy, the Norwegian government might have used very low discount rates so that average long-term profits from public oil and gas investments weighed favorably against alternative short-term reinvested profits from immediate exploitation. This would have conserved resources and thus alleviated the need to pay higher prices later to import substitute quantities of oil and gas. However, although the government might have preferred to increase the role of national companies by using state companies in oil and gas production and distribution, its every move would have increased the political leverage and, consequently, market shares demanded by domestic industries such as shipping or labor groups. Pressure would probably have continued from Conservative opposition in the Norwegian Parliament as well as from labor union influence on the Labor government. Thus, the government might have had to concede increasing shares of operations to private industry and/or labor groups while still retaining control for Statoil.[59] In this way the Norwegian government might have been obliged to shift from global or national analyses of profitability or efficiency toward more fragmented political analyses that account for profitability and efficiency in subunits: the government, Statoil, foreign oil companies, fishermen, shipping companies, and other domestic groups. By pinpointing relationships between these groups and entities, efficiency and fair compensation (equity) trade-offs might have been made among actors over long-term resource exploitation periods.

In so using notions of the "general welfare," there would increasingly be a shift from global to actor-specific efficiency and profitability criteria tied to long-term plans for domestic industry participation and the development of national capacity. Instead of paying domestic groups the minimum necessary to quell their opposition, calculations and compensation would approach truer Pareto optima reflecting "parity norm" or "split the difference" payoffs.[60] Despite these payoffs, however, groups using domestic politics to prevent environmental disruptions or the local destruction of industry (fishing) would probably continue to impede short-term profit maximization of national resources, because those groups' economic gains might never completely offset their losses in terms of livelihood, environmental quality, and other values. Although such opposition efforts might be successful only in delaying government energy policies, this would prove costly in terms of both suboptimal timing of investments and electoral votes. Furthermore, the domestic opposition might not be satisfied merely with a fair financial share. The government might have to develop specific locational or seasonal policies in order to accommodate broader demands of such groups concerning environmental preservation or the protection of industries such as fishing.

In contrast, although Britain is also likely to follow a conservation policy, the restrained Conservative government will probably take an approach that utilizes resources optimally in the short-term economic sense. As in Norway, continuing high oil prices (on average), future scarcity of supply, and the conservation strategies of other governments will persuade the British government to conserve its reserves despite its more general commitment to short-run efficiency and market forces. In addition, despite its North Sea oil exports, a continued worsening of the U.K. balance of trade owing to the relative strength of the British pound (reducing other British exports such as manufacturing) may force the government into a conservation strategy as a way of delaying until a better trade situation appears. The combination of these factors accounts for government projections that 1984 oil production will be down 27 percent from what it was projected to be in 1975 and for the fact that 1981 production was substantially less than either projection.[61]

Even though conservation may prevail as a policy, the British government's general commitment to market efficiency should ensure a "global" or "national" (rather than any subunit) analysis of optimal resource exploitation. This approach would favor the existing multinational oil companies as the most profitable and most efficient producers, transporters, and marketers of British oil and gas. The Conservatives will convert state companies into joint ventures between state and private interests by injecting private capital and limiting those companies to domestic production on a purely competitive basis. For instance, by 1982 the British government was giving multinational oil companies ownership shares and exclusive marketing privileges in the government-planned gas-gathering system. Because BNOC has become so profitable—its profits had quadrupled by 1980[62]—the extent to which the government devolves BNOC operations to private interests in the future will be determined by how much income the government may lose owing to reduced operations. Thus, even the Conservatives seem destined to create more complicated partnerships between multinational oil companies and the state monopoly.[63]

A passive British government response to pressure from domestic industry and labor opposition groups may either lead to pivotal domestic opposition or repress it through unyielding government positions regarding suboptimal compensation policies. In either case, if the government increases production levels or its revenue share, the ensuing taxes and royalties may be used to provide domestic firms with incentives to form joint ventures or to enter specialized oil and gas service markets related to production. Alternatively, government policies may appease British interests by encouraging low levels of participation in offshore oil production by domestic industries (such as fishing, food, and tractor manufacturing) in joint ventures with major and independent oil companies.[64] It may also use those revenues to create more sophisticated compensatory schemes to handle possible damages to the local environment or employment base.

In sum, powerful international and domestic forces will continue to reorganize and control the oil and gas industry in both Norway and Britain during the 1980s. In contrast to Odell's thesis, I have argued that the politics of conserved resources and fair shares, more than market fluctuations, are molding government policies in the North Sea. This perspective takes Noreng's analysis of public and private control a step further by focusing on the political bargains that resulted from a convergence of foreign and domestic state and private industry interests.

Complex trade-offs among multinational oil companies, state oil and gas firms, domestic companies, and pivotal interest groups will increasingly intervene in economic determinations of how much to produce, how revenues and operations will be divided in aggregate, and what forms the shares will take (control, profits, operations, oil in kind). In general, even with a Conservative government, Norway is likely to expand the role of state companies more aggressively, at the same time conceding shares of national operations to other domestic groups. Britain is clearly committed to restricting the government's entrepreneurial role. But in a country where the state has had full or substantial ownership in two large oil companies and a gas utility, a laissez-faire policy may be too tough a trick to learn. Finally, despite the initial efforts of state and domestic companies in both countries to erode the control of the major multinational oil companies, the latter continue to have the upper hand in international operations.

Notes

1. The research draws from a larger study of inter-industry conflict among oil, shipping, and fishing interests in Norway, Britain, Indonesia, and Malaysia. See Merrie Klapp, "Inter-Industry Conflict in the North Sea and South China Sea: A Comparative Analysis of Oil, Shipping, and Fishing in Four Nations," Ph.D. dissertation, University of California, Berkeley, 1980.

2. Peter Odell, "The Economic Background to North Sea Oil and Gas Development," in Martin Saeter and Ian Smart (eds.), *The Political Implications of North Sea Oil and Gas* (Guildford, England: IPC Science and Technology Press, Ltd., 1975); idem, *Oil and World Power: Background to the Oil Crisis* (New York: Taplinger Publishing Co., 1975), pp. 103–104.

3. Oystein Noreng, *The Oil Industry and Government Strategy in the North Sea* (London: Croom Helm, 1980), pp. 30–34, 75, 110–111, 214–229. In a recent article Noreng has, however, described the emergence in Norway of a "petrolized foreign policy." This reflects the unresolved political dilemma in Norway between those domestic groups interested in sustaining the moderate rise of oil and gas prices in accordance with a prosperous political economy and those groups interested in high prices and slow extraction in order to maximize the economic rent returning to Norway. Oystein Noreng, "The International Petroleum Game and Norway's Dilemma," *Cooperation and Conflict, The Nordic Journal of International Politics,* Vol. 17, no. 2 (1982):90–91.

4. British Petroleum (BP), a British-based and partly government-owned multinational oil company, is an integral part of the international oil oligopoly.

5. Noreng has pointed out, however, that although the international market is oligopolistic, having few sellers but many buyers, the Western European international gas market has only a few sellers (of which Norway is an important one) and a single cartel of buyers on the Continent. Noreng, "International Petroleum Game," pp. 85–86.

6. Returns to scale provide savings on marginal unit costs because the size of operations and size of markets are both large, reducing respectively the inputs per unit of output and transportation costs. Transfer-pricing increases profits because companies are able to shift prices among various operations in order to apply what would otherwise be revenues against costs in other countries rather than have them taxed. Optimization of vertically integrated operations refers to the profitability resulting from the effective management of operations across multiple markets.

7. *The Norwegian–United Kingdom Agreement Relating to the Delimitation of the North Sea Between the Two Countries* (Cmnd. 2757) (London, March 10, 1965).

8. Norwegian Ministry of Industry, *Report No. 76 to the Norwegian Storting (1970–71): Exploration For and Exploitation of Submarine Natural Resources on the Norwegian Continental Shelf* (Oslo, April 30, 1971), p. 32; Norwegian Central Bureau of Statistics, *Industrial Statistics, 1976* (Oslo, 1978), p. 19.

9. Norwegian Central Bureau of Statistics, *Industrial Statistics, 1976,* p. 21.

10. M. M. Sibthorp (ed.), *The North Sea: Challenge and Opportunity,* David Davies Memorial Institute of International Studies (London: Europa Publications, 1975), p. 263–264; Keith Chapman, *North Sea Oil and Gas: A Geographical Perspective* (London: David and Charles, 1976), pp. 129–130; Louis Turner, "The Oil Majors in World Politics," *International Affairs* (Chatham House), Vol. 52, No. 3 (July 1976):99.

11. Respectively, 208 million Norwegian kroner and 42 million Norwegian kroner. All currency conversions are calculated at the par value rate of exchange for that year. Rates are quoted from the American International Investment Corporation, *World Currency Charts,* 8th ed. (San Francisco, 1977); the International Monetary Fund, *International Financial Statistics,* Vol. 31, No. 10 (Washington, D.C., 1978); and Norwegian Central Bureau of Statistics, *Industrial Statistics, 1976,* p. 15.

12. Norwegian Central Bureau of Statistics, *Industrial Statistics, 1976,* p. 33; Norwegian Ministry of Industry, *Report No. 76,* p. 32.

13. Norwegian Ministry of Industry, *Report No. 30 to the Norwegian Parliament (1973–74)* (Oslo, 1974), pp. 43–44.

14. Interview #128 with official, Public Affairs and Information Department, Statoil, Stavanger, Norway, 1978.

15. Norwegian Ministry of Industry, *Report No. 30,* p. 35.

16. Sibthorp, *North Sea,* pp. 262–263.

17. Interview #135 with high-level official, Economics and Legal Division, Petroleum Directorate, Stavanger, Norway, 1978; Norwegian Ministry of Industry, *Report No. 30,* p. 50.

18. Norway's fleet was fourth largest in the world. Norwegian Shipowners Association, *Review of Norwegian Shipping, 1977* (Oslo, 1977); *Norwegian Shipping News* (Oslo), No. 9–16, 1977; interviews #135–139 with high-level official, Ministry of Commerce and Shipping, Oslo, Norway, 1978.

19. Norwegian Ministry of Industry, *Report No. 30,* p. 78.

20. Katherine Huger, "North Sea Oil Development Policy: A Case Study

of the Government-Industry Relationship in Norway and the United Kingdom," *Fletcher Forum,* Vol. 1 (Fall 1976):49, 135.

21. Interviews #35 and #39.

22. The 1972 "full and fair competition" clauses of the national continental shelf regulations (Degree 8.12.72, section 54) were the channels for Norwegian private-sector participation in markets offshore.

23. Interview #147 with high-level official, Petroleum Legislation Division, Petroleum Directorate, Oslo, Norway, 1978; Interview #141 with executive, R. S. Platou A/S (shipping brokerage firm), Oslo, Norway, 1978.

24. Statoil, *Annual Report and Account, 1976* (Oslo, 1976); Norwegian Central Bureau of Statistics, *Industrial Statistics, 1976,* pp. 19, 31, 35; *World Oil,* August 15, 1980, p. 53. The Norwegian government's share of oil and gas production value in 1980, however, was substantial: 25 billion kroner in taxes out of a total of 43 billion kroner. Gunnar Gjerde, "Norwegian Petroleum Policy: Factors of Importance When Deciding the Extraction Rate," *Cooperation and Conflict, The Nordic Journal of International Politics,* Vol. 17, No. 2 (1982):96.

25. *World Business Weekly,* October 13, 1980, pp. 15–16, and ibid., May 5, 1980, p. 14.

26. *Petroleum Intelligence Weekly,* January 5, 1981, p. 7. By 1982 Norway was gaining significant market power by becoming both the only gas-exporting country and net exporter of oil in Western Europe. Martin Saeter, "Natural Gas: New Dimensions of Norwegian Foreign Policy," *Cooperation and Conflict, The Nordic Journal of International Politics,* Vol. 17, No. 2 (1982):141.

27. Interview #157 with a former high-level minister (until 1981) in Norwegian Labor government, April 22, 1982; *Financial Times,* June 9, 1981, p. 3, and June 19, 1981, p. 8; *Wall Street Journal,* November 24, 1981, p. 31.

28. Sibthorp, *North Sea,* p. 11; Directorate of Fisheries, "Fiskerirrettlederen i Haugesund-Bokn-Tyvaer-Utsina," internal document, Bergen, 1978; interview #19 with high-level official, Legal Division, Directorate of Fisheries, Bergen, Norway, 1978; Interview #125 with high-level officer, Sor Norges Tralerlag (trawlers association for the North Sea), Karmoy, Norway, 1978.

29. This amount covered slightly more than 1,145 claims (out of 1,645 total) by fishermen for compensation (Directorate of Fisheries, internal documents).

30. Interview #124 with high-level official, Rogaland District Fishing Organization, Karmoy, Norway, 1978, "North of 62—Ready for 1978 Action?" *Noroil,* No. 1 (January 1978).

31. *World Business Weekly,* May 5, 1981, p. 14.

32. OECD, *Review of Fisheries in OECD Member Countries, 1976* (Paris, 1977), p. 186.

33. However, in 1980 drilling had begun on two fields north of the 62nd parallel. By 1981 three additional blocks had been licensed in the north. *Petroleum Intelligence Weekly,* April 6, 1981, p. 10.

34. Chapman, *North Sea Oil and Gas,* pp. 129–136.

35. Ibid.; European prices were also regulated by governments and at the time were higher than world market prices.

36. Ibid.

37. By 1971, the first year of production, the government had received a total of 1.37 million Norwegian kroner ($89 million) in initial payments from oil companies. Ibid., p. 14; D. I. MacKay and G. A. MacKay, *The Political Economy of North Sea Oil* (London: Martin Robertson, 1975), p. 25; Sibthorp, *North Sea,* pp. 255–258.

38. Alan Budd, *The Politics of Economic Planning* (Manchester: Manchester University Press, 1978), p. 122.

39. Ewan Brown, "Finance for the North Sea: A Matter of European Concern," Royal Institute of International Affairs, Oslo, Norway, February 1975.

40. BNOC was involved in thirteen of the seventeen oil fields under production or development in the British sector by 1978. Among the international oil companies involved in these production agreements were Gulf Oil, Continental Oil, BP, Occidental, Tenneco, Shell, and Exxon. U.K. Department of Energy, *Development of the Oil and Gas Resources of the United Kingdom, 1978,* Report to Parliament by the Secretary of State for Energy (London: HMSO, 1978), p. 21.

41. U.K. production in thousand barrels per day was the following:

1973	8	1977	770
1974	9	1978	1080
1975	20	1979	1570
1976	245	1980	1619

U.S. Department of Energy, Energy Information Administration, *Monthly Energy Review,* April 1981, p. 93; the 1977 price of British crude oil is not available, but the 1978 average f.o.b. price (including insurance and transportation costs) was $13.62 per barrel. Ibid., January 1981, p. 79; U.K. Department of Energy, *Development of Oil and Gas Resources,* p. 20; MacKay and MacKay, *Political Economy,* p. 28.

42. Board of Trade, U.K. Ministry of Trade, *Report* presented to Parliament May, 1970, by the Committee of Inquiry into Shipping (London: HMSO, 1970), p. 429; Ignacy Chrzanowski, *Concentration and Centralization of Capital in Shipping,* S. J. Wiater (ed.) (Lexington, Mass.: Lexington Books, 1975), p. 30; Central Office of Information, *Shipping* (London: HMSO, 1974), p. 4.

43. *Economist,* May 9, 1970; Board of Trade, *Report,* p. 160.

44. U.K. Department of Energy, *Memorandum of Understanding* (London: HMSO, 1975); and idem, *Code of Practice* (London: HMSO, 1975).

45. *Banker,* May 1977, p. 89.

46. However, this supplementary tax was installed only for eighteen months. *Petroleum Intelligence Weekly,* May 4, 1981, p. 8; *World Business Weekly,* October 1, 1979, p. 21.

47. Britain's North Sea oil production was 1,570,000 barrels per day by 1979. U.S. Department of Energy, Energy Information Administration, *Monthly Energy Review,* April 1981, p. 93; *World Business Weekly,* July 7, 1980, p. 16, and October 27, 1980, p. 16; *Financial Times,* October 12, 1981.

48. *World Business Weekly,* October 27, 1980, p. 16; *Business Week,* October 20, 1980, p. 51.

49. *Financial Times,* June 9, 1981, p. 3.

50. The resulting loss of catches (in 1976 prices) was assessed at between £150,000–£460,000 ($90,000–$828,000) in 1976, rising to between £170,000–£600,000 ($126,000–$1,080,000) by 1986. U.K. Department of Energy, *Development of Oil and Gas Resources,* pp. 20, 29–30, 37; interview #161 with an editor, *Fishing News,* London, 1978; University of Aberdeen, *Loss of Access to Fishing Grounds due to Oil and Gas Installations in the North Sea,* Department of Political Economy and the Institute for the Study of Sparsely Populated Areas, Research Report no. 1 (Aberdeen, 1978), pp. 126–128.

51. Participants included the English and Scottish fishing organizations; UKOOA, the oil company operators' association; MAFF and DAFS, the ministries of agriculture and fisheries for the U.K. and for Scotland; and the Department of Energy.

52. *Economist,* January 21, 1978.

53. Interview #167 with a high-level official, Scottish Fishermen's Federation, Scottish Division, Aberdeen, Scotland, 1978; and page 3 of a letter from Gilbert Buchan to the Fishing and Offshore Oil Consultative Group, 1978.

54. Interview #157 with a high-level official, FOOCG and Ministry of Agriculture, Fisheries, and Food, London, 1978.

55. Norway is a relatively marginal supplier in the world market, and would have a difficult time stepping up its output suddenly because it lacks spare capacity. Noreng, "International Petroleum Game," p. 91.

56. Klapp, "Inter-Industry Conflict," p. 168; *Banker,* May 1977, pp. 77, 95.

57. *Banker,* February 1975, p. 127.

58. The articles by Noreng, Bergesen, Østreng, and Saeter in the 1982 issue of *Conflict and Cooperation* explain the evolution of Norwegian oil and gas policy as a commercial rather than foreign policy of the Norwegian government. These authors do not see Norwegian policy in terms of a response to the structure of international oil and Western European gas markets. I agree with the commercial policy explanation and seek merely to demonstrate how domestic and multinational corporate politics contributed to and may continue to influence the outcomes of government policy. See particularly Noreng, "International Petroleum Game," p. 91, and Helge Ole Bergesen, " 'Not Valid for Oil': The Petroleum Dilemma in Norwegian Foreign Policy," *Conflict and Cooperation, The Nordic Journal of International Politics,* Vol. 17, No. 2 (1982):113, 115.

59. In the three northern blocks licensed in 1981, Statoil had a 50 percent equity holding, with the possibility of escalating that share to 80 percent depending upon future output. However, in one of these blocks (Tromsoe), Norsk Hydro was given 20 percent and Saga 5 percent, while in another block (Holden Bank), Saga got 10 percent and Norsk Hydro, 5 percent. Foreign equity holdings were between 25 and 35 percent. *Petroleum Intelligence Weekly,* April 6, 1981, p. 10.

60. "Parity norm" payoffs would give industry groups such as fishing an amount that represented a fair assessment of their losses owing to oil production

offshore. "Split the difference" would instead give them a share of the *total* fishing and oil profits produced offshore.

61. By 1981 the British government appeared to be cutting back production on major fields as a way of leveling out the U.K.'s peak production curve for purposes of national self-sufficiency. Government projections for that year were only 80–90 million tons, down from 1975 estimates of 125–160 million tons. Projections for 1984 were 90–120 million tons. *Petroleum Intelligence Weekly,* March 16, 1981, and April 13, 1981.

62. More than half this profit increase came from exchange-rate gains on a $825 million advance crude oil sale in 1977. Its net profit was £88.1 million ($193 million) in 1980. *Petroleum Intelligence Weekly,* April 27, 1981, p. 12, and June 20, 1977, p. 12.

63. For example, the need to profit from oil and natural gas in order to help finance other failing nationalized industries such as British Steel Corporation is one reason the government is unlikely to cut back the role of state utilities. In 1979 nine nationalized industries relied upon government funds for 23 percent of their financing. *Wall Street Journal,* October 16, 1980.

64. In its seventh round of licensing in 1981, the British government awarded eighty-two British companies (comprising diverse domestic industries such as fishing, food, and tractor manufacturing) stakes in offshore licenses. *World Business Weekly,* March 30, 1981, p. 15.

5
The Energy Utilities: How to Increase Rewards to Match Increasing Risks

Kermit R. Kubitz

On the one hand, profit is in fact bound up in economic change (because change is the condition for uncertainty), and on the other hand it is clearly the result of risk, or what good usage calls such, but only a unique kind of risk, which is not susceptible of measurement.

—Frank H. Knight

Introduction: Change and Challenge for Energy Utilities

The energy utilities, suppliers of electricity and gas for one hundred years in the United States, have been buffeted by a tidal wave of change. They were, naturally, hugely affected by the multiple facets of the revolution in world energy economics that began in 1973–1974. These changes created both problems and opportunities for the energy utilities. Economists argue about the price-elasticity of demand for industry products. Politicians and regulators debate the legal structure that has governed these businesses since the early twentieth century. Managers of energy utilities, who must answer to existing shareholders for the financial performance of their companies while convincing new investors to provide funds, believe problems and opportunities have combined to make the energy utility business much riskier today than it was in the past.[1] Utility planners and managers seek to understand how to plan and operate to restore a balance between risks and rewards, whether it can be accomplished within the existing regulatory and industry

Views expressed are those of the author and do not represent the views of any utility company.

structure or will require the creation of new structures (both regulatory and within the industry).[2]

In this context, possible solutions for the financial and service problems of the energy utilities can be related to each other in terms of their effects on risks and rewards. Some sources, principally within the industry, advocate reforming the regulatory procedures of existing institutions in light of such economic realities as continuing high inflation, increased construction costs, and the disproportionate increase in fuel costs. The extreme variant of this trend toward regulatory reform is deregulation, which would either remove entirely or loosen substantially present regulatory limits on financial rewards from supplying energy. A second major option for increasing rewards and possibly lowering risks would be for utilities to pursue a strategy of diversification. Diversification assumes that the fundamental economic viability of providing energy services is greater than that of continuing to provide just gas and electricity.[3] A third option open to the utilities is pursuing greater demand management and redefining the obligation to provide services in a more flexible way. Conservation, load management, and conditions of service would all be part of this risk-allocating process.

The advocates of all three approaches have seemingly sound reasons for their positions. Some utilities may adopt hybrid strategies that include elements of several approaches phased in over time as conditions make different actions feasible.[4] The question of how to achieve adequate rewards has arisen, however, because of the fundamental changes in the business environment of energy utilities. Before we examine these approaches, it is useful to explore briefly the current circumstances of the utility industry.

Utilities and the Energy Crisis: Four Impacts

The energy utilities are perhaps the most interested business observers of the multiple transitions under way on the world energy scene. For decades, the energy utilities expanded their investment, met the service needs of their customers, and reduced or maintained the level of rates. These achievements produced congenial relationships with regulators and investors. The 1970s produced a reversal of favorable relationships with customers and investors. The OPEC price increases suddenly raised the industry cost of production. Oil-based generation became increasingly expensive; natural gas also increased in price and suffered periodic shortages of supply. Meanwhile, the very affluence of U.S. society made it hard to generate political support to accept the risks and impacts of other sources of centralized generation of power—coal and nuclear

Table 1
Cost Components of Electricity in 1969 and 1979

	1969	1979
Fuel	18%	41%
Non-Fuel	27%	24%
Capital	55%	35%

Source: Stephen P. Reynolds, "Marginal Cost Methods in California," p.1, a paper presented at National Economic Research Associates, Inc., PURPA Section 133 Workshop, Los Angeles, California, February 26, 1981.

plants. Environmental regulation permitted new plant construction only with costly and complex safety and emission controls.

The massive escalation in fossil fuel prices in the 1970s thus revolutionized the national and international economic marketplaces as well as the energy utilities that operate within them. Four of the changes in the business environment are particularly significant for this analysis. First, higher fuel prices have dramatically reordered the components of the cost of supplying electricity. The cost components of electricity in 1969, the year of lowest cost, and in 1979 are shown in Table 1.

Even this dramatic reorientation in the costs of production masked the true impact of the problem of fuel-price escalation. Because cost increases were rapid, uncertain, and huge, they were unmanageable by traditional regulatory processes, which provided for lengthy hearings, few time limits for decision, and a lag between the time costs were incurred and rates were revised. Thus, the first impact of the energy crisis was to degrade the financial performance of the energy utilities by creating all the conditions for inadequate rate relief. And where fuel costs were fully recovered, their magnitude prompted increasing reluctance by state regulatory agencies to permit full recovery of other utility expenses, such as cost of maintenance or capital.[5]

The second impact was to increase the level of utility charges for customers and raise the corresponding cost-effectiveness of a variety of energy-conserving options. The continuing effects of price increases have led to reduced demand for electricity and a substitution of other means of providing energy where possible. Economists refer to these phenomena as the onset of price- and cross-elasticity. The level and extent of this substitution process is a matter of great debate today. It

Table 2
Oil Prices Compared to Fuel Cost per Kilowatt-hour[a]

Year	Oil Price per Barrel	Fuel Cost per Kilowatt-hour
1973	$3.00	$0.005
1979	$18.00	$0.03
1981	$36.00	$0.06

a. Numbers are illustrative based on assumption of 6 x 10^6 Btu/bbl and heat rate in text.

may be increasingly important for the gas industry if further decontrol of gas prices narrows the cost advantages of gas over electricity or oil as sources of energy services to consumers. The electric industry has already experienced most of the consequences of higher prices. In a typical power plant of moderate efficiency, with a heat rate of 10,000 Btus per kilowatt hour produced, the OPEC price increases are directly translatable into increased electricity prices, as shown in Table 2.[6]

This escalation of fuel prices and electricity rates has made a number of conservation options economical for residential, commercial, and industrial consumers.[7] They are being adopted at an accelerating pace as new business entities are formed to exploit these possibilities. This continuing trend must be a major element in the analysis of options to restore utility profitability.

The third major impact of the energy crisis is the macroeconomic impact of energy prices on inflation, investor expectations, and the availability of capital.[8] There is convincing evidence that we are witnessing a historic redistribution of profits and concomitant capital investment in the U.S. economy. The energy companies as a group now account for 40 percent of all manufacturing profits in U.S. business. Similarly, energy investments constitute an increasingly disproportionate share of all capital investment.[9]

A number of industries, including airlines, automobiles, and primary industries such as cement and aluminum, face a massive task of replacing present products or processes with more energy-efficient ones. For industry, cogeneration, waste-heat recovery, pipe insulation, and energy-efficient process redesign are all necessary steps in achieving competitiveness and controlling costs. But, like the energy utilities, although to a lesser degree, these industries lack the financial strength to make the necessary investments.

The difficulty all these industries and utilities face is that they must compete with the unregulated energy sector for funds in the capital markets.[10] If the marginal efficiency of capital investment in the energy utilities is substantially less than that of other equally or less risky opportunities, investment funds simply will not be available to utilities. The profitability of fuel exploration and development and the built-in competitive advantage of frequent price increases by OPEC means that the underlying asset value of the oil industry also contributes to its ability to raise capital.[11] This advantage does not exist for utilities.

A fourth impact, this time in the economic policy area, is the increasing application of marginal or value-based pricing to a widening number of energy commodities by an increasing variety of institutions. The decontrol of new oil and unconventional gas and the possible accelerated decontrol of all gas supplies contribute to this trend. A major question for the future, for example, is whether the price of coal will be increasingly decoupled from its energy value in oil-equivalence terms or whether it will follow the price of oil.

A similar question is the extent to which utilities will move away from their traditional approach of pricing on the basis of average or embedded costs toward marginalism in both the structure and level of rates. Marginal cost principles have been increasingly adopted in rate structures through such devices as time-of-use rates or peak-load pricing, inverted rate designs, and alternative fuel-price ceilings for natural gas to industries that have the ability to convert to other fuels. A more fundamental question, however, is whether the level of revenues provided to the industry will reflect the costs of developing new supplies or the costs incurred in the existing system.

Section 210 of the Public Utility Regulatory Policy Act, which provides for avoided or marginal cost purchases of cogenerated electricity or the output of other qualifying small power production, is an initial step in this direction. The trend toward marginal pricing is a response to the first three impacts in that the shift in world energy-market forces has dictated a more realistic pricing structure for all energy transactions and in all segments of the production and distribution chain. But questions remain about how quickly this reform will spread because of the complex interplay between market forces and regulatory realities. Moreover, although this reform potentially increases the rewards of supplying utility energy, it also entails new risks. Whether the risks and rewards will be balanced can be determined by further experiments in this area.

In summary, these four impacts—the need to recover increasing fuel costs, the rapidly rising level of rates, the increased demand and competition for capital, and the trend toward marginal pricing of energy—have all revised the outlook for which utilities must plan. These impacts are, in many ways, national energy-policy issues as well as problems that utility management must face, but their cumulative effect is to present an array of risks, some opportunities for increasing rewards, and a dynamic market for both the supply of and the demand for energy. Before we discuss utility approaches to planning, it is useful to categorize the risks that face managers of utility industries.

Issues, Risks, and Alternatives

The energy utilities face a series of critical questions as they consider their future role, including how to improve financial performance, how to provide future service to customers, and how to deal with regulation.

These issues reflect the interplay between economic, technological, and political forces that will determine this industry's future. The issue of improved financial performance is central to any continued role for energy utilities, but the route to that improved performance is not clear. If private industry cannot obtain adequate rewards for providing energy utility service, then some form of direct government intervention may become necessary because of the industry's crucial role in the U.S. economy.

The issue of service to customers is critical to maintaining any degree of political support for fair treatment of the energy utilities. Customers may accept, to a limited degree, increased energy costs if they are justified but are unlikely to accept both increasing costs and decreased service, at least in essential areas of energy use. Widespread unmanaged failures of electrical supply or reductions in levels of gas service will be attributed to the utilities, whatever the real cause.

Ultimately, the degree and form of regulation affect both financial performance and the future provision of service. Preferences of regulatory agencies among alternative means of restoring financial vitality and providing service will influence utility approaches to these issues. The regulatory process, however, is responding to the impacts of escalating fuel costs as well as to the perception of the local political establishment of its adequacy to provide required service by, and financial returns to, the energy utility industry. As each state's regulators learn from their own and other states' experience, we can hope that good regulation will drive out bad. However, the lead times for energy decisions are generally longer than the tenure of regulatory commissioners.

Each of these issues involves assessment and allocation of risks and rewards. In order to understand how proposed solutions to the industry's problems affect finance, service, regulation, and the risk-reward balance, it is necessary to survey the variety of risks faced by the energy utilities. The number of risks exceeds those facing other U.S. businesses because of additional uncertainties arising from the existence of regulation and the dynamics of energy markets. A comprehensive discussion of utility risks is found in the work of Kahn, Benenson, and Brown.[12] These risks include business or competitive risk, which is the ability to make sales at a profit; market risk, which is uncertainty associated with returns on common equity; financial risk, which stems from the fixed obligations of bonds, debentures, and bank debt; inflation risk; interest-rate risk; and regulatory risk, which is the risk that future regulatory requirements will be different from today's.

These risks are interrelated. The escalation of fuel prices has increased the business risk of electric utilities by increasing the uncertainty of demand growth and the likelihood of substitution of other products. It has similarly increased market risk because of the regulatory pressure on other utility costs stemming from the need to pass through fuel-purchase expenses. Indirectly, by providing a significant incentive to build long-lead-time, oil-displacing generation, fuel prices increase the inflation risk. Long-lead-time plants and continuous-financing requirements also enhance interest-rate and regulatory risk. Similarly, past and possible future gas-price escalation in response to decontrol increases the business and market risk of gas utilities. Rate structures that allocate costs more heavily to one customer segment than another (such as incremental pricing or lifeline rates) can affect business risk as well.

More important, *treatment of risk under current regulatory procedures is asymmetric.* Savings from utility industry resources that prevent costs from escalating as fast as oil prices are generally passed through to ratepayers, but costs of developing new resources are not generally recovered in rates until the new projects are placed in service, and utilities may never recover all costs incurred for projects that do not come into operation. These factors contribute to a general pessimism about regulatory risk and explain some of the momentum behind alternatives to present forms of regulation.

Alternatives for Utility Profitability and Service

Clearly, the energy utility business is today a far riskier one than it was a decade ago. Rewards have not increased with the pace of economic change in energy markets or the increasing uncertainty of these businesses. However, there are a variety of alternatives for restoring the financial integrity of these companies, including

- Demand management, including conservation, load management, and redefinition of the service obligation
- Regulatory reform within existing regulatory structures
- Deregulation in conjunction with industry reorganization
- Diversification into new energy sources and customer services

Each of these alternatives must be evaluated for its impact on financial performance, future service, and regulatory and political practicality. These alternatives do not directly revolve around future technology choices. Technology affects the course of utilities, but the issues faced by utility management are broader than any choice between hard and soft technologies. Both can be embraced under proper circumstances, but not unless the financial integrity of utilities is restored.

These alternatives all must deal also with the fact that utilities are nearly unique among privately owned businesses in being both regulated and obligated to expand service to meet customer demand. Most other regulated industries, such as trucking and airlines, have more limited commitments. Communication utilities have the most similar obligations but do not face the same size, length, or riskiness of required future capital commitments. The alternatives may be considered singly or in combination. They may, as well, represent different phases of an overall approach that varies with time as conditions change. However, all these approaches are being considered seriously.

Demand Management and Redefinition of the Obligation to Serve

Several factors encourage the consideration of increasing management of demand as a means of improving financial performance. One factor is the current financial status of the industry, in which bond-coverage ratios are declining and stock is selling well below book value. Under these circumstances, capital investment in excess of those funds provided from earnings and depreciation tends to dilute the ownership value of existing shareholders. Restricting growth in capitalization mitigates such earnings and asset dilution. Demand management also makes sense when some fraction of sales is unprofitable. If costs are not being recovered for various market segments, further growth in these markets only damages financial performance.

Demand management, however, is not a simple matter. It embraces a spectrum of operating tactics ranging from pricing decisions, to implementation of new technologies for affecting customer end use, to renegotiating at the regulatory level the implicit, and often ambiguous, technical and legal requirements for service to new and existing customers.

Pricing is one obvious form of demand management. Electrical utilities have with increasing frequency adopted peak-load pricing practices for large industrial loads. Big users often already have sophisticated metering, and their energy bills are significant enough to make them responsive to price signals. European utilities have successfully adopted such pricing strategies, and early U.S. experiments have yielded similar results.[13]

At the residential customer level, price signals alone may not be enough to provide an adequate response or reliable load shifts, so many experiments with direct appliance controls are under way. These are usually accompanied by some form of economic incentive or rate discount in order to encourage customer acceptance of load controls. Cycling off air-conditioners, hot-water heaters, or other major energy-using appliances for a few minutes every half hour can contribute to a significant reduction in total system peak demand. Such actions can avoid the need for incremental capital investment solely to meet peak-demand growth or system reliability requirements. However, they may not alter the need for baseload generation sources.

Similarly, for gas utilities the problem is to meet overall energy needs, rather than merely peak requirements. Avoiding the risks of developing major new increments of gas or electrical supply is the essence of the demand-management option, and to do this, a major effort to reduce the growth in total gas or electric energy demanded, not merely peak-shaving, is necessary.

Both conservation and load management have favorable regulatory impacts. Many programs of improving end-use energy efficiency or shifting the timing and extent of customer demands can be expensed and recovered in current rates rather than capitalized for future recovery. Similarly, many regulatory agencies find it difficult to resolve power-plant-siting questions for a variety of technical and political reasons. It may be easier to solve even difficult questions of equity and structure of conservation programs, which can be continuously adapted to social and political circumstances. In addition, demand management through conservation makes economic sense. The escalation of fuel prices and the inflation in overall costs of providing utility service mean that many means of conserving energy are less costly than some forms of additions to energy supplies, particularly oil-fired electric generation. Some of those who have studied conservation opportunities have constructed supply curves beginning with the least costly measures and moving to the more complex and costly techniques for improving energy efficiency. Insulation, low-flow showerheads, weather stripping, and set-back thermostats can all help moderate customer demands and costs for energy services.

There is debate about the proper role of utilities in encouraging conservation. At one extreme is the provision of conservation services directly to customers by utilities, about which more will be said in discussing diversification. At the other extreme is total reliance on proper price signals and information to customers about present and future energy prices and the relative cost-effectiveness of various options. This, in general, is the approach adopted by the federally mandated Residential Conservation Service (RCS) program, which requires gas and electric utilities to offer audits of customers' residences.

Beyond conservation and load management is the option of redefining the obligation to serve.[14] If present utility financial circumstances continue, it will be neither profitable nor economically feasible to make major investments in improvements or additions to service without special rate treatment of these additions. The alternative is to make utility service available on a basis that reflects the overall decreasing ability of energy utilities to meet an unlimited obligation. Some forms of this redefinition of service are already under consideration. One form is the possibility of mandatory load management for future requests for new service. Another is the assessment of charges or fees for customers' requests for new service. These fees may be based on the marginal costs of the energy resources required to meet additional load, including improvements or extensions of the local distribution system. The gas industry underwent a period, before the partial decontrol of gas prices, when new service connections were severely limited. This approach has been tried, but with little practical or legal acceptance of such an extreme revision of the utility obligation.

In summary, the approach of demand management is finding increasing acceptance among utility managers. Some utilities have adopted explicit goals or principles for limitation of future customer demands; these types of programs are clearly a growth industry within the energy utility sector.

Regulatory Reform Within the Existing Framework

The most common prescription for restoration of financial health and profitability to energy utilities still appears to be reform of the ratemaking procedures of existing regulatory institutions to allow industry revenues to match increased costs more closely. This approach has been advocated variously by representatives of the financial community, government officials concerned about energy supply, and utility executives.[15] Some forms of procedural innovation merely shift the time of receipt of utility revenues to increase the financial flexibility of the industry; others are designed to increase the basis on which total revenue level is determined.

The existing scheme of utility regulation has a rational economic basis, which is described in the key legal cases about a state regulatory agency's duty to fairly balance the interests of ratepayers and investors.[16] The rate-setting process must estimate the rate base or capital investment, determine a fair return on that investment, and based on projected expenses, set rates at a level high enough to provide sufficient growth of revenue and net income to provide a fair return. The technical legal duty of a public utility commission is not to follow any given methodology in any of these intermediate steps, but, as described by Justice Douglas in the *Hope* case,[17] to achieve an end result that fairly compensates investors for risks assumed and allows the company to maintain its financial integrity and attract capital.

It is hard to argue that regulation has fulfilled its obligation to maintain the financial integrity of the energy utilities under the existing scheme of regulation. Overall returns of the energy utilities were comparable to those of industrial companies during the 1940s and 1950s,[18] but during the 1970s while risks increased substantially, returns were essentially flat, averaging about 10–11 percent for electric utilities and 12–14 percent for gas distributors.[19] In the meantime, interest rates in the economy at large rose dramatically. By the beginning of the 1980s, interest rates for risk-free government securities and money market funds available to broader segments of the public had reached 12–14 percent, while the prime lending rate had risen even higher. Members of the financial community judge financial integrity in terms of standards for internal cash generation, a widely acceptable bond rating, and an ability to sell new common stock with proceeds above the book value per share. The capital markets' negative verdict about the financial health of utilities is reflected by the fact that most utility stocks sell at 20–30 percent below book value. Wall Street knows that costs are outpacing revenues and rewards are lagging behind perceived risks.

Regulatory reforms seek to alter the end result of the ratemaking process to permit the utilities to regain financial integrity. But the process of changing ratemaking is essentially fractionated because each state has its own commissioners' preferences, regulatory policy precedents, and staff positions. There is little leverage or motivation for adoption of uniform methods or procedures of ratemaking. Despite these problems, some regulatory innovations have become widely accepted; others have met widespread resistance.

When the first wave of fuel price increases hit in 1973–1974, regulatory commissions were generally ill prepared procedurally to deal with the flood of requests for rate relief. Rate cases were lengthy, time limits were few, and the resulting lag was great. By the late 1970s, however, many regulatory jurisdictions had fuel-adjustment clauses, which provided for cost recovery of increased fuel expenses based on amounts expended by utilities. Often these adjustments included balancing accounts to track expenses and revenues accurately.

The upward pressure on rates from fuel costs, however, meant that commissions increasingly scrutinized and reduced allowances for other costs. Since then, the industry has searched for a comprehensive package of ratemaking procedures that will ensure that the result of rates is full recovery of costs. That package has various possible components, including time limits on hearing decisions or suspensions of proposed rate schedules, fuel-adjustment clauses, inclusion of construction work in progress or bond-interest costs, normalization of taxes, and adjustment of rates through indexing.

In addition to these procedural requests, the substantive issues of a fair return on investment and the valuation of the rate base are also being debated. It was the practice in the past to compare returns with those of other utilities, on the theory that these were the enterprises of comparable risk. Now, aggressive utilities are going beyond this intraindustry comparison and suggesting that the risks of utilities are increasingly comparable to those of industrial or high-technology companies and that they should be given the opportunity to earn comparable returns.[20]

Utilities are also seeking greater freedom to adjust rates to reflect the continuation of high underlying inflation in the U.S. economy. Some jurisdictions, such as New Mexico and Michigan, have accepted the indexing of rates to provide for cost increases in areas such as maintenance and administration. In addition, recognition of inflation appears to be finding legal acceptance by courts sympathetic to the proposition that these general cost increases will affect utility expenses and earnings in a manner detrimental to financial integrity if they are not accounted for in the rate-setting process.

Thus, reform of existing regulator institutions and procedures offers some promise of improved financial performance for utilities. Utility management can be expected to endorse new procedures necessary to generate revenues that permit recovery of costs. The political acceptability of such reforms, however, will vary from area to area and will depend, in large part, on the underlying cost trends in fuels and operations, over which management can exert only limited control. However, improved procedures for adjusting rates would have the salutary effect of contributing to the demand-management objectives previously discussed.

Deregulation and Reorganization

The previously discussed deficiencies in regulation have triggered some recent calls, generally originating outside the ranks of utility management, for deregulation of the utility industry.[21] The reasons for deregulation are as varied as the advocates. Utility commissioners have called for deregulation because of what they see as an unhealthy trend of increasingly shifting risks from investors to ratepayers. Others call for relaxation of some regulatory controls because of the decline of the natural monopoly status of the energy utilities. The decline of natural monopoly comes about not because competition between two or more electrical or gas distribution companies has become more feasible, but because the rising cost of fuel has made it increasingly possible to make capital investments in conservation as a substitute for generating energy. Deregulation, in this sense, is possible because competition now exists at the consumer level of use.[22]

Deregulation, as generally conceived, would be implemented by encouraging competition at the generation stage of electrical power utilities. Rather than having either a guaranteed return or a regulatory limit on earnings, generation entities would produce power as economically as possible under the spur of competition from other producers and would sell to some purchasing agent (possibly a regulated transmission network) at whatever the competitive market could bear.

Section 210 of the Public Utilities Regulatory Policy Act (PURPA) is one step toward deregulation. As implemented by the Federal Energy Regulatory Commission, it provides for the sale of certain types of electric generation based not on the producer's costs but on the value, expressed at the avoided cost, of the energy to the local utility company. These avoided costs vary substantially across the country but are generally higher where significant amounts of oil- and gas-fired generation are used. Thus, this form of deregulation tends to increase the trend toward marginal valuation of energy resources.

Utility management has viewed the alternative of deregulation, at least as currently proposed, with skepticism. Deregulation of generation, although theoretically desirable, may pose significant problems when applied to the problem of financing large or even moderate-sized generation facilities without an assured revenue stream.[23] Furthermore, the application of principles of deregulation to certain types of technologies has contained restrictions on utility involvement in or ownership of these resources. If the economics favors deregulation, utility managers may ask, why not deregulate thoroughly and completely.

It is more likely that rather than accepting these proposals for deregulation, skillful managers will justify regulatory reforms such as indexing or allowances for construction work in progress as a more efficient alternative to deregulation. Greater flexibility in the ratemaking process is a partial step toward a deregulated energy-supply system. At the same time, utility executives will fight to ensure that utilities share at least equally with other entities in whatever competitive and financial advantages follow from deregulation of segments of the business.

Whether deregulation, either partial or complete, is adequate to stimulate major energy-supply investments in technologies perceived as risky will be a continuing question.[24] The implications of deregulated markets for industry organization—in sharing risk and reducing financial stress—may be as important as deregulation itself. In a deregulated market, the setting of prices would be a continuous function involving the dispatching and evaluation of resources over a wide area on a bidding and selling basis. This could eventually lead to a system of feedback between customers and energy producers on a real-time basis in which supply and demand would be continuously balanced. One such proposal for a real-time energy market has been described as a system of homeostatic utility control. In this conceptual outline, a utility makes the market for energy in its area by simultaneously providing buyers and sellers with the current costs of energy. Increasing demand leads to increasing prices, which ration energy until the system is once again in balance. Although this proposal is not likely to be implemented fully in the near future, it will undoubtedly influence the course of the debate about deregulation.

Diversification of Resources and Services

One of the impacts of the fundamental shift in energy economics previously discussed was to make a number of substitutes for gas and electricity cost effective. This increased competitiveness of substitutes is also an issue in possible utility deregulation. A direction different from improvement in utilities' financial position in the supply of solely energy commodities is diversification into providing multiple services and products to customers. This option has been encouraged by numerous studies of the cost-effectiveness, environmental desirability, and financial attractiveness of providing such expanded services. In addition to providing means of improving end-use energy efficiency to customers, many analyses have suggested that utilities should experiment with a variety of novel energy sources whose fuels are renewable or whose efficiency is greater than that of conventional sources.

Studies of industry trends in diversification reveal a great variety of enterprises.[25] Most of the revenue, however, seems to be concentrated in those utility subsidiaries that previously developed fuel and resource exploration and development assets. Companies such as Montana Power and Pacific Power and Light have significant earnings streams from these sources. The greatest impediment to accelerated utility exploration of this type of diversification appears to be fear of regulatory recapture of any increased earnings, while investors alone would face any losses.

Some utilities have already diversified into customer services of nontraditional types. There appears to be a substantial barrier, however, in the perception, fostered by present suppliers of conservation services and dispersed energy systems, that utility participation in these markets offers substantial opportunity for unfair competition. This tendency is reflected in the initial prohibition in the National Energy Conservation Policy Act against utilities' providing the kinds of services recommended by their energy audits.[26] Subsequently, sober second thoughts about the desirability of utility participation resulted in partial removal of this restriction.

There is at the state level, however, a residual reluctance to permit utilities to engage in delivery of conservation services in competition with existing suppliers.[27] This hesitance may mean that the rate of penetration of some conservation technology may be slowed by the cottage-industry form of delivery that currently characterizes some developing energy conservation systems. Like the reluctance to permit utilities to utilize fully the incentives of PURPA Section 210, regulatory reluctance to encourage in the face of opposition direct utility participation in delivery of conservation improvements and dispersed energy systems may impede utility consideration of this option. Strict regulatory controls on utility diversification would also enhance fears of regulatory recapture of earnings, thereby removing the basic incentive for pursuing this course in the first place.

Utilities that wish to diversify will have to find niches that represent areas of technology where they will be welcomed by existing purveyors or where a competitive position has not yet been staked out. The alternative, which is distinctly possible, is that utilities might, in the search for profitability and secure fuel supplies, become a second tier of competition for the major oil companies in the development of oil, gas, and coal resources.

Diversification may not do much to decrease the risks of the energy utilities unless it contributes to meeting load and customer demands for service with less capital-intensive services than is traditional. However, some dispersed energy resources and alternative energy technologies may be more expensive, in terms of up-front investment per unit of energy produced, than conventional utility projects.[28] One analyst, for example, reported that while conventional generation and residential weatherization are of about equal capital intensity, solar energy systems are today twice as capital intensive.[29]

A program of diversification, therefore, would have significantly stricter financial controls than a program merely of demand management. The objective would be to establish a profit center in the supply of nontraditional services, not merely to match the costs of providing load-reducing measures to customers. Whether this can be achieved throughout much of the industry is questionable in view of regulatory reluctance and supplier opposition.

Summary: Trade-Offs and Transitions

Each of the options discussed for improving utilities' financial performance is limited by the pace of regulatory understanding and acceptance of the need for revision of traditional conceptions of utility operations and regulation. There is a tremendous impetus for change because of increasing concern about the capabilities of these industries to meet the economy's energy needs and recognition of the fact that the long lead times of energy decision making mean that actions now will affect the adequacy of energy supplies in the 1990s.

The industry has the task of developing effective plans for restoring some semblance of the financial strength that characterized the utilities from the 1940s through the 1960s. This may include a period of retrenchment and restructuring of the traditionally open-ended service obligation of energy utilities. At the same time it will seek to make the regulatory process more realistic in matching revenues to the pace of increasing costs, as well as to employ other measures to improve the competitiveness of the industry in capital markets.

There may be experiments with radical revisions of traditional regulation, including attempts to remove regulation and increase competition in some segments of the business. Preferential deregulation of some technologies may stimulate utility interest in such areas as cogeneration or wind energy production, but limitations on utility involvement will dilute this interest unless they are removed. Similarly, although there are obvious incentives for utility diversification to mitigate risks and increase rewards, particularly in view of the attractive economics of some resource development and customer service business opportunities, uncertainty about regulatory treatment of earnings and opposition to competition in expanded markets by the energy utilities will limit involvement in this area. The 1980s will see experiments in each of these areas carried on in different states, with no clear resolution of appropriate roles until later.

None of the utilities will be able to play a vigorous role in the supply of future energy needs unless, in cooperation with responsible state regulators, they are able to develop a practical plan for achieving financial integrity. This in practice means convincing regulators and the public they represent that the risks of the energy utilities are the risks of society in general and that the reward of future supplies of gas and electricity and other energy services that are reliable, safe, and economic is worth some revisions of historical regulatory procedures that do not adequately reflect the risks of the current dynamic markets for these commodities.

Notes

1. See "A Dark Future for Utilities," *Business Week*, May 28, 1979, p. 108.

2. For another discussion of the interplay between industry and regulation, see Mason Willrich and Kermit R. Kubitz, "Organizational and Regulatory Alternatives for the Energy Utility Industry," *Public Utilities Fortnightly*, June 18, 1981, p. 21.

3. See "Energy Conservation: Spawning a Billion Dollar Business," *Business Week*, April 6, 1981, p. 58, for an estimate that investments in energy conservation may be a $30 billion market by 1985.

4. See Don C. Frisbee and M. Eugene Akridge, "The State of the Utility Management Art: Emerging Utility Strategies," *Public Utilities Fortnightly*, March 12, 1981, pp. 15, 20, for a description of a variety of strategies and how they may be combined.

5. Paul L. Joskow and Paul W. MacAvoy, "Regulation and the Financial Condition of the Electric Power Companies in the 1970s," *American Economic Review*, 65, 2 (May 1975):295, 301, described the effects of regulation and predicted substantial capital shortages if existing regulatory procedures continued.

6. For oil prices during the period covered by Table 2, see the table on landed cost of Saudi crude oil, *International Energy Indicators* (U.S. Department of Energy), July 1981, p. 21; see also *Business Week*, June 1, 1981, p. 57.

7. Alan Meier, Arthur H. Rosenfeld, and Janice Wright, "Supply Curves of Energy for California's Residential Sector," Lawrence Berkeley Laboratory–13608; Barry R. Sedlik, "Industrial Energy Planning: Building a Strategy for the 1980's and 1990's," *Dames & Moore Engineering Bulletin*, No. 56, July 1981, p. 23.

8. "A Breather for Oil Prices," *Business Week*, May 25, 1981, pp. 104, 106.

9. "America's Restructured Economy," *Business Week*, June 1, 1981, pp. 56, 58; "The Implications of Oil Company Profits," *Business Week*, August 18, 1980, p. 84.

10. See "Energy Outlook: The Efficiency-Investment Tradeoff," *Annual Report of the Thermo Electron Corporation*, 1981, pp. 17–19, for the proposition that a lowering of inflation and interest rates will release a pent-up demand for industrial investments in energy efficiency.

11. In 1979 the net income of fifteen oil companies, totaling $20.2 billion, was dwarfed by the $57.4 billion gain in oil reserve value of these same companies. *Business Week*, August 18, 1980, p. 87. This factor appreciation of the value of energy production assets as energy costs rise is not applicable to utilities but might be under deregulation.

12. Edward Kahn, Peter Benenson, and Burnett Brown, "Commercialization

of Solar Energy by Regulated Utilities: Economic and Financial Risk Analysis," Lawrence Berkeley Laboratory–11398, October 1980, pp. 17–32.

13. Bridger M. Mitchell, Willard G. Manning, Jr., and Jan Paul Acton, *Peak Load Pricing—European Lesson for U.S. Energy Pricing* (Cambridge, Mass.: Ballinger Publishing Co., 1978). See especially Chapter 5, pp. 89–120, and Chapter 8, pp. 151–189, for descriptions of the responsiveness of European and U.S. industry to peak-load pricing.

14. See Stephen P. Reynolds and Paula G. Rosput, "The Obligation to Serve: Do Utilities Have a Choice?" paper presented to the Institute of Public Utilities conference, Williamsburg, Va., December 15, 1981.

15. W. S. White, Jr., "A Closer Look at Electric Utility Deregulation," *Public Utilities Fortnightly,* January 21, 1982, p. 19.

16. Alfred E. Kahn, *The Economics of Regulation* (New York: John Wiley and Sons, 1970), pp. 3–14, 42–53.

17. *Federal Power Commission* v. *Hope Natural Gas Co.,* 320 U.S. 591 (1944).

18. See Table 2, Average Rates of Return on Net Worth of Leading U.S. Corporations, 1947–1964, in Harold H. Wein, "Fair Rates of Return and Incentives—Some General Considerations," in Harry M. Trebing (ed.), *Performance Under Regulation* (MSU Public Utility Studies, 1968), p. 60.

19. Remarks of Charles Benore, first vice-president, Paine Weber, Mitchell and Hutchins, Inc., in Steven Westly (ed.), *Energy Utilities—The Next 10 Years,* A Symposium at Stanford University, March 27, 1981 (Sacramento: California Public Utilities Commission, 1981), pp. 20–31.

20. This is equivalent to the use of the "lending rate" as the cost of capital as described in Alexander Barges, *The Effect of Capital Structure on the Cost of Capital* (New York: Prentice-Hall, 1963), p. 3, citing Harry Roberts, "Current Problems in the Economics of Capital Budgeting," *Journal of Business,* January 1957, p. 14, for a definition of the lending rate as "the expected rate of return on equity investments outside the firm that appear to the entrepreneur to involve a degree of riskiness similar to those contemplated within the firm."

21. See statement of John E. Bryson, president, California Public Utilities Commission, before the Committee on Energy and Commerce, Subcommittee on Energy Conservation and Power, U.S. House of Representatives, April 6, 1981; Alvin L. Alm, "Deregulate Electricity," *Washington Post,* April 22, 1981, p. A23.

22. For a detailed description of end-use substitution possibilities, including conservation measures, solar energy use, and appliance efficiency improvements, see Henry Kell and Karl Gawell (project leaders), *A New Prosperity—Building a Sustainable Energy Future, The SERI Solar/Conservation Study* (Andover, Mass.: Brick House Publishing, 1981).

23. See Joe D. Pace, "Deregulating Electric Generation: An Economist's Perspective," paper presented to the International Association of Energy Economists Third Annual North American meeting, Houston, Tex., November 12–13, 1981.

24. A wind turbine manufacturer withdrew from a $350 million planned

Hawaii wind power project because the developer had difficulty in arranging financing with a rate of return to project participants that was "commensurate with the risk involved." United Press International wire story, September 28, 1981.

25. An Edison Electric Institute survey showed that seventy-nine electric utilities were involved in 247 nonutility business ventures. "Utilities Search for a New Revenue Source," *Electrical World,* July 1981, pp. 39–44.

26. This ban on utility participation in the conservation delivery business has been criticized by Daniel Yergin, who wrote, "One way to speed up retrofit is to give utilities a stake in it." Robert Stobaugh and Daniel Yergin (eds.), *Energy Future: Report of the Energy Project at Harvard Business School* (New York: Random House, 1979).

27. See "Can Advance Approval Control Diversification," *Electrical World,* July 1982, p. 25.

28. See James H. Malinowski and Kermit R. Kubitz, "Looking Toward the Future, Building on the Past: Developing New Energy Sources," *Abstracts of Selected Solar Energy Technology (ASSET),* July/August 1981, Special Conference Issue for the United Nations Conference on New and Renewable Sources of Energy. The table shows that the capital costs of saving one barrel of oil per year through a variety of conservation and alternative energy measures range from $76 to $905. This is based on work of Sam V. Shelton of Georgia Institute of Technology.

29. Kahn, Benenson, and Brown, "Commercialization of Solar Energy," p. 25, in their work on solar energy commercialization found that capital intensity was a critical factor.

6
Financing Synthetic Fuels Investments in the United States: Public Support and Private Investment

Zvi Adar
Tamir Agmon

The development of energy sources within the United States has been a major policy goal of the U.S. government since the radical change in the price of oil in 1973. These efforts have been focused recently on the production of gas and liquid fuels from coal. The abundance of coal in the United States and the availability of proved liquefaction and gasification processes make this "synfuel" industry a focal point for a massive joint venture of the public and private sectors.

The concept of a cooperative effort by the government and the business sector with regard to the production of synthetic fuel was implemented by the Carter administration in 1979. The process culminated in 1980 with the establishment of the U.S. Synthetic Fuels Corporation (SFC) as the linchpin of the Energy Security Act. Following the presidential elections in 1980, the Reagan administration indicated a preference for relying more on the private sector to solve problems associated with consumption and production of energy in the United States. This transition has provided an opportunity for examining the major premises underlying the participation of the federal government in financing the development and the production of energy in the United States. The first premise is that the United States needs a substantial capacity for producing synthetic fuel in the next decade and, furthermore, the investment itself will have an immediate beneficial effect for the U.S. consumer. Second, the necessary investment, given the target level of production, is too large and the risks involved too great to be undertaken by the private sector alone. It follows, according to this view, that without some form of support by the federal government, this investment will not be undertaken.

The purpose of this chapter is to examine these premises and their policy implications. The first part of the analysis explores whether or not the nature of the synthetic fuel project makes investment or other financial help by the federal government necessary and desirable. More specifically, where does the advantage of the public sector lie? Is it in the nature and the size of the required outlay? Is it in the cash flows to be generated by the project? Do the risks associated with the project vary when evaluated by the public or the private sectors? Assuming that private-sector support will not be forthcoming, will the project be abandoned, delayed, or undertaken on a smaller scale?

In the rest of the chapter, we look at whether the development of synfuels warrants a support program by the federal government, and if so, what is the best way to provide this support? In order to choose among such options as direct grants, matching grants, loan guarantees, and other insurance schemes, we develop a model of risk sharing based on the goals of a representative firm and a representative government agency. This model shows that the optimal form of support is a function of the technology to be developed, the phase of the process, the type of developer, and the nature of the "market failure" that justifies public-sector intervention.

Risk, Return, and the Role of the Government in Synfuel Projects

Ever since the radical increase of oil prices in the 1973–1974 period, the U.S. government has emphasized the need to develop additional energy sources within the United States. The United States has a substantial reserve of stored energy in the form of some 3 trillion tons of coal. Measured by its energy content, this reserve may be sufficient for up to 300 years of consumption. However, in its current form, the coal reserve cannot satisfy many of the energy needs of an advanced and sophisticated economy like that of the United States. The way to bridge the gap between the existing reserves and market needs is by converting the coal into more usable fuels. The transformation of coal to fuels is the main part of a new industry in the United States—the synfuels industry. The conversion of coal is not a new process. The German economy during World War II and the South African economy today are two examples of large-scale users of coal-based synthetic fuels. However, these two cases cannot be used as evidence for the economic viability of the synfuels, as economic considerations were dominated by national security issues.

The Carter administration embarked on a large-scale attempt to produce substantial amounts of coal-based synthetic fuels by using investments by the federal government to spur development. This attempt received considerable support from private developers, who argued that a federal program was a financial necessity and a proper exercise of the government's obligation to override the marketplace in order to protect national security.

The involvement of the federal government in this field started with financial support from the U.S. Department of Energy (DOE) for single projects. Coal gasification and liquefaction plants were initiated by the oil industry and by the utilities. The Solvent Refining Coal II (SRC II) Project initiated by Gulf Oil Corporation is an example of the former; the Great Plain Coal Gasification Project (which is sponsored by five utilities) is an example of the latter. As the projects moved from the research to the development and commercialization phases federal support increased. It peaked in 1980 with the enactment of the Energy Security Act and the creation of the Synthetic Fuel Corporation. This policy of massive investment of public funds through a variety of support schemes has been questioned by the Reagan administration, which argues that government investment in what is seen as a commercial enterprise is both wasteful and unjustified.

The opposing points of view of the Carter and Reagan administrations can be better understood against the profile of a typical synfuel project. The typical coal-based synthetic fuel project is characterized by large initial outlays and highly risky cash flows. The risks are of two major types: technological and market risks. The technological risks are associated with the fixed as well as the variable costs of production. The market risks focus on the market price of a barrel of oil equivalent (BOE) once a given plant starts producing. For example, the Treasury Department has estimated the construction costs of a coal-based liquid-fuel plant with a capacity of 50,000 BOE per day to be $4.5 billion (in 1981 dollars); the actual costs may differ substantially. Once the plant is producing, the costs of production may vary. Although the basic technology is known and is working, the various projects entail different specifications designed to reduce costs and to produce higher-grade fuels. Prior to the construction of the demonstration plants, substantial uncertainty exists about the actual costs of production.

These risks are internal to the projects and, to some extent, can be controlled by effective management. The market risks are more troublesome. The market for energy is oligopolistic. The actual path prices will follow in the future is uncertain. Moreover, it is not independent of what happens in the synfuel industry. (This point will be discussed more fully later on.) This risk cannot be controlled by the producers of synfuel; thus it is external to the project. Given all these risks, the private sector has not demonstrated a willingness to fully finance investment projects in the synthetic fuel industry. The lack of private-sector investment does not necessarily justify a public-sector investment. Many will argue, in fact, that the public sector should offer support only where it can be shown that a desirable investment, from a public point of view, will be forfeited without such support. The next section examines a typical coal-based project in this light.

Market Failure and Government Support in Energy Projects

The rationale for government intervention in the capital market, or in any other market, usually rests on a "market failure" argument. It assumes that under existing conditions, private-market forces alone cannot bring about the "socially desirable" outcome and that intervention can yield a *net* gain in social welfare, taking into account the direct and indirect costs of intervention.

The synfuel effort, as formulated by the Carter administration, is one of the largest examples of planned government intervention in U.S. history. It includes many research, development, and commercialization projects, some very costly and all with varying degrees of uncertain costs and benefits.

Despite this inherent uncertainty, we first examine the case of a synfuel development project under certainty. The private firm considering this project will make a decision based on the net present value of the net benefits to the firm over time (i.e., revenues less costs, discounted at the firm's cost of capital). A case for government support to the project can be made if

- the social benefits generated by the project exceed the revenues captured by the firm
- the project's social costs are lower than the cost to the firm
- the cost of capital used by the public sector to discount net future certain benefits is lower than the firm's cost of capital (this is the normative argument that the current government should care more than the private sector for the welfare of future generations).

A discussion of the generalities of these arguments can be found in any traditional cost-benefit-analysis text. For our purposes, it suffices to point out the possible divergences between the privately and publicly evaluated net present values of such synfuel projects.

The social-time-preference issue is common to any public investment decision and of no special importance here. Of the possible divergences between public and private costs and benefits, the following are pertinent:

1. Because the price of oil is affected by the OPEC oligopoly, a major synfuel effort yielding future energy alternatives may affect current (and future) oil prices. Estimates of this link may differ, but a link exists. The associated benefits (or costs) in terms of changes in consumer surplus are very high. For example, if the price of oil in world markets declines by $1.00 per barrel for any barrel sold in the United States over the next five years, the *direct* benefits to consumers would be about $1.97 billion, which is certainly comparable to the order of magnitude of the investment considered. Clearly these benefits cannot all be captured by the private firms that engage in synfuel R&D and commercialization. For those who are on the supply side of the current energy market, their *producer* surplus (in the current production of oil or coal) may actually drop; for the projects financed by the utilities, this type of benefit will be shared with the final consumers.
2. In any future price-structure scenario the development of energy alternatives reduces U.S. dependence on foreign oil. This consideration, which played a definitive role in South Africa's synfuel efforts, is not easily translated into money terms in the U.S. context, and we shall not attempt to do so. It seems, though, as in the previous argument, that the social benefits are generally a function of the *output* of the proposed projects. Some guidelines for the perceived value of lowering U.S. dependence on foreign oil can be derived from the current government policy to increase the exploration and production of conventional oil sources in the United States.
3. Oil and gas from shale, coal, or tar sands may have environmental effects different from those of any current energy sources, both in production and consumption. Where such externalities exist, and if there are no means to tax/subsidize the production/consumption of synfuels directly, a case can be made for reflecting these externalities by government intervention in the investment decision.
4. As with many other R&D efforts by the private sector, not all the economic payoff of a successful invention accrues to the developer. Imperfect patent protection and other factors may

cause a significant difference between private and social costs and benefits. To the extent that such conditions prevail, the ratio between the social and private net benefits should be estimated and used to calculate the direct subsidy to the research effort.

5. Finally, private costs and benefits may diverge from social costs and benefits as a result of current government intervention in fields related to synfuels. This is a "second-best" argument for intervention if the current resource allocation in energy is already distorted by regulation of the coal, gas, or oil industries or other intervention. For example, if certain other investment expenditures of a firm are heavily subsidized, the firm will tend not to undertake investments in synfuel R&D even if these have net positive social benefits.

At least some of the above considerations may be present in the context of specific synfuel projects. If so, the form of government intervention (e.g., subsidizing the synfuel output or the R&D input expenditures) should reflect the reason for intervention. Differences among specific projects and among the firms involved in the synfuel effort (e.g., oil producers versus oil consumers) probably dictate a discriminatory approach rather than a unified scheme.

Synfuel projects are risky. Once we relax our simplifying assumption of certainty and allow for the risk, the following question arises: Should the government subsidize projects because they are too risky for the private sector? This question has been dealt with extensively in recent years, but there is still no agreement on the answer.[1] Before discussing our approach, it may be helpful to characterize and classify the economic uncertainties associated with a typical synfuel project, beyond the common dichotomy between project risk and market risk.

In each of the research, development, and commercialization stages of a synfuel project the first risk is that of *technical* failure: a failure to deliver a product/process that can be further developed or commercialized. Even if a certain stage in the process is technically a success, the investment of resources (*fixed cost*) is a random variable. The *variable cost* of synfuel production resulting at the commercialization stage is an uncertain variable a priori, depending on both technological (process efficiency) and market (cost of raw materials) uncertainties. Finally, the *price* that the synfuel product will command in the uncertain markets of the future, for the duration of its economic life, is also a random variable. Some of these risks can be controlled by the firm, the government, or both. When this is the case, "moral-hazard" on the part of the firm *or* the government cannot be ruled out.

Who bears the various risks associated with a large synfuel R&D

project? The answers to this question, and their normative implications, would dictate the policy of risk-induced government intervention.

The traditional finance literature focuses on the firm's owners—its shareholders—and the constituents of the government—the taxpayers—as the ultimate risk bearers and on the existence of capital and insurance markets in which risks can be traded.[2] According to this approach, in a world of perfect capital markets, in which all investment projects are perfectly divisible, the only risk that matters is what is known as "nondiversifiable risk." In such a world, firms are assumed to act as if they are maximizing the market value of the representative shareholder. The shareholder is assumed to hold a fully diversified portfolio of assets. The relevant measure of risk, in that world, is the contribution of the project in question to the risk of the investor's portfolio. The goverment is assumed to behave as if it represents the typical taxpayer. Like the shareholder, the typical taxpayer holds a well-diversified portfolio of government projects (the returns of which reduce his tax liability) and other assets. It follows that in such a world the risk associated with any one project will be spread among a large number of investors or taxpayers, whether the project gains government support or not. Within that paradigm, a case for government support of private synfuel R&D projects must rest on the covariance between the project returns and the returns on all other assets to investors and taxpayers at some future state of the world. The relevant social risk is only the contribution of the project to the total risk of representative taxpayers. In other words, investing in synfuels has elements of insurance because it may provide returns even when investment is in a project that fails.

The preceding analysis assumes that firms do behave according to the paradigm of a perfect capital market and that only nondiversifiable risk matters. The observed behavior of most firms (including those associated with synfuels) differs from this model.

Managers are evaluated and compensated on the basis of the actual business results of the units for which they are responsible. Similarly, public-sector decision makers are responsible to their superiors and to Congress. These sensitivities to the *total* project risk (rather than to the nondiversifiable portion alone) affect the project-selection decision of the firm and therefore should be incorporated into government policy. In many cases, a large enough firm can hedge against some R&D risks by diversifying its own portfolio of R&D (and other investment) efforts. To a limited extent, the insurance market can provide limited coverage against specific R&D risks. But because the typical synfuel project is very large compared even with the resources of the largest U.S. firms, the residual volatility of net economic profit is still very significant, possibly exposing the firm to risks and the costs of takeover or bankruptcy.

The government, in this case the DOE, SFC, and other agencies, can finance or support many independent projects simultaneously. The agencies' success will be judged by the outcome of the total synfuel effort, not that of one particular project. It is fair to assume, therefore, that the aversion to risk of the government agency is, and should be, lower than that of the firm. The asymmetry in attitudes toward risk drives a wedge between the socially desirable set of synfuel projects and the set of projects that will actually be selected by the firms. Some worthwhile but risky projects will not be executed at all, others will be postponed or slowed down, and low-risk, low-social-returns projects will be pushed forward. To close this gap, government intervention is needed. As the next section shows, merely compensating the firms for undertaking R&D risks may not be the optimal form of intervention; because the case for intervention is a failure of the insurance (and capital) market(s), the support itself has to be state-contingent.

Finally, the question of moral hazard in the behavior of the firm and the government cannot be ignored. One common argument against government support to private-sector projects is that the very possibility of obtaining this support will induce the firm to select undesirable courses of action.[3] Examples are

1. applying for government funds when even without any support the same project would be undertaken. Here the claim is that in many cases government support to R&D is a pure transfer
2. using government funds for purposes other than those for which they were intended
3. deliberately altering the apparent outcome of a project to qualify for support funds

The management of firms can make equally strong claims of possible moral hazard on the part of the government. Many risks that face the individual synfuel project, especially market risks, are controlled by government. The recent experience of the U.S. coal and natural gas industries provides a good example of inconsistent and oscillating government behavior that created uncertainties concerning future support and the regulatory environment. Part of the insistence by private firms on government support for R&D projects may be explained as an attempt to secure stability in this environment. Plainly stated, the firms would rather finance and insure their projects with a government agency (even when capital and insurance market tools are available) to guarantee that the government does not *cause* the failure of these projects, if future governments' preferences change.

Notice that the two opposing moral hazard arguments deal with different sources of uncertainty. Moral hazard in the behavior of the firm is associated with the project risk (i.e., its technical success and total capital expenditure); moral hazard in the behavior of the government, as perceived by the firm, is associated with market risk, or the uncertainty in the environment of the project. This asymmetry points toward a possible risk-sharing arrangement between the firm and the government. In principle, any risk-sharing arrangement should be constructed to avoid a situation whereby the firm's value will increase by not performing its task. On the basis of the externality arguments and the risk-bearing discussion already presented, we conclude that the *form* of government intervention seems to be of utmost importance. With significant externalities and uncertainties present, there exists justification, in principle, for government support of private synfuel R&D efforts.

Optimal Instruments for Government Support

Granted the rationale for government support to synfuel R&D, we pose now the problem of selecting the optimal financial support instruments. Using known results from the optimal contracts literature[4] and additional analysis, we rank alternative support instruments for given types of firms and projects. Although one firm may propose and execute several R&D projects simultaneously, and the government faces an industry of many synfuel developers, we base the analysis on a model of one project, one firm, and one government agency. This model can be easily generalized. The model contains the following elements and assumptions:

1. *The Project.* At the time of decision, the project has a stochastic outcome. The firm's decision variables are the accept/reject variable, and the investment in the project is X dollars. R, the private gross returns, and S, the social gross benefits, are random variables of known distribution Recalling from the previous section the different types of risks present in R&D projects, the expressions for R and S may include several random variables and relationships and may be quite complicated. Rather than deal with unspecified joint probability distribution, we treat first each source of uncertainty separately and then integrate the normative results. Furthermore, for our purposes it suffices to reduce the range of possible outcomes to two: "success" and "failure," with probabilities P and (1 − P) respectively. The generalization to a larger number of outcomes (or states of nature) is straightforward. Each type of risk, R and S, obtains different

values depending on success: R_1 (or S_1) at probability P, and R_0 (or S_0) at probability (1 − P). The event "success," and the probability associated with it P, have different meanings for different types of risk. With pure technological risk, (1 − P) is the probability that the project (or the project phase) will fail, i.e., yield no output at all. Cost overruns for obtaining a specified result can be described as a reduction in R (again at probability (1 − P)), as can pure market risks (variation in input or output prices). Finally, P and R (or S) may or may not depend on the firm's research effort X. This possible dependence turns out to be important.

2. *The Government Goal.* The analysis is carried out from the point of view of one government agency (e.g., DOE or SFC). The agency is endowed with a given budget and uses it in various support instruments to maximize a given goal function. Because many projects will be supported simultaneously, the agency will be judged according to the sum of the resulting synfuel developments. To the extent that there remains any residual risk aversion in the choice of alternative projects to be supported, we make the normative assumption that such risk aversion should not be permitted *in the selection of instruments.* Hence, the agency is assumed to maximize, subject to budget constraint, the mathematical expectation of net social benefits (given as $\bar{B}(x)$) from the project

$$\bar{B}(x) = P(x)\, S_1(x) + ((1 - P)(x))\, S_0(x) - x \qquad (1)$$

over the set of feasible support instruments.

3. *Instruments.* The financial support instruments at the disposal of the agency are assumed to be equally politically acceptable and administratively feasible. Following the short experience of the DOE, the Energy Security Act of 1980, and the longer history of federal support to R&D in other fields, we include in the list

- Direct grants (conditional, unconditional, lump-sum, or matching)
- Joint ventures: direct government investment in the project
- Direct loans
- Loan guarantees
- Purchase agreements
- Price guarantees

4. *Firm Behavior.* At the center of our analysis is a model of the private-sector firm that invests in synfuel R&D and owns (all or part of) its commercial outcome (a plant, a process, a patent).

The model hinges on the firm's attitude toward risk. Recalling from the previous section the importance of properly defining the risk *as perceived by management,* we have selected a framework in which aversion of management to total project risk is possible. In this framework, risk neutrality of managers, as in the perfect capital market paradigm, is allowed as a special case.

In the general case, aversion to risk can be formalized in several ways. The simplest (and strongest) is the assumption that the firm makes R&D decisions that maximize the expected value of a well-behaved concave Von Neumann–Morgenstern "managerial" utility (of wealth) function. For example, given this function U(w) and a project where both P and R depend on project cost X, the model predicts that the firm will choose activity level X that maximizes EU(w), the expected utility of wealth:

$$EU(w) = P(x)\,U[w - x + R_1(x)] + (1 - P(x))\,U[w - x + R_0(x)] \qquad (2)$$

where w is the firm's (certain) wealth if the project is not undertaken.

With this set of assumptions, we focus now on the problem of the agency. Suppose that initial studies have shown that the project is scientifically and technologically sound, and $\bar{B}(x)$ in equation (1) is known to be positive and increasing in x over the relevant range. Hence, given its limited budget, the agency searches for the instrument that will induce the firm to adopt the project and execute it at the highest-scale x.

This model can now be used, first to classify the various instruments in an economically meaningful way and then to compare the effect of different instruments on firm behavior, given the project's "production relationships" R(x) and P(x). Classification of support instruments by their technical forms (grants, loans, guarantees, purchase agreements) sheds little light on the question of which instruments are effective. Clearly, we must be able to represent instruments within the behavioral model. If firms behave so as to maximize (2) (the utility of wealth function), we must add in each state to the wealth levels the cash flow of support in that state. Hence, a useful way to classify instruments is by examining the level of support given for any possible outcome of the project. Using this classification, the instruments to support synfuel R&D programs fall into three groups:

1. Those in which the amount of money received by the firm is independent of the project's outcome, e.g., matching grants. We label this type of support "unconditional." Obviously, this type of support is always preferred by the firm.

2. Those in which the firm receives support mainly if the project fails, e.g., loan guarantees or joint ventures in which the government agency recovers its investments only if the project succeeds. We label this type of instrument "insurance."
3. Those in which support is conditional mainly on the project's success, e.g., transferring patent rights or federally funded projects to the firm. We label this type of support "prize."

Although, in reality, instruments may be found that are hybrids of two of the above types, we use this classification to determine the major effects of government intervention on the behavior of the firm. Hybrid instruments are interpreted as government mixed strategies, with results that combine the effects of the basic unconditional, prize, and insurance elements.

Should the government agency act as an insurer, decreasing the difference (in a firm's wealth) between success and failure, or should it do the opposite by rewarding only successful projects? Should government subsidies depend on a firm's efforts (e.g., matching grants) or not (lump-sum grants)? These questions are not new; our model has similar structure and therefore yields some results that are similar to those in the optimal contracts literature. However, some important differences remain between the problem of optimizing government support to R&D and problems such as the design of an optimal insurance policy. Unlike the situation with an insurance policy, we assume that the subsidies to the firm are nonnegative in all states of nature. More important, whereas most insurance models assume the probability of loss to be given exogenously, separating "objective" risk from moral hazard, R&D risk in our model may be a decision variable of the firm, when $P = P(x)$. We should, therefore, distinguish between different R&D technologies, or project types:

1. Projects of fixed size, $R = \bar{R}$ *and* $P = \bar{P}$. These are rather uninteresting projects from our point of view, as the firm's decision is limited to accepting or rejecting the project.
2. Projects of variable size, $R = \bar{R}(x)$ *and* $P = \bar{P}$ (development type)—a continuum of alternative projects of Type 1, characterized by a fixed probability of success P and a technology in which higher investment in the project yields higher gross revenue. Mathematically, we assume R(x) to be continuous, increasing, and concave in X (decreasing returns to scale). This technology may prevail at the development and commercialization end of the synfuel R&D spectrum. At this stage the probability of failure is rather constant (and presumably small) but the firm can increase

R by increasing the scale of the project, improving product quality, and advancing completion dates. In addition, to simplify increasing the present discounted value of the project, an earlier completion date may increase R also if competing R&D efforts by other firms are a threat.[5]

3. Projects of variable size, $P = P(x)$ *and* $R = \bar{R}$ (research type). Again, this technology may be viewed as a continuum of projects of Type 1, in which an increase in x increases the probability P of obtaining a given result valued at $\bar{R}$. Typical of the research phase of the R&D process, projects of this kind have a risk-return structure different from that of insurable risks. Because P is bound from above by certainty, we assume P(x) also to be increasing and concave in X; additional effort (e.g., number of research teams assigned to solving the problem) increases P at a decreasing rate.
4. Projects of variable size, $P = P(x)$ *and* $R = R(x)$, combine the dependence on x of the two polar project types.

In summary, our framework consists of the following elements:

1. R&D projects, with polar types being
   - development type: $R = R(x)$, $P = \bar{P}$
   - research type: $R = \bar{R}$, $P = P(x)$
2. A government agency with a given expected budget that uses support instruments to maximize the net social benefits of the synfuel program. Although the possibility of overinvestment in synfuels should be considered, for a given project this goal amounts to maximizing x.
3. A set of feasible instruments, classified by their dependence on firms' reaction to
   - Lump-sum support that does not depend on x
   - Matching support that depends on x

   and by their dependence on projects' outcomes to their polar cases:
   - insurance
   - prize

   with outcome-independent support treated as a combination of the above.

4. A firm that may be assumed to be

   • neutral to project risk and selecting projects by their expected net returns
   • risk-averse and maximizing the expected utility derived from projects.

In an earlier paper, one of us showed that different combinations of assumptions on firm behavior, R&D technology, and government goals yield different optimal incentives.[6] Rather than repeat the proofs, we provide the intuitive explanation of the results (see Appendix, p. 176).

The simplest of all cases is that of a fixed-size project. If the agency wants to induce the firm to undertake it, the form of optimal subsidy depends on the firm's attitudes toward risk. If the firm is risk neutral, it judges all incentives by their expected monetary value. Because the agency's budget is also given in expected value terms, all incentives are equivalent, and the problem does not exist. If the firm is risk averse and the agency is risk neutral, we obtain the familiar insurance-theory result, i.e., the agency should bear all the risk. Risk aversion implies that the firm's utility (of wealth) function is concave; hence, sums of money received from the government when failure occurs have higher impact on expected utility (which determines project acceptance) than sums of money (of equal expected value) conditional on success. As we shall see presently, this dominance of insurance over prize instruments characterizes all the cases in which a risk-averse firm has no control over the probability of success P (i.e., development-type projects). With projects of variable size, the analysis becomes more complex. As a general rule, matching grants have a bigger effect on firm behavior than lump-sum grants, as they affect marginal considerations. Nevertheless, the crucial difference between insurance and prize supports exists in both lump-sum and matching grants.

Consider first the simplest case of lump-sum grants, where the firm is risk neutral. If the project in question is a research project with $P = P(x)$ and constant R, in the absence of government intervention the firm will select project size x that maximizes its expected profits. A government agency with $\bar{B}(x)$ (i.e., the net social benefits) that increases with x over the relevant range obviously wants to induce the firm to spend a higher x, thereby increasing P(x)—the probability of success. Should it use a lump-sum insurance or prize support? A prize support increases $(R_1 - R_0)$, the dollar difference between successs and failure, and an insurance support decreases it. Hence, the marginal contribution of an extra dollar spent by the firm to expected profits (the increase in P(x) multiplied by $(R_1 - R_0)$) increases as $(R_1 - R_0)$ increases. The immediate conclusion is that prize support should be preferred. Moreover, since insurance reduces $(R_1 - R_0)$, lump-sum insurance grants will decrease the firm's efforts in comparison to the nonintervention status quo. If matching grants are used with research-type projects, the positive effect of prize support increases because of the additional incentive effect of the matching feature. If insurance-type matching grants are used with research-type projects, the two incentives work in opposite directions: The insurance element reduces the firm's effort, while the matching element increases it.

With development-type projects ($R = R(x)$, $P = \bar{P}$) and a risk-neutral firm, we recognize that we are in the domain of the neoclassical theory of the firm. The firm judges all incentives by their expected value. Lump-sum grants of both the insurance and prize variety will have no effect at all on the R&D level x but can induce the adoption of an (otherwise losing) R&D project. Matching grants of both varieties do affect the firm's marginal consideration, having an equal positive effect on x.

Now, consider again the risk-averse firm. As stated before, risk aversion alone would cause all parties to prefer insurance-type incentives and shift all or most R&D risk to the government. However, this obvious result should be modulated by the two other factors mentioned above.

With development-type projects and risk-neutral firms we found that insurance has the same effect as a prize. It comes as no surprise, therefore, that with risk-averse firms, insurance-type support should always be preferred. Moreover, the concavity of the firm's utility function (risk aversion) causes the strong result that a lump-sum prize will actually reduce the R&D effort x of firms: Without intervention, the firm will select a project level equating the expected marginal utility of gains to that of costs. In the Appendix we show that a prize, for given project level x, decreases the marginal expected utility of gains by more than the reduction of the marginal utility of costs, thereby reducing the optimal project size for the firm. Again, this negative effect may change when matching grants are used, because these universally increase x in comparison to lump-sum grants. However, the dominance of insurance prevails with matching grants also, so that when the agency faces risk-averse firms with development-type projects, insurance-type support (and matching) should *always* be used.

With research-type projects ($P = P(x)$, $R = \bar{R}$) and risk aversion, our results are considerably weaker, because of the presence of opposing effects on firm behavior. Clearly, matching grants dominate lump-sum grants whenever the agency tries to induce an increase in x. Beyond that, our results become ambiguous because the concavity of the firm's

TABLE 1
The Impact of Prize and Insurance Subsidies on the Maximization of Private-Sector Investment in Research and Development Type Projects

	Prize Mechanisms	Insurance Mechanisms
Research Type Projects	If firms are risk neutral, investment will increase. If firms are risk averse, investment will increase.	If firms are risk neutral, investment will decrease. If firms are risk averse, the outcome is uncertain.
Development Type Projects	If firms are risk neutral, the go/ no-go decision will be influenced but not the magnitude of investment. If firms are risk averse, investment will decrease.	If firms are risk neutral, the go/ no-go decision will be influenced but not the magnitude of investment. If firms are risk averse, investment will increase.

utility function (risk aversion) points to the superiority of insurance, while the concavity of P(x) (decreasing marginal increases in success probability) points to the superiority of prize incentives. In the Appendix we show that while a prize-type incentive still increases firm effort, insurance incentives have uncertain results that depend on the degree of risk aversion and on the sensitivity of P(x) to increases in x. It is shown that if the firm has low aversion to risk (in terms of the Pratt-Arrow measure of absolute risk aversion) and P(x) is relatively sensitive to x, insurance may still reduce the firm's research effort (as in the risk-neutrality case). The superiority of prize-type incentives, although weaker than before, is still present when the firm is risk averse.

These results, which are summarized in Table 1, were derived with a model using strong simplifying assumptions. We, therefore, consider now the effect of relaxing some of these assumptions.

Perhaps the most disturbing assumption used is that of a two-state world (and project). However, all our results generalize to projects with several outcomes (at different probabilities) as long as the basic assumptions of concavity are maintained. The notations and structure of proofs become much more complicated (e.g., we must deal with joint-probability distributions of outcomes that may depend on x), but the intuitive explanation of the results stays intact.

Increasing the number of projects (R&D activities) per firm and the number of firms facing the agency does not create additional difficulties. The firm's utility (or profits) represents a portfolio of cash flows from different projects by the same firm (e.g., due to external effects of some) that require more complicated, conditional support instruments. Increasing the number of firms involved in synfuel R&D may actually simplify the problem of the agency: A "one on one" world may lead to strategic behavior on the part of the firm—ignored in our model—typical of bilateral monopoly situations. Competition among bidders for the agency's support reduces or eliminates the possibility of wrong signals in bargaining contexts.

"Wrong signals" are one variety of the general moral hazard problem that is present whenever the government supports risky private activity. Our model has eliminated the moral hazard present in many insurance contracts by explicitly including the control by the firm of the probabilities of success and failure. The remaining sources of moral hazard are partially treated by the agency's assumed knowledge of the general form of the R&D process subsidized and by competition among firms. It is well known that matching grants introduce risks of deliberate inflation costs (i.e., diversion of funds to other projects), but these types of moral hazards are not specific to the selection of optimal incentives to synfuel R&D.

U.S. Synfuel Policy

The U.S. synfuel effort could yet be one of the largest R&D efforts in history. It remains, even with the Stockman cuts, one of the largest and most controversial parts of the government's participation in financing U.S. energy needs. Plans for synfuel R&D and commercialization cover a wide range of sources, technologies, and stages of development. Some, like coal gasification, are well-known processes awaiting commercial-scale application. Others are still in the laboratory stage. Given this heterogeneity, the analysis in previous sections implies that no general, across-the-board policy recommendation can be made. The justification for government support, and the selection of support instruments, should be made on a project-by-project basis.[7]

This diversity has already surfaced in the policies of the relevant government agencies, mainly the DOE and the SFC. The DOE undertook major revisions in the instruments used to support mainly research-type projects. In contrast to the traditional contract research that characterized most federal support to R&D, innovative instruments have been introduced by the Office of Industrial Programs and the Office of Advanced Technology Projects. The main changes were the following:

1. The 1974 law that created the Energy Research and Development Administration (ERDA) allowed the government to waive the patents rights for a (partially) funded innovation, thus reversing a major characteristic of traditional R&D support.
2. In return, contracts may now stipulate a sharing of the revenues from a successful project. The role of government was thus changing from buying R&D to providing venture capital as an investor.
3. Less rigid cooperative agreements replaced the standard contracts. While still ensuring that the resulting innovations would be utilized by the firm, or sold at "reasonable" prices to other responsible parties, these agreements allowed flexible sharing arrangements without many constraints on firm behavior.

It is still too early to evaluate the success of these new instruments or how they might be used if the Department of Energy is dismantled by the Reagan administration, but our model suggests some possible outcomes. The release of patent rights to the firm is an excellent example of a prize-type instrument. Faced by technological risk in a research-type project, a firm is expected to react to this by increasing its research effort, i.e., accepting a marginal project and increasing its own investment. The shift toward joint ventures has the effect of an insurance-type support.[8] As we have shown, insurance may decrease firms' efforts on research-type projects unless the matching element in the joint venture is sufficient to counteract this effect. The net result is ambiguous. On the other hand, this change is expected to increase the R&D effort of firms at the final development and commercialization stages of R&D.

The Energy Security Act, signed into law in June 1980, established the SFC and empowered it to support R&D-type synfuel projects. According to the original plan, $20 billion was to be spent during the first four years, concentrating on research and pilot plants. The most successful projects completing the first phase would then compete for a total of up to $68 billion, which would be used in the development and commercialization stages of these projects during the second eight-year period.[9] The prize element in the first period of a research-type project is explicitly built into the combined support programs, as our model would recommend. As with DOE support, the law specifically authorized the SFC to enter into joint ventures for the *demonstration* of synthetic fuel models (i.e., development-type projects), while limiting the support to 60 percent of the total funds. We have argued in favor of this insurance-type support for development projects as a preferred support scheme compared to unconditional grants. The law also specified other instruments to be used and the order of priority in which they should be applied. These were, in descending order of priority:

- price guarantees
- purchase agreements
- loan guarantees
- direct loans
- joint ventures

and, if all these fail to generate a desired result,

- government-owned R&D enterprise(s).

The classification of price guarantees and purchase agreements in our model depends on the type of uncertainty involved. With research-type projects, in which the main concern is technological success, these instruments are certainly prize-type: If the project is a success (that is, ends with marketable output), the government will "buy or pay," thus increasing firms' revenue in that state. If the project fails (technologically), the instruments are meaningless. However, when market risks (e.g., selling price or input prices) are of major concern, these instruments provide insurance. For example, if alternative fuel costs decline, thus causing a synfuel plant to fail commercially, the government comes to the rescue. This approach is utilized in the Union Oil purchasing agreement. Loan guarantees, to an extent, have the same effect in the "loss" scenario and should therefore be classified as insurance. Two such loan guarantees were approved in 1981. Government loans should be regarded as unconditional unless they have special features (i.e., payment depends on success). Given the existence of a capital market, the implicit subsidy contained in them can be treated as a grant. We conclude that the order of priority of the SFC instruments generally moves from prize-type support to insurance.

Notes

1. Joram Mayshar, "Should the Government Subsidize Risky Projects," Hebrew University, Department of Economics, Research Report No. 86, March 1976.

2. Kenneth Arrow and R. C. Lind, "Uncertainty and the Evaluation of Public Investment Decisions," *American Economic Review* 60 (1970):364–378.

3. A. Raviv, "The Design of an Optimal Insurance Policy," *American Economic Review* 69 (1979):84–96.

4. For a discussion of this concept see H. E. Leland, "Theory of the Firm Facing Uncertain Demand," *American Economic Review* 62, 3 (1972):278–291.

5. It may also be possible for a firm to raise its return by speeding completion of a project while decreasing the social rate of return. This phenomenon has frequently arisen in North Sea oil field developments.

6. Zvi Adar, "Optimal Government Incentives to Industrial R&D," Interdisciplinary Center for Technological Analysis and Forecasting, Tel Aviv University, mimeo, 1978.

7. For a summary of the debate leading to the creation of the SFC see *The Pros and Cons of a Crash Program to Commercialize Synfuels,* Report prepared for the Subcommittee on Energy Development and Applications of the Committee on Science and Technology, U.S. House of Representatives, 96th Cong., 2nd sess., February 1980. On the state of the development of U.S. synfuel projects and technology as of mid-1981 see "Synthetic Fuels Report," *Oil & Gas Journal,* June 29, 1981, pp. 71–128.

8. Joint ventures may have additional costs due to the need to coordinate activities among many participants. For more analysis see Peter Cowhey's discussion in Chapter 8.

9. Robert Stobaugh and Daniel Yergin (eds.), *Energy Future,* rev. ed. (New York: Ballantine Books, 1980), p. 122.

Appendix

This appendix includes the proofs of the less intuitive results in the third section, thus illustrating also the general method of that section.

Lump-sum Grants to a Development-Type Project

With a prize-type grant, (2) becomes

$$((1)) \quad E\ U(w) = P[U\ \hat{W} - x + R_1(x) + G_1] + (1 - P)\ U\ [\hat{W} - x]$$

The optimal project level can be derived from the first-order condition for maximum E U(w)

$$((2)) \quad \partial\ \bar{B}(U)\ /\ \partial x = P\ R_1'(x)*U'[\hat{W}-x^*+R_1(x^*)+G_1]\ -$$

$$[P\ U'(\hat{W}-x^*+R_1(x^*)+G_1) + (1-P)U'(\hat{W}-x^*)] = 0$$

where the first term can be interpreted as expected marginal utility of gains and the second as expected marginal utility of costs, both resulting from a $1 increase in the scale x. Denote that optimal level by x*. With all other parameters and relationships constant, this first-order condition can also be written as

$$((3))\quad h(G_1, x^*) = 0$$

by the concavity of U(w) and R(x)

$$((4))\quad h'_x(G_1, x^*) < 0 \qquad \text{[the second-order condition for maximum E U(w)]}$$

Denoting a positive increase in the prize-type grant dG_1, the comparative static result is

$$((5))\quad \frac{dx^*}{dG_1} = -\frac{\partial h(\ \ )}{\partial h(\ \ )} \Big/ \frac{\partial G1}{\partial x^-} = -\frac{1}{U'(\ \ )}\ [P(R_1'x-1)$$

$$U''(\hat{w} - x + R_1(x) + G_1] < 1$$

which is negative by $(R'_{1(x)} - 1) > 0$ and the concavity of U( ). Therefore, an increase in a lump-sum prize-type grant to a development-type project reduces the research effort.

Lump-sum Grants to a Research-Type Project

With a prize-type grant (2) becomes

$$((6))\quad E\ U(w) = P(x)\ U\ [\hat{w} - x + R + G_1] + [1-P(x)\ U\ (\hat{w}-x)]$$

The first-order condition for maximum E U($\hat{w}$) is, therefore,

$$((7))\quad \frac{\partial E(U)}{\partial x} = P'(x)\ [U(\hat{w} - x + R + G_1) - U(\hat{w}-x)] -$$

$$[P(x)U'(\hat{w} - x + R + G_1) + (1-P(x))U'(\hat{w}-x)] = g(x, G_1) = 0$$

Denoting the optimal x for given G_1 by x*, the comparative statics result here is

$$((8))\quad \frac{dx^*}{dG_1} = -\frac{\partial g(\ \ )/\partial G1}{\partial g(\ \ )/\partial x} = -\frac{1}{\partial g(x)/\partial x}\ [P'(x)U'[\hat{w} + x + R + G_1] -$$

$$P(x)U''[\hat{w} - x + R + G_1]] > 0$$

which is positive, since $\partial g(\ )/\partial x$ is the second-order condition for internal maximum of ((6)), $U'(\hat{w}) >$ and $U''(\hat{w}) < 0$.

We conclude that a prize lump-sum grant should increase the scale of a research-type project.

With an insurance-type grant ((6)), ((7)), and ((8)) are replaced by

$$((9))\quad E\,U(w) = P(x)\,U[\hat{W} - x + R] + (1-P(x)\,U[\hat{W} - x + G_0]$$

$$((10))\quad \frac{E(U)}{\partial x} = P'(x)\,[U(\hat{w} - x + R) - U(\hat{w} - x + G_0)] -$$

$$[P(x)U'\,(\hat{w} - x + R) + (1-P(x)U'(\hat{w} - x + G_0)]$$

$$((11))\quad \frac{\partial x^*}{\partial G_0} = -\frac{1}{j(\ \ )/\partial x}\,[-P'(x)\,U^1(\hat{W} - x + G_0) -$$

$$(1-P(x)\,U''(\hat{W} - x + G_0)]$$

the sign of which is ambiguous.

Let $R_1^A = -U''(\ )/U'(\ )$ be the Pratt-Arrow measure of absolute risk aversion. Then, ((10)) can be rewritten

$$((12))\quad \frac{dx^*}{dG_0} = \left[\frac{(1-P(x))\,U'\,(\hat{W} - x + G_0)}{\partial j(\ \ )/\partial x^*}\right]\left[\frac{P'(x)}{1-P(x)} - R_1^A\right]$$

Since the first term is negative,

$$\frac{dx^*}{dG_0} \gtrless 0 \text{ if } R_1^A \gtrless \frac{P^1(x)}{1-P(x)}$$

Part 3

Market Competition and Risk

7
Insurance, Risk Management, and Energy in Transition

Jonathan David Aronson
Charles Rudicel Proctor

Two oil price shocks and persistent inflation in most of the industrialized nations revolutionized the international energy scene during the 1970s. In less than a decade the potential profits or losses at stake in large energy projects increased by almost an order of magnitude. High energy prices made previously inaccessible fields and exotic energy sources commercially more viable. As the size and diversity of energy projects expanded, political, economic, technological, and geological risks proliferated in parallel. In response, insurance markets adapted to new realities and began to cover large, complex risks on which no loss records were available.

This chapter examines the diversity of insurance coverages available for fortuitous risks associated with large and innovative energy projects.[1] We analyze the ways insurance underwriters determine the pricing of their coverages, sometimes providing the insured with bargains and sometimes carefully matching the risks to the premiums to the extent that uncertainty allows.[2] We then discuss the application of risk-management techniques as an approach capable of facilitating otherwise unviable projects by identifying, evaluating, and eliminating or modifying risks. More broadly, we are concerned with the possibility that the functioning of the insurance industry—a group not generally considered in depth by energy analysts—may in some instances influence the selection and viability of new energy projects. If that is so, it would suggest that a new level of complexity is necessary in the interplay

The authors extend thanks to August Ralston, Serge Taylor, and particularly Ward Ching for their comments and assistance.

between markets and regulations in the pursuit of sensible energy policy and development.

In the first section we examine insurance provisions currently in force for several large and innovative energy projects. The discussion stresses two points. First, suppliers of insurance can be grouped according to their approach to managing risks. Although one insurance group may perceive a project as unique and analyze and manage it accordingly, another may fit the same risk into existing categories by using intuitive, traditional approaches. Second, although a project may be large, *all* its assets may not be simultaneously subject to the same risk of loss. Therefore, the insurability of a project need not be inversely proportional to its total value.

The next section investigates competition within insurance markets and suggests how this competition might alter the markets' functioning. One view of insurance contends that the premiums paid should be determined by the probability of loss. As the frequency or likelihood of losses increases, the level of premiums should increase proportionately. (Your insurance rate rises after a claim but falls again after a significant loss-free period.) If the prudent deserve lower premiums, at the extreme, insured parties who are grossly unsafe should have to pay such high rates that they are forced to improve the safety of their operations. If insurers could calculate the probability of all losses, the setting of premium rates would in fact be as boring as it is sometimes alleged to be.[3] In reality, some underwriters have always been willing to accept risks for which no loss data are easily available and intuition must suffice (e.g., on the probability of a baseball strike or of the withdrawal of the United States from the Olympic games). Other insurers have attempted to analyze new risks "scientifically" and assign premiums as best they can. Each of these methods, but particularly the latter one, may help to promote innovative, expensive investments in energy and other fields that investors would not generally enter into without insurance coverage. Competition among insurers using different styles is an ongoing process. Moreover, the dynamics of this competition may significantly influence the structure of industry and the type and extent of benefits accruing to society. The functioning of the insurance market in handling different-sized energy projects may actually alter the need for government supervision of these projects.

We believe that the impact of this competition may be capricious. Therefore, in the third section we discuss applying risk-management techniques as one way to smooth the functioning of the insurance market. We examine whether it may prove possible for insurers to escape from the ironic situation of managing the ups and downs of others' businesses while being unable to manage their own risks. Briefly, we also speculate on some of the possible impacts of the functioning of insurance markets on government policies designed to promote a more stable energy situation in the coming decades.

The Management of Fortuitous Energy-Related Risks

Insurance companies have shown a willingness to cover large projects involving new technologies; they are, however, not monolithic. Let us begin by describing differences in insurance treatment for various large-scale energy risks. Different segments of the insurance market act differently. The experience of those needing LNG insurance is indicative. The marine insurance market has apparently provided adequate capacity for insuring the LNG carrier fleet at low rates, which continue to decline despite a record of frequent payouts. In contrast LNG land-based facilities, which have experienced a superior safety record, often have capacity problems, and rates have, on average, climbed somewhat since the mid-1970s. Although this situation seems to make no sense on the surface, it exists because the two risks were underwritten by different segments of the insurance market, each of which used a different approach.

The marine market is the oldest segment of the market, tracing its beginnings back to the Phoenician traders. Lloyd's of London began as a market to insure marine risks,[4] and although marine risks account for only about 8 percent of world insurance premiums, it is still the most romantic of markets. More important, the marine markets have remained more intuitive in their approach to risk while nonmarine markets have moved more toward quantification. An example is the marine market's traditional reluctance to update policy language because, over the centuries, every essential word and phrase in standard marine wordings has been interpreted in the courts. It is easier to leave in such perils as "Pirates, Rovers, Assailing Thieves, Jettisons, Letters of Mart and Counter-Mart" than to adopt new marine wordings that would have to be completely reinterpreted in the courts over a period of decades.[5]

When LNG carriers first appeared, the marine market accepted them easily despite their sophisticated, relatively untested technology and their astronomical price tags (up to $250 million apiece). The marine insurance market was so vast that, rather than set up new criteria for LNG carriers, insurers for the most part simply insured them as part of existing tanker fleets. Shipowners and insurers perceived LNG carriers as being no more hazardous from the point of view of explosion liability than ordinary crude carriers and considerably less vulnerable to pollution risks because LNG vapors dissipate rapidly.[6] In the vastness of the marine market, the inclusion of less than one hundred LNG carriers caused scarcely a ripple. Rather than worry about possible problems with these new carriers, all of which were operated by prestigious owners on long-term charters with highly trained crews, the Lloyd's market simply added coverage of the tankers as part of an owner's fleet.

LNG carriers normally are insured to protect against (1) war risks, which are usually handled separately from hull and machinery coverage; (2) loss of time and earnings occurring when cargoes cannot be delivered because the carrier is under repair or idled by breakdowns at the liquefaction or reception facilities; and (3) business interruption or consequential losses sustained when LNG facilities on either end are shut down for a prolonged period.[7] In contrast to projections on the proposed Alaskan gas pipeline, however, insurers are unwilling to provide insurance protecting LNG carrier owners against delays in the initial start-up of LNG facilities.[8]

For their part, cargo owners insure separately the value of the LNG carried. LNG as a cargo presents a special problem because between 0.13 and 0.25 percent of the cargo must be allowed to boil off each day to prevent pressure from building. (The vapor can be used to partially fuel carriers.) Cargo owners are able to insure against excess boil-off caused by bad weather or unforeseen circumstances. Until recent gas price rises remedied the disparity, cargo owners feared that, because the value of an LNG cargo was substantially less than the value of the tanker that transported it, in an emergency a ship's master might vent the LNG into the atmosphere prematurely.

Integrating the new and expensive LNG carriers immediately into the existing world fleet ensured that sufficient insurance capacity would be available. But several major losses have occurred because of technological faults that would not have taken place on other crude carriers. For example, gas pressure was inadvertently allowed to build on one tanker while in port at Newport News, and one of its tanks buckled. Even more devastating to the insurers was a claim of \$300 million they were forced to pay after three newly launched LNG carriers built for El Paso Natural Gas at the Avondale shipyard failed to meet Coast Guard specifications (the cryogenic systems allowed an excessive temperature drop on the outer shells). The timing was fortunate for El Paso because, although the faults might have been corrected (for about \$300 million) at the Mitsubishi yard, the ships had actually become redundant. By that time the Algerian–U.S. East Coast LNG runs over which they were supposed to operate were in jeopardy, and the carriers would have had to be placed in mothballs.[9] On the operational side, LNG carriers have thus far escaped all incidents in which LNG was inadvertently released. In late June 1979, however, the *El Paso Paul*

Kayser ran aground near Gibraltar, sustaining substantial damage but not rupturing her storage tanks.[10] Insurers paid out something in excess of $50 million.

In light of the problems just described, the wisdom of current premiums on LNG carriers can be questioned. Nonetheless, despite serious losses, insurers apparently are still offering lower and lower premium rates for LNG carriers. Ample capacity to write such risks remains because underwriters are eager to collect premiums and because fewer carriers are in service due to difficulties in the LNG markets. No price incentive exists for LNG carrier owners to take further precautions. One LNG carrier underwriter commented, "We've given them quite a deal to get this trade off the ground and we're still giving it to them."[11]

The separation of marine and land-based LNG markets is complete. The Lloyd's LNG underwriter quoted above never dealt with the major insurers of LNG liquefaction and reception facilities. In contrast to the surplus capacity and falling rates in the marine market, it does not appear that there is adequate capacity available to cover the largest existing land-based LNG risks, and prices may have increased for this coverage. Those concerned with land-based risks did not lump LNG facilities with other types of petrochemical plants but developed separate plans to handle them. Owner-operators of LNG facilities and natural gas pipelines may purchase a full range of coverages during construction and operation of the facilities. The concentration of values and the possible maximum loss in any single incident are so large, however (several billion dollars in some cases), that capacity does not exist to cover most plants at full replacement value. Further, the competition for existing capacity, coupled with the occurrence of a major liquefied petroleum gas accident in Qatar in 1977, may have persuaded underwriters to raise the premiums charged.

The size and uniqueness of land-based LNG risks discouraged all but the most sophisticated underwriters from entering this market. As a result capacity was initially lacking and underwriters could, for the most part, unilaterally dictate prices on the basis of their perceived risk exposure. Capacity developed slowly but continues to increase because the operating results of LNG facilities have for the most part been excellent. In contrast, the tanker coverage was provided too easily and capacity was made available quite generously. Competition ensued that pushed rates well below the level that objective underwriters believed to be viable over the long term.[12]

Thus, insurance markets may treat large energy risks in distinctly different ways. However, even when standard underwriting approaches are applied to huge energy projects, results are not always uniform because equal investment in projects does not necessarily lead to equal exposure to risk. For example, single energy facilities and transmission systems are extremely costly. However, the entire asset is not likely to be subject to the same risk at the same time. Risk managers identify potential losses and their economic consequences and establish a maximum likely value for such losses, sometimes called "probable maximum loss" (PML). Project planners work with engineers to segment any large project into smaller units to avoid high PMLs without impairing operational efficiency. But this procedure cannot always eliminate high PMLs for every peril on every project. Insurance is obtained accordingly.

A sharp contrast can be drawn, for instance, by comparing the insurance requirements for the Alaskan oil pipeline with those of an offshore oil platform. The 1,500-mile Alaskan oil pipeline cost $7.7 billion to build. However, the entire pipeline is unlikely to be destroyed by catastrophe. If the pipeline is damaged, or a pumping station is put out of operation, repairs are made. Physical damage is likely to be quite small and rapidly repairable except at the two ends of the line. Each of the members of Alyeska, the consortium that owns and operates the pipeline, has determined that its portion of such direct losses can reasonably be retained for its own account without purchasing insurance.

A more serious problem could be caused by a catastrophic event such as a repetition of the March 24, 1964, earthquake and tidal wave near Valdez, the southern terminal of the pipeline, or a major calamity striking the primary gas separation station at Prudhoe Bay. A lengthy halt in the flow of oil would impair the income of those deriving revenues from the pipeline. The first entity to consider protecting its operating income was the state of Alaska, which in 1980 derived 80 percent of its revenues ($6 million per day) from the tax on the oil flowing through the pipeline. A significant halt in this income stream could create serious financial problems for state-funded programs and projects. Alaska, therefore, considered purchasing contingent business-interruption insurance to cover its insurable interest.

While the state was considering arrangements for this coverage, Atlantic Richfield (Arco), one of three oil companies that participates in Alyeska, decided to purchase similar coverage. A large portion of Arco's total income is derived from its Alaskan operations. It purchased much of the capacity then available in the world market. In the event of an interruption of flow, Arco would absorb the first 15 days of lost earnings, and the insurance policy would cover the next 150 days of loss. In contrast, neither Exxon nor Standard Oil of Ohio, the other two pipeline owner-operators, sought business-interruption insurance. This difference highlights the fact that each company follows a risk-management philosophy that is appropriate for its own style, exposure to risk, and willingness to absorb short-term balance sheet losses. After Arco purchased its coverage, the state of Alaska evaluated both the purchase of similar coverage and the issuance of general obligation bonds. With some difficulty, an additional $250 million of insurance market capacity was found so that in the event of an interruption of flow, the state would absorb the first 30 days of impaired income, after which its insurers would begin to pay out against a $250 million limit.

The intense debate over the possible environmental damage resulting from a major oil spill has focused popular attention on this as another major risk. To handle this exposure, companies can purchase pollution coverage that allows for the recovery of costs incurred in the removal of unauthorized discharge of oil and other specified hazardous substances. However, the owner or operator cannot be held liable if it can be proved that the discharge was caused exclusively by an act of God, an act of war, negligence on the part of the U.S. government, or the omission of a third party.[13]

In sharp contrast, oil platforms are far less expensive than the Alaskan oil pipeline or the projected gas pipeline, even though their values are in the billion-dollar range. No catastrophe is likely to destroy an entire pipeline transmission system, but total losses of oil platforms do occur. A major storm or a "hundred-year wave" can put out of commission or sink an entire structure. For example, on February 15, 1982, one of the world's largest semisubmersible offshore drill rigs, Hibernia J-34, leased to Mobil Oil Canada Ltd., was sunk in a heavy storm approximately 165 miles east of Newfoundland. All eighty-three workers perished. The Mitsubishi-built rig cost $120 million when it was constructed in 1978; its replacement value was far higher. Platform losses could be compounded because there are many of them in relatively small regions off the East Canadian coast, in the Gulf of Mexico, and in the North Sea; thus is it conceivable that multiple losses could arise from a single natural disaster. Further, the concentration of highly valuable equipment and technology in the small space of a drilling platform means that even a partial loss can be substantial, due to what is known as interdependency among the different elements of the platform exposed to risks and due to the limited availability of replacement equipment adapted to the specialized needs of the platform.[14]

All interested underwriters with the daring to participate in such risks have done so; thus, the insurance industry's capacity to cover these risks is limited. One consequence is that, with rare exceptions, only major companies or state-subsidized firms capable of tolerating huge losses will attempt to undertake the construction and operation of such platforms. (This restricts competition in offshore production; indeed, governments could discourage entry by foreign firms into their offshore fields by creating new risks for which there is insufficient insurance capacity.[15])

In summary, analysts and project managers must distinguish between the total investment in a project and its probable maximum loss. Moreover, project planners and financiers may enhance the insurability of their projects by focusing attention on designs that allow risks and exposures to be segmented. But unless insureds begin to understand the differences in the way various sections of the insurance market function, they may not be able to plan and undertake the best strategy of insurance of their exposure available to them.

The Dynamics of Insurance Industry Pricing and Capacity

The comparisons of risk situations already provided, when augmented with some analysis of the effectiveness of the insurance marketplace, may help us to assess the likelihood that insurance actors will promote large-scale, innovative energy projects during the 1980s and 1990s. First we must address two areas of debate within the insurance community. One, how can we begin to account for the prevalence of the underwriting cycle within the insurance profession? Two, is there enough capacity in the world market to insure major risks?

With respect to the first area, most analysts tend to categorize insurance industry participants in terms of their functions, e.g., as insurers, reinsurers (frequently lumped with insurers), and brokers. For our purposes a more useful view of the industry can be gained by examining those participants within a structure defined by two functional dimensions: (1) degree of entrepreneurship: the willingness to take on new risks about which a history of underwriting results is unavailable or rapidly changing; and (2) breadth of knowledge: the scope of experience and depth of management expertise over a wide range of insurance areas. Table 1 summarizes the industry when viewed in these dimensions.[16] Note that insurance actors may move along one or both dimensions from time to time. In addition, breadth of knowledge is very often highly correlated with a wide range of high-quality specialized services. Further, an actor may be found in one quadrant regarding certain risks and in other quadrants regarding other risks.

Old Pros are the established insurance companies, brokers, and industrial risk managers[17] who possess substantial knowledge about the risks with which they deal and choose to act conservatively. They adapt slowly to changing conditions but do so very competently. The Innovators see change more as an opportunity than as a danger. They are the more aggressive risk takers and managers who venture into new risk

Table 1
Classification of Insurance Entities

		Degree of Entrepreneurship	
		Low	High
Scope of Knowledge	High	OLD PROS	INNOVATORS
	Low	FOLLOWERS	SPECULATORS

areas when they believe they have the competence and techniques to do so. They are, in fact, very pure innovators. Because they require large amounts of knowledge, Old Pros and Innovators need longer underwriting planning horizons than Followers or Speculators. The former two must anticipate new developments in order to adjust their knowledge base. They also plan how to adapt their operations in the face of changing information.

Followers are the bedrock of the insurance market in that, by imitating (with a time lag) or by participating concurrently in risks taken by Old Pros and Innovators, they provide additional insurance capacity for the market. Reinsurers and Lloyd's of London names (i.e., members), who participate in risks proportionately to the lead insurer or name, are often Followers; in a sense they underwrite the original underwriter of the risk or of a group of risks. (A Lloyd's of London syndicate lead underwriter would be an Old Pro or an Innovator.) Followers need an excellent knowledge of whom to follow in order to compensate for their weaker and narrower knowledge of risks and hazards.

Speculators look to Old Pros and Innovators to see what kinds of risks are currently being written with apparent substantial underwriting profits. Frequently they see themselves as Innovators rather than as Speculators.[18] Their pricing is more likely to be established on an intuitive rather than a "scientific" basis. Neither Followers nor Speculators have to absorb the expenses incurred by those needing to gather large amounts of information about risks. Because their operating costs are lower, they are frequently able to undercut prices offered by Old Pros and Innovators. Thus, Followers and Speculators may divert profitable business from Old Pros and Innovators, forcing them to consider a comparable price reduction to retain their insureds. Not all clients, however, are perfectly price sensitive, because Speculators and Followers cannot generally offer the same quality and scope of needed services. While Followers may adjust their prices to the extent that they have cost advantages, Speculators will also take into account any perceived "overpricing" of risks. Speculators drive down prices until results demonstrate that risks are underpriced; then they rapidly withdraw from the market because they do not understand how to correct their own pricing. Further, Speculators are more likely to rely heavily on investment income to support the underwriting profitability of risks than are other groups. For these reasons speculative activity may exaggerate the amplitude of underwriting cycles.

This classification of insurers helps us begin to explain why great tension exists between the social function of insurance and the pursuit of profit. As noted earlier, insurers help manage risk and allow the private sector to regulate hazards without government control.[19] But they also seek to maximize profits through some mix of premiums and investment incomes. Under normal conditions the price-cutting activities of Followers and Speculators drive down the prices of insurance until underwriting losses chase them from the markets and allow Old Pros and Innovators to reestablish profitable rates. Unfortunately, in recent years high investment earnings achieved in inflationary times hid the down-turn in underwriting profits. Speculators, in particular, were willing to cut rates dramatically even for questionable risks, presumably in order to ensure increasing premiums for investment. The great bulk of all insurers' earnings came from investments, not from underwriting profits. Unless stability of some form is reasserted and the pricing cycle is leashed (if not tamed), difficulties are almost guaranteed in the future if investment prospects abate. The cash-rich positions of many insurers, which has allowed them to rush into acquisitions of brokerages and other companies providing financial services, disguise a deeper weakness. A McKinsey and Company report summarizes the situation succinctly:

> Given that all of the parties to the insurance transaction are hurt by the cycle and the cycle is largely driven by those parties, the opportunity to get the recovery process started sooner, rather than later, is there. The key is not to expect a single player to take major risks by going it alone but rather for all players—companies, producers, and regulators—to take some low-risk actions that are in the best long-term interest of all.[20]

But getting such a process going has always proved extraordinarily difficult. As noted earlier, one of the ironies of the insurance market is that, while managing risks for insureds and allowing them to conduct business on a more orderly basis, the insurance market has never been able to impose such discipline on itself. Indeed, one possibility is that the process may continue in the future, but that coming cycles will fluctuate around return on equity, not around combined ratios (losses plus expenses, divided by earned premiums). One observer has suggested "a combined ratio of 105 percent to 110 percent being tolerable and of 115 percent not out of the question."[21] In other words, insurers could still make a profit while paying out 5, 10, or even 15 percent more in claims than they took in in premiums.

Underwriting results and investment results have covaried recently. Generally favorable underwriting results in the mid-1970s were offset by realization of the impact of the stock market decline. Insurers were required to recognize immediately the erosion of their invested assets because insurance company investments are always valued at market value (in contrast to the more common accounting practice of selecting the lower of original cost or market value).[22] Conversely, since the onset of poor underwriting results in the late 1970s, investment results have been excellent and investment income obscured underwriting income. The high investment results diverted attention from underwriting criteria. Speculators became more willing than ever to cut margins.

This analysis leads us to two suppositions about the operation of the insurance markets. First, contrary to popular opinion, the insurance industry may be better at handling extremely large risks than small and medium-sized ones. Only the Innovators and Old Pros have the technical expertise and skills required to manage giant, complex risks sensibly. Followers may provide additional capacity but cannot easily provide the skills and services necessary to serve as leads. (Followers, however, could lead on large but not complex risks.) So long as the client perceives substantial value in the knowledge and services received, Speculators have little hope of substantially influencing the pricing or handling of these risks, although they may be early contributors of capacity for innovative risks. On the other hand, when huge values and complexity are not involved, Followers and Speculators may try to act as lead managers. They have an advantage wherever the purchaser of insurance does not perceive significant utility in the insurer's knowledge and services. Then, Followers and especially Speculators are likely to reduce prices in order to write this business.

Second, it may be useful to view the capacity issue as dichotomous. Because the insurance marketplace is segmented, surplus capacity in some lines of insurance can coexist with a shortage of capacity in others. Most insurers diversify their risk portfolios because they realize that each line will have its own fluctuating range and that by holding a wide variety of risks, their underwriting portfolio will be less volatile.

Conversely, this preference for heterogeneous risk portfolios means that less capacity will be available for innovative projects than for known risks. Innovators will lead the initial underwriting and may find some early support from Speculators. Old Pros and Followers are generally slower in lending their capacity to new risks. Speculators are less likely to behave this way and prefer to enter and leave specific lines rapidly.

Our assessment leads us to suggest that Innovators employing techniques to manage risks "scientifically" are more likely to underwrite large risks involving innovative techniques and equipment, but that available market capacity (which includes Speculators and Followers) may initially be quite limited. Risks for which routine underwriting approaches have been established (whether or not these routines improve the quality of the underwriting decision) are more likely to find ample capacity at relatively inexpensive rates, particularly when Speculators seek those risks because they perceive a greater opportunity for underwriting and investment profits. When these circumstances are fully developed, insureds will receive "bargains" at the moment from their insurers, which will reduce their incentive for effective loss control. When insureds become inattentive to loss control, their insurers are threatened with unexpectedly high losses. In short, the insurance industry is functioning smoothly as a social institution when it tackles new large risks rather than known ones.

When Speculators provide surplus capacity they may distort underwriting cycles by rapidly pushing them from profitability to loss and back again. Keen competition for premiums may very well take precedence over the sound underwriting of risks. At the outset, when a new technology most desperately needs careful attention, it is likely to find available expertise even if capacity is somewhat lacking. Over time, as the insurance marketplace's competitive urges take precedence, more capacity will appear, but the careful attention to sound underwriting principles will diminish and the loss-control services available from Followers and Speculators may prove less than adequate; the risks of a technology are likely to become subject to the insurance profit cycle. The risk-management process discussed below is one way to counteract this process and make new energy projects viable. Even with this process, however, once the novelty wears off and the insurance industry becomes familiar with a class of risks, distortions may creep in.

The Risk-Management Process

Most of our personal experience with insurance is with familiar risks that are easily comprehended and treated in standard fashion. For instance, anyone buying personal automobile insurance knows that insurers rigorously apply sets of rules and formulas to determine whether they will accept a risk and what the premium will be. Office buildings are subjected to similar standard underwriting procedures; further, underwriters normally insist on installation of a sprinkler system and on periodic inspections to ensure its ability to perform adequately. Even the typical independent refinery is a risk that can be handled by underwriters in a routine way; the process and components are familiar, and many insurance company engineers know how to minimize or eliminate hazards. But when technologies are new and untested and values are large, there are no standard underwriting routines for underwriters and insurance company engineers to apply to the risks.

Rather than waiting for experience to accumulate concerning a new technology, risk-management techniques have been developed by risk managers, brokers, and insurers to facilitate innovative processes and projects.[23] We argue that not only does this process promote innovation on a large scale, but it may also help to moderate the instability of the insurance pricing cycle. In its simplest form, risk management consists of three principal activities: risk identification, risk control, and risk financing.

Risk identification is the deliberate review of a project to pinpoint and to measure the amount of economic loss likely to be incurred from a specific peril occurring at a particular part of the project (e.g., a fire in the storage area) or due to a specific kind of event (e.g., an oil spill while unloading a crude carrier).

Risk control is the elimination or modification of a hazard to improve the quality of a risk, such as moving a highly volatile storage area away from the principal control station for an automated facility, reengineering a very large risk into a number of smaller units by physically isolating each step of the process, or implementing a safety program to improve a risk through a system of procedures and controls.

Risk financing is the determination of how much risk should be retained by a project or its owners and how much should be transferred to insurance companies. Retained risks may be funded or not; and the retention program may be formal and highly structured (with a contracted administrator and many purchased services), or it can be simple and self-administered. There will be an *optimal* risk retention/risk transfer level that can be determined by considering the specific risks at issue, management's ability and willingness to control the risks, and the insurance underwriters' pricing aggressiveness; the optimal level will change as the determining factors vary. When actual loss data are available from the risks being considered, they are analyzed; otherwise, data are used from similar risks operated by other firms, or surrogate information is developed for novel projects. A simulation analysis can be used to forecast expected losses and their variability at some desired level of confidence. These forecast data can be used to test the operation of various combinations of risk retention and purchased insurance to identify an optimal retention level.[24] Selection of a specific insurance plan will be significantly dependent on the plan's ability to satisfy other financial requirements, such as accelerated tax recognition of expenses, deferrals of cash outflows, and present-value costs.

The risk-management technique originated in the United States at the turn of the century and has grown continually more scientific. It was championed mainly by some U.S. brokers and was long resisted by insurers and reinsurers because they feared it would drain premium dollars away from them and leave their capacity underutilized.[25]

Over time, application of the risk-management process to a technology enables that technology and its risks to be understood by many underwriters and leads eventually to the development and application of underwriting routines. For instance, the typical automated oil refinery owned by an independent operator was once an unusual and difficult risk to place, but it can now be handled comfortably by a wide variety of risk managers, brokers, and insurance companies. All the main risks have been identified and are common knowledge. Safety engineers understand how to minimize the hazards of such plants. Plant owners are aware of the costs and benefits of transferring part or all of the remaining risk to insurance companies so that the decision concerning the amount of risk to retain can be made with relative ease.

Today, risk managers are increasingly able to work with project managers to disaggregate large risks into smaller ones, even for projects involving new, unique, or esoteric technologies. They thereby enhance the insurability of a new project, in turn substantially improving the prospects that the project will be feasible and will not suffer a major setback or premature termination due to a fortuitous loss. As new technologies become known and standardized, the market for underwriting such risks expands, and capacity increases.

The advantages of the risk-management process can be illustrated by examining recent synfuel projects in the planning, construction, or operational phases and showing how this approach has been successfully applied. These projects involve coal liquefaction, coal gasification, gas-to-methanol-to-gasoline, tar sands, and shale oil.

Before construction begins, plans can be easily modified with minimal disruption and added expense, so this is the period when great care and expertise in risk identification and measurement is more readily applied and when risk can be more easily abated or eliminated. Construction plans, timetables, logistics, and contracts must be reviewed as well as the product flow, plant operating capacity in contrast with expected load, spare parts, sources of supply, and expected earnings. Hypothetical losses should be evaluated to determine their probable cost in property damage, loss of earnings, workers' compensation, and liability.

As a property damage example, one proposed coal gasification project had a total expected plant value of $1.11 billion, and the initial plans showed that the greatest PML was on the order of $600 million. The project management and its loss-control consultants made changes that brought the highest PML down to $191 million and resulted in the project's consisting of more than sixty-five operating units engineered so that forty-four units would have PMLs averaging $2 million, seven units averaging $19 million, five units at $40 million, eight units averaging $71 million, and a single unit at $191 million.

During the planning period, there should also be an assessment of the impact of large amounts of retained loss expense on the prospects for continued project viability. Normally, a project manager would prefer to have low retentions until an operating record has been established and to obtain insurance limits high enough to respond fully to any likely loss. (Note that the amount of coverage needed is determined by PMLs rather than by the total value of the project.) In fact, underwriters should have no unusual difficulty in accommodating low retentions during the course of construction for all risks, and subsequently during operation for all but the risks related directly to the uniqueness of the technology, because in its construction phase a synfuel facility is much like any other large construction project. The principal risks are property damage, workers' compensation, liability among contractors, and delays in completion. These risks can be handled in standard ways.

The chief difficulties would arise as the project became operational and would concern the risks related most directly to the novelty of the project's technology. For example, specialized electrical equipment, high-speed centrifugal equipment, and specialized pressure vessels (including portions of the process conducted under pressure) must be specially underwritten. These risks can be more satisfactorily presented to underwriters if loss-control experts participated in all engineering meetings, helped to set spare parts inventory levels and to obtain second sources of supply, established a sound preventive maintenance program, arranged a vibration monitoring procedure for the centrifuges, and the like.

Similarly, the project would be critically dependent on the sophisticated use of computers for operations and control functions. Attention should be given to their location, operations, and security; contingency plans should encompass the possibility of their failure. Underwriters would then be more willing to provide the desired coverage limits at reasonable retentions.

The most difficult risk to assess would be pollution—focusing both on the public and on the employees. The most elusive risk is the prospect that emissions now believed to be safe would later be found to be the cause of injuries or property damage. Loss-control efforts must provide for application of state-of-the-art monitoring devices. An especially thorny problem is that pollution policies often exclude certain injuries, thereby motivating the leading innovators in the insurance industry to explore new ways to provide more complete coverage. One approach includes a major loss participation by the project operator (say a $25 million retention with a $100 million limit of liability); in another approach, insurers would also have a financial interest in the project; in a third one, insurers and project managers would form underwriting pools, much as was done for the nuclear risks of electric utilities.

Specific environmental concerns in a coal gasification project include air quality, water quality, coal-slurry pipelines, employee health and safety, and environmental impact. Air quality could be impaired by emissions from an operating unit or construction equipment; problem emissions would be more likely to come from traditional sources (such as coal dryers) than from the gasification step itself, so preventive maintenance assumes great importance because of the need to keep all equipment operating properly. Water quality can be maintained by designing the facility to achieve a zero-aqueous-discharge level, but doing so creates a solid waste problem. Further, certain of the potential air pollutants may affect groundwater quality. Again, state-of-the-art monitoring and environmental engineering must be applied. The coal-slurry pipeline would be subject to its own catastrophic failure at a weak spot or to external damage (such as earthquake or landslide), so design engineering should incorporate loss-control considerations. Employee health and safety concerns would arise in many of the areas with which loss-control experts are familiar and effective in traditional industrial settings, including noise, superheated steam, and dust. A more difficult aspect of the problem is the possibility that a fugitive chemical would be carcinogenic or toxic. Adverse environmental impacts can be minimized, again, through careful planning.

Project management should establish overall project loss-control guidelines and specific ones for each operating unit and should subject each unit to a periodic loss-control audit. Management should also identify specific problem areas for engineering or safety attention by collecting loss statistics for the entire project in a data base and immediately using them to identify trends. Prompt attention should be given to claims as they arise so that small losses and claims do not develop into large ones due to inattention. Project management must also keep abreast of all scientific, engineeering, and regulatory developments that would have a bearing on its ability to operate and to monitor the facility at the state-of-the-art level. Finally, as experience is developed in operating the facility, underwriters should be able to increase any coverage limits that were restricted earlier because of limited capacity. A project's management may determine that more risk can be retained without jeopardizing the project.

Conclusions and Observations

Our discussions of the operations of the insurance market, the handling of several large and innovative energy projects within the insurance markets, and the process of risk management lead us to close this chapter not with a firm conclusion but with a hypothesis. We believe that in those lines of insurance in which risk-management techniques are becoming more widely used there may be less volatile swings of the underwriting cycle in the future. Although Speculators will always return (and prevent any oligopoly from charging excessive prices over the medium and long term), the widespread adoption of risk-management techniques can provide both insureds and insurers with more stable pricing over the duration of a project. Such stability will allow greater smoothness and predictability for energy projects and within the insurance markets and the economy.

This analysis of the availability and functioning of insurance markets in meeting the demands of large, innovative energy projects also leads to some intriguing possibilities. The difficulty of planning and mounting huge new projects, particularly in the wake of the recent dip in energy prices and of lower projections for energy demand, has forced and will continue to force insurers to react creatively in support of largeness and innovation. The best of the Innovators and Old Pros are using risk-management techniques to aid the developers of giant projects without having to worry immediately about price-cutting competitors.[26] Insurance coverage is likely to be provided only at costs reflecting perceived risks to the underwriters. At least for a time, owner-operators will not have the capacity to insure against all perils and will be forced to assume much of the risks themselves. This indicates that only large companies could take on large projects; it also imposes care and discipline on developers. Once technologies have been successfully demonstrated, then Followers and Speculators will participate and allow insurance to be purchased more cheaply and in abundance.

In contrast, smaller projects using either new or known technologies are less likely to be subjected to risk-management processes. The older-style, intuitive approach is likely to predominate. It simply may not be worth the time, trouble, or expense to subject projects with PMLs of less than $100 million to arduous risk-management techniques, particularly where the projects outwardly resemble known risks. If an inexpensive new technology proliferates, the insurance market is likely to provide new capacity as necessary without rigorously applying the risk-management process. The pricing is likely to be less rigorously set and will be adjusted only as underwriting results become known. Furthermore, when redundant capacity is available, there is likely to be a bias toward a softer price. Thus, at first it may be cheaper per unit of exposure to insure new, smaller projects. Insurance reverts in these instances to its traditional passive role. Insurance will minimize the variability of project costs and may thereby make the project more viable. Less government support will be necessary to get such small projects off the ground, because the underwriters may flock to them and even effectively provide short-term subsidies. In fact, the variability of the projects' risks actually have been transferred from the owner to the insurer. Although an incentive to start up projects of this sort may be present, the risks and other associated costs for the public have not been reduced or eliminated. On the other hand, applying the risk-management process to a large project may reduce or eliminate some of the overall risk of the project to the public but may slow the process of development substantially.

Although societal decisions regarding the selection of large, innovative projects versus smaller ones cannot and should not be made on the basis of risk-management and insurance considerations alone, it seems clear that the insurance market is better at promoting small projects than large ones, but better at monitoring large ones than small ones. Small projects are likely to attract ample capacity at reasonable rates because underwriters often fit such risks into familiar categories using common underwriting routines. Underwriters are less likely to employ sophisticated loss-control services to reduce the inherent risks associated with small projects; thus, government intervention may be necessary because the risks remain for society as a whole. Insurers will protect the public to the extent that their own assets are at risk; they are less capable of monitoring society's exposure to risk when they perceive that they have less to lose themselves. In contrast, large projects command the risk-management approach and careful attention to loss control no matter how much insurance capacity is available. Therefore, they are likely to require less government involvement in risk management and control. It appears that the risk-management approach is likely to motivate self-correction of disequilibrating tendencies when dealing with very large, innovative projects. There may be a greater need for government supervision of risks associated with smaller projects that are widely replicated, because the self-regulating and monitoring incentives within the insurance market are less effective. At the same time, government subsidies are almost certain to be more necessary for the larger, innovative projects.[27]

When government intervenes, it applies its own version of the risk-management process. Governments wishing to minimize their regulatory intervention and supervision of energy projects may choose to favor large projects structured to ensure self-regulating tendencies. This is not to say that society as a whole benefits more from one size of project than from another or that a multitude of small projects will not often work more effectively and productively than large ones. It does imply that the structure and functioning of the existing international insurance marketplace provides private developers of complex and expensive new projects with a stronger incentive to ensure that their operations are safe and profitable than it does to developers of smaller projects in the absence of government regulation.

Notes

1. "Fortuitous risk" may be defined as uncertainty of financial loss due to an unforeseen event. Other key concepts used in this article include "capacity," which is the amount of insurance that the insurance market is able to provide on a single loss exposure, and "underwriting cycle," which describes the intertemporal price fluctuations for a given line of insurance motivated by the supply and demand conditions within a given market. A hard market indicates limited capacity. A soft market indicates abundant capacity.

2. We are acutely aware of the difficulties of determining what would constitute "efficient" or "optimal" operation of the insurance market. Throughout this analysis we adopt the perspective that the benefits that may be passed on to the insureds when underwriters do not know the probability of losses and therefore "underprice" their services are outweighed by the disruption such pricing promises for the insurance markets in the medium term. Further, we have accepted the normative position that the greater good of society may be diminished when insurance markets systematically and inappropriately favor one type of new project over other possible competitors.

3. For a discussion of the propensity of insurers to "gamble" in recent years, see Hazel Henderson, "Risk, Uncertainty and Economic Futures," *The Geneva Papers on Risk and Insurance,* No. 9 (July 1978), pp. 9–12. It is striking that in marketing Andrew Tobias's look at the domestic insurance industry, *Invisible Bankers* (New York: Simon and Schuster, 1982), the publishers felt it necessary to constantly refer to the myth that all things dealing with insurance are inherently routine and boring.

4. Standard histories of Lloyd's of London include: D.E.W. Gibb, *Lloyd's of London* (London: Macmillan, 1957), and C. Wright and C. E. Fayle, *A History of Lloyd's* (London: Macmillan, 1927). Also see: H.A.L. Cockerell and

Edwin Green, *The British Insurance Business 1547–1970* (London: Heinemann Educational Books, 1976).

5. The perils clause in the American Institute Hull Clauses issued on June 2, 1977, was as follows:

> Touching the Adventures and Perils which the Underewriters are contented to bear and take upon themselves, they are the Seas, Men-of-War, Fire, Lightning, Earthquake, Enemies, Pirates, Rovers, Assailing Thieves, Jettisons, Letters of Mart and Counter-Mart, Surprisals, Takings at Sea, Arrests, Restraints and Detainments of all Kings, Princes, and Peoples, of what nations, condition, or quality soever, Barratry of the master and mariners and of all other like Perils, Losses and Misfortunes that have or shall come to the Hurt, Detriment or Damage of the Vessel, or any part thereof, excepting, however, such of the foregoing perils as may be excluded by provision elsewhere in the Policy or by endorsement thereon.

In fact, insurers will normally pay out on almost any other loss not included on this list except for war damages, which must be insured separately.

6. Interviews conducted by one of the authors, Lloyd's of London, 1979.

7. Samir Mankabady, "Insurance and Reinsurance Requirements of LNG," *Marine Policy* 2, 4 (October 1978):332.

8. The Malaysian operations have experienced this problem of carriers' being completed well before the liquefaction facilities.

9. Alexander Stuart, "El Paso Comes in from the Cold," *Fortune,* March 23, 1981, pp. 55–56.

10. E. F. Shumaker, "Ship-to-Ship Transfer of LNG, the *El Paso Paul Kayser/ El Paso Sonatrach* Gas Transfer Operation," *Gastech Houston: Proceedings Gastech 79 LNG/LPG Conference,* November 13–16, 1979 (Rickmansworth, Herts.: Gastech Ltd., 1980), pp. 173–175.

11. Interview, Lloyd's of London, spring 1979. Also see A. M. Platt, "Insurance of LNG Vessels," *Tanker and Bulker International,* January/February 1976, p. 29.

12. These two LNG examples were selected to illustrate the differences in underwriting approaches but were not intended to imply that the results of the intuitive approach are often or necessarily inadequate. Any seasoned underwriter of either school knows to trust his instincts about a risk. Further, the profitability of the marine segment over the long term affirms the viability of the intuitive approach.

13. Water Quality Improvement Act (WQIA), 84 Stat. 91 33 USCA Sec. 1161.

14. Standard coverages available to platform owners and operators include physical damage, earthquake, wind storm, and general liability. Special coverages available include redrilling, blowout, and seepage and pollution.

15. We thank Peter Cowhey for this point.

16. Characterizations of members of each of the four categories necessarily apply to actors located well within their respective quadrants; an actor possessing slightly above-average scope of knowledge and degree of entrepreneurship would

perhaps be characterized as traditional with an innovative inclination. This matrix has been tested to a limited extent with executives within the insurance industry; interestingly, those consulted generally agree on how a few notable firms should be identified. Steven Resnick's discussions with one of the authors over recent years were helpful here.

17. Many organizations have a staff executive designated "risk manager" who is responsible for identifying, measuring, and controlling the organization's fortuitous risks and for stabilizing the potentially adverse financial impact of losses from these risks.

18. We thank Peter Walker for this point.

19. For more analysis on this point, see Jonathan David Aronson and William Westermeyer, "US Public and Private Regulation of LNG Transport," *Marine Policy* 6, 1 (January 1982):19–24.

20. McKinsey & Company, *First Quarter Update Property-Casualty: Comparative Performance Data,* 1981, "McKinsey Perspective," "Mounted a Concerted Attack on the Cycle," p. 6.

21. Charles McAlear, "E/S Industry Feels the Pinch . . . But Admitted Markets Surge," *Business Insurance,* August 10, 1981.

22. What happens here is that the stock market at its higher level caused insurance companies to recognize the value of their invested assets at prevailing higher levels. When the market declined dramatically, insurers were forced to recognize that investment loss at the end of the calendar year; and that investment loss had to be expensed against income that same year. That event, added to a reduced investment income, caused a real problem. Further, the eroded asset base meant that insurers could not maintain the same premiums-to-surplus (equity) ratio at the former premium levels. So, the regulators allowed the insurers to write at higher ratios—which, in the past, had always been a signal that a company was in shaky financial condition.

23. Standard risk-management texts include C. Arthur Williams and Richard Heims, *Risk Management and Insurance* (New York: McGraw-Hill, 1976); Philip Gordis, *Property and Casualty Insurance,* 26th ed. (Indianapolis: The Rough Notes, 1980); and Norman A. Bagliani, *Risk Management in International Corporations* (New York: Risk Studies Foundation, 1976). Also see David Holbrook, "Risk Management Needs of the Energy Industry," *Viewpoint,* The Marsh & McLennan Quarterly 10, 2 (Fall 1981):21–23; Gary Bergstrom, "A New Route to Higher Returns and Lower Risks," *Viewpoint,* The Marsh & McLennan Quarterly 4, 3 (Winter 1976):1–9.

24. For an example of the application of this technique, see "The Marsh & McLennan Case," Chapter 10, cases 10-3A, 10-3B, in Paul A. Vatter et al., *Quantitative Methods in Management* (Homewood, Ill.: Irwin, 1978).

25. A 1901 proposal appears in "Pioneering the Risk Management Trail," *Viewpoint,* The Marsh & McLennan Quarterly 11, 1 (Spring 1982):1–3. Until recently groups such as Munich Reinsurance opposed the adoption of risk-management techniques, arguing that it would cut down premium income of the insurers and reinsurers.

26. Bankers seek similar sophisticated customers who understand that a dif-

ference in interest of one-half of one percent is not a good reason to abandon a bank that provides excellent services and is willing to support a customer over the long term.

27. The experience of the Diablo Canyon nuclear power station would tend to support this point. Although environmental groups under the banner of the "Abalone Alliance" delayed the plant's licensing and opening, their massive demonstration in early 1982 did not force corporate or governmental authorities to halt the plant's start-up. However, when safety engineers required by the government and the insurers discovered design faults, the plant was closed down immediately. It is disturbing, however, that the environmental protesters may eventually prove correct in their assertion that the technology is so complex and the workmanship so shoddy that the plant should never be allowed to open.

8
The Problems of Opportunistic Behavior and the Future of Energy Investments

Peter F. Cowhey

In Chapter 1, I argued that the international majors' power in world energy markets has slipped substantially since 1973. In response they have initiated a major shift in strategy designed to limit increasing economic and political risks. I concluded that these changes would directly influence the security of consumers in industrial nations, particularly if some companies are markedly more successful in executing the shift than others. This chapter identifies snags that the majors may run into as they pursue their new strategy and concludes by suggesting the need for a different approach to analyzing government policies concerning all phases of the energy sector.

To simplify my task and to draw attention to aspects of the strategy that are less commonly analyzed, I shall make two assumptions: (1) Fundamental trends in prices and demand make a strategy of diversification feasible (even if delayed by several years and reduced, as I pointed out in Chapter 1), and (2) understanding the risks that are unique to each project is less important than uncovering systematic patterns of risks arising as a result of the total portfolio of projects.[1] In order to identify unforeseen risks I have tapped the rich literature on the relationship among legal contracts, vertical integration, and opportunistic behavior in the marketplace. In this literature it is argued that each party to any economic relationship has a constant temptation to cheat or to demand a reworking of an established bargain on more advantageous terms. Economists call this phenomenon "opportunistic behavior." In a highly volatile marketplace, actors must develop an adroit mixture of incentives and penalties, including new forms of legal contracts and partnerships, to reduce the likelihood of opportunistic behavior.

The Determinants of Opportunistic Behavior

When firms make investments that are tailored to the needs of specific users (such as custom-designed machine tools) or for specific locations (such as refineries), they confront risks of opportunistic behavior by other actors in the marketplace. Because the firm cannot redeploy the investment for other uses without substantial losses (if it can salvage anything at all), others may try to coerce the firm by limiting its return on the investment. For example, a government may threaten to expropriate a mining smelter or a customer may try to renegotiate a purchase contract. These losses are especially serious for firms like the majors because they operate on the principle of linking an integrated network of projects designed to optimize production and delivery of a product or products to the customer. Disruption of one project can upset profits of many other related projects. (This remains largely true even if the majors do not emphasize balanced vertical integration as much as in the past.)

Willful distortion of information, false promises, threats, and violations of contracts (formal or informal) in order to exploit the possibility of redistributing profits are examples of opportunistic behavior.[2] Such behavior raises the costs of economic transactions and, as economists have pointed out repeatedly in recent work, thereby produces some unusual outcomes in the behavior of the market. In particular, firms have strong incentives to eliminate conventional arms-length relationships and create partnerships, vertically integrated firms, or other hierarchically coordinated relationships in order to ensure good faith, obtain more accurate information, and improve efficiency. Indeed, many of the responses resemble the exchanges of hostages associated with warfare in earlier times more than the textbook ideals of the classic firm.

Two sets of factors determine the vulnerability of any party to opportunistic behavior in a major business relationship involving substantial capital investments.[3] One is the degree of *specificity* of the investment. Specificity is a function of (1) the degree to which there are other users who are willing to pay similar amounts for the product of the investment and (2) the ability of the investment to be made physically available to the alternative users. The other dimension is the *cost of enforcement*. Enforcement costs are determined by (1) the legal/political tradition of the country, (2) the degree of uncertainty limiting the detail of contract terms, (3) the frequency and duration of transactions between parties, and (4) the extent to which mutual hostages exist between contracting parties.

I have already noted that specificity is a function of the level of loss incurred by having to find new users for an investment. The other factor affecting specificity is the ease of physical transferability. In general, drilling rigs for exploration can be withdrawn and put to other uses, although some of the custom-ordered equipment for frontier areas may not have ready use elsewhere. But permanent production platforms, pipeline systems, and refineries are highly specific investments; so also are LNG facilities and pipelines for natural gas, as Aronson and Cragg showed in Chapter 2. The accumulation of expertise and technology for synfuel projects may also have to be discounted heavily if switched to another project.

The first element influencing the cost of enforcement is the *legal and political tradition* of the country. The countries that present the lowest risks have legal traditions that share the Anglo-American emphasis on the sanctity of contracts. In practice, most OECD nations honor contracts between parties in the private sector, but their willingness to use the power of the state to force renegotiations of contracts on behalf of the public interest varies. France is more willing to do so, for example, than is West Germany. And, as Chapter 4 has shown, the balance of political forces can shift frequently even within a single nation. For example, Australia has grown more insistent on foreign oil companies' giving local partners more than half the equity in new projects. As a result, a few of its largest mineral corporations may command especially favorable investment terms because they are large enough to be particularly attractive partners in major projects. At the high end of the risk spectrum are many developing nations that have neither the political stability nor the ideology necessary to maintain contracts with a high degree of assurance.[4]

A second factor influencing enforcement costs concerns *uncertainty.* The less standard is a product, the process for making it, or the nature of the business venture, the harder it is to write a detailed contract to cover relevant risks; the parties must rely increasingly on "good faith" cooperation to work out unanticipated problems. Under these conditions one party can more easily cheat on a contract because obligations are harder to pin down. This is a major difficulty for all research and development projects (such as synfuels) and for assigning responsibility for failure to meet delivery dates on risky new energy sources (such as coal or LNG). Moreover, it may be hard to distinguish a dispute about a particular item from a broader venture. Thus the party that has a grievance may feel constrained in the remedies that it seeks unless it is willing to terminate the venture altogether.[5]

A third element determining enforcement costs is the *frequency and duration of transactions* among the relevant parties. This factor can make enforcement either harder or easier. A firm may not pursue legal or other avenues of enforcement because it expects to continue to do business frequently with the other party and does not want to escalate hostilities. But if relationships are frequent and entail continual renewal and initiation of contracts, many agreements can become "self-enforcing" because firms rarely want to be considered unreliable.[6] If, however, the contract is close to a "one shot" affair, reputation means less. And, too, the importance of reputation obviously depends in part on how much firms consider themselves to be part of a uniform class. For example, if all oil companies view themselves as being roughly equivalent in their interests and liabilities, then bad faith bargaining with one company causes a loss of credibility with all firms. But if oil companies do not view themselves as part of a uniform class, then the loss may be with only a segment of the industry.

A final factor determining the cost of enforcement is the presence or absence of *mutual hostages.* When parties to an agreement jointly hold outside assets or exercise power over the same assets, they may become mutual hostages. For example, if Saudi Arabia unilaterally changed the ownership arrangements on some of the petrochemical plants it has built jointly with oil companies, the firms could retaliate by abrogating their agreement to sell Saudi petrochemicals in their European markets. Kuwait Petroleum Corporation's major investments in oil exploration and production in the United States and Australia may make it more vulnerable to counterpressure by OECD nations when negotiating about oil markets.[7] More generally, oil companies consistently act to develop interdependent interests in order to create mutual hostages.

In short, opportunistic behavior by countries and by firms becomes more probable as investments become specific and the costs of enforcement rise. When opportunistic behavior is frequent, risks for individual firms are much higher, and the economy as a whole suffers from suboptimality in investment choices.[8]

Applications to Overseas Investments

This section begins with four hypotheses about risks for the majors in conventional oil and gas projects outside the United States that follow from the above discussion of opportunistic behavior.[9] Then it sets out two hypotheses applying to investments in synthetic fuels and coal.

The first hypothesis is that there is a trade-off between security and market share; under the economic and political conditions assumed in this chapter, third-party guarantees increase security in one country at the cost of global autonomy and market share. The best illustration of this hypothesis is the continuing debate concerning the role of the World Bank in energy projects. One obvious method of reducing risk when operating in a developing country is to find a third party to enforce agreements concerning oil and gas projects. Unless an oil company can "call the marines," it may bring into the picture international institutions with substantial influence over host governments. The World Bank has expressly justified its growing involvement as a funding partner in oil and gas projects as a form of guarantee to encourage investment by oil companies.[10] The bank argues that no one reneges on its projects because bank lending support is too crucial to a developing nation. (Although a bank guarantee is not decisive for extremely large oil fields, it could make the difference in many smaller ones.) Ironically this method of increasing security also reduces the leverage of big oil companies as financial risk takers. Accordingly, the greater the involvement of the World Bank, the easier it is for other investors to bear the risk of a project and the harder it is for the majors to retain the competitive advantage and increased security they enjoy when they are indispensable sources of financial risk taking. Thus the role of national oil companies may increase more rapidly if the majors choose to support a program that could expedite their diversification by lowering risks in a specific project. Increased security of individual projects may lead to worldwide erosion of the majors' market share.[11]

The second hypothesis is a logical corollary to the first: Entry into joint ventures in country B with a local partner from host nation A increases corporate bargaining power in country A, but it lowers the majors' bargaining power globally. For example, by inviting parties threatening their interest in one project to join with them in investments elsewhere (thereby creating a mutual hostage situation), the company's risk in the initial project drops. If the other party then tries to take advantage of the major on its home ground, the firm can take reprisals on jointly held assets elsewhere. However, crossinvestments of this nature may reduce the autonomy of the corporations' global operations, particularly by linking them too closely to a specific supplier or corporate partner with quite different interests. As noted earlier, under the market conditions assumed in this chapter, the majors prize autonomy as a source of global leverage in energy markets.

Even though it reduces autonomy and power in a general sense, many majors have entered into widespread partnerships with national oil companies (NOCs) along the lines just outlined. For many years, Compagnie Française des Pétroles (CFP) was strongly linked to British

Petroleum in many operations, but their strategic interests clashed severely in their Iraqi holdings. Negotiations over these policies often reached byzantine proportions. At present, several of the majors have entered into joint ventures along the lines described in the second hypothesis. (None has reached the degree of cooperation exhibited by, for example, the Socal-Texaco partnership in Asia or the Shell-Exxon ventures in the North Sea.) In these cases of extensive joint ventures they have sacrificed some autonomy for the benefits of secure working relationships with a partner holding special advantages in a particular segment of the world market. Thus, the way to interpret the application of the second hypothesis is that the majors will favor a few local partners as collaborators in many overseas ventures and try to avoid such arrangements to the greatest extent possible otherwise.[12] This understanding of the second hypothesis opens the way to a third proposition.

The third hypothesis underscores the dangers of arms-length relationships: Short-term brinkmanship and haggling endanger long-term cooperation. Students of game theory argue that the rationality of adopting cooperative strategies rises as the value actors assign to gains and losses in future transactions increases. If projected exchanges are more numerous and of longer term, cooperation is more likely. In the past, the majors' habit of building long-term partnerships with specific countries and the need for continual rounds of new investment in order to meet the rapidly growing demand for energy helped enhance cooperation. Today the situation differs. As the energy demand sags and the majors attempt to retain their autonomy, the need for frequent, long-term exchanges of critical value to both sides is diminished. Thus, the majors' strategy of moving more freely from country to country undercuts the probability of voluntary cooperation in any particular country.[13]

The fourth hypothesis about risks for the majors relates to the decline of homogeneity among oil companies: As the goals and needs of the oil companies become more diverse and their interests diverge, the security of each oil company declines. As more independents, particularly state-subsidized oil companies from industrial and developing nations, grow more active in the energy trade, corporate interests begin to diverge. Many newcomers are more sympathetic to government-regulated trade in energy tied to other economic arrangements than are the majors. Their economic missions also differ. For example, they are more interested in procuring secure sources of oil for the state than are the international majors. As a result, they sometimes deem the problems concerning reneging on contracts faced by the majors as less pertinent to their prospects. Whether or not their reasoning is sound, it lowers the cost to a host government (or its NOC) of breaking a contract with a major and thus lowers the security of the major.[14]

The four hypotheses presented so far suggest sources of increasing risks for the majors in conventional oil and gas projects in which the technology is well defined and the world markets are rather thoroughly established and integrated. The last two relate to risks that develop in industries in which neither the technology nor the markets are well developed.

The fifth hypothesis is a corollary to the fourth. It applies to situations, like synthetic fuels, in which lead times are very long, technological development is subject to many risks, and markets are not absolutely certain. In this situation, even if the types of companies are similar, adding more partners in order to spread the project's risk increases the chance that one or more partners may engage in opportunistic behavior. Let us examine the reasons in more detail.

A substantially larger pool of partners (especially when it entails a wider variety in the types of firms, such as small and large) is desirable only if markets are well defined and all the relevant risks can be written into a contract for a joint venture. But the nature of many technological projects and the difficulty of matching production capacity and uncertain market demand in coal and other new sources makes such contracts impossible. Accordingly, a wider array of partners makes it more likely that the special problems of each partner may create risks for the stability of the project at a later date. Current protection raises future risks.

Even excluding the dangers of future disputes, at the outset the partners also must invest considerably more in time and bargaining costs in order to work out the details of larger syndicates. Thus factors pertaining to future risk and current bargaining costs lead one to expect small numbers of partners in the major synfuel projects currently moving toward commercial development. This has, in fact, proved to be the case. A corollary is that smaller partnerships to share the risk would mean that fewer projects will be undertaken on a slower schedule, even if prices justified a synfuel project.[15]

The final hypothesis is that as risk increases, companies sometimes spread their exposure so widely as to affect efficiency adversely. In a similar vein, Samuel Popkin noted that peasants "scatter" their plantings over many fields to reduce the risk of being wiped out by a disaster in any particular field.[16] Unfortunately, scattering also reduces efficiency substantially. Similarly, oil companies have often kept spreading their bets rather than moving quickly to major commercial plants on new technologies. Under these circumstances majors could also rely increasingly on a "global averaging strategy." For every investment that is liable to one type of risk, the firm may try to match it with one that will benefit it if the risk materializes. For instance, in synfuels the majors turn to scattering and averaging to make themselves less vulnerable to the risks of geographic concentration, especially the dangers of having virtually all the shale mining projects in one section of Colorado.[17] Companies might move into Utah, even if the quality of the shale deposits is inferior, as an offsetting venture. By slowing the pace of Colorado projects and speeding up the pace elsewhere, the companies might gain additional bargaining leverage with local governmental authorities. But such averaging may be severely suboptimal from the viewpoint of society because new supplies would materialize more slowly. (Again, this assumes that prices justify the investments.)

Implications for Government Policies

The proper business of business may be the taking of risks in the pursuit of profit, but entrepreneurs rarely accept their lot with silent good grace. Frequently they seek government assistance to cushion the burdens of risk. Thus we should be careful not to confuse the existence of risk with a strong case for government intervention. But most economists agree that the type of strategic risk being discussed here can produce inefficiencies in the marketplace. Thus, the problems of strategic risk open up some uncomfortable questions for the Reagan administration's rather single-minded devotion to reliance on the private sector for the solution of energy problems.

This section explores specific changes in U.S. policy that might be necessary to cope with these risks. However, it narrows its search for policy options by trying to conform as much as possible to the Reagan administration's professed devotion to maximum reliance on the private sector and marketlike approaches to regulation.

The basic lesson of this and the other chapters in this volume is that the government should broaden its approach to assessing the impact of its policy on industry. There are inevitable and legitimate tensions between the concerns of society (such as the lowest prices for energy, environmental protection, and good diplomatic relations with particular nations) and the (perfectly proper) priorities of the corporation. One such divergence is that what maximizes security (and profit) for the firm may not do so for society as a whole.[18] Yet the measures that government takes to address this problem may actually deepen the tensions between the private and public sectors, thus hurting both. In the future the government must think more carefully about how the overall impact of its policies alters corporate strategies for managing risk and thus the future security of consumers. Such an approach would not lead uniformly either to a laissez-faire or a dirigiste policy. Instead, it could help government to lay out policies for corporations that narrow the gap between the interests of the firm and the priorities of the government.

How could we begin to broaden the approach to analyzing policy? Exhortation alone rarely works. Someone in the government must focus on the exercise as part of its bureaucratic self-interest. When a new purpose is carefully melded with a juggling of operational responsibilities, innovation may occur. In the case of the United States this would require a departure from the emerging distribution of bureaucratic power concerning international energy markets.

If the Reagan administration abolishes the Department of Energy (DOE), analysis of the energy industry, especially the majors, will revert to three groups. Leaving aside questions of antitrust policy, the axis of the Treasury Department and Office of Management and Budget will focus on implications for tax and spending policy (such as the size of public stockpiles of oil or World Bank lending for oil projects); the Commerce Department will focus on market shares and profits of the oil companies; and the State Department–National Security Council (NSC) nexus will worry about general diplomacy with other governments about particular aspects of the oil trade. The latter policy nexus might house the work advocated here, but the tradition of the State Department on these matters would spur doubt about its ability to do so on a sustained basis. During the lengthy discussions concerning the price of LNG (see Chapter 2), the DOE was the one place in the U.S. government that undertook a sustained (if controversial) analysis of the implications for the global energy market of natural gas price and regulatory decisions. Unless a vehicle, such as the NSC, is mandated to force government agencies to think about the relationship between the emerging commercial strategy of an industry and the problems of strategic bargaining that affect the public interest, such considerations are likely to remain largely ignored in Washington.[19]

Although new review processes (to assess environmental and regulatory costs) are a popular solution to complicated problems, they provide no panacea. But the point at this stage should not be the search for quick solutions. Instead, large doses of antidotes to the naiveté that plagues U.S. predictions about the interactions of politics and economics in the world energy system are required. Predictive errors will always occur, but better analysis can reduce U.S. vulnerability to surprises emanating from entire classes of risks that are too frequently ignored.

What might new thinking about risk and regulation eventually produce? We can distinguish between improved understanding of the dynamics of the marketplace that would help guide the forecasts of policymakers and the possible changes in specific policies.

With a keener understanding of the phenomenon of opportunistic behavior, the government will recognize that a change is taking place in the relative importance of the majors and that the independents will play an important role in the world energy trade. Small U.S. firms and the national oil corporations of other countries will play a more prominent role in the future. By pinpointing and entering risky situations where large firms would rather not gamble (because the scale of the ventures is not worth the trouble for them), the "new" independents could earn handsome profits and carve out a substantial niche in the market. In addition to refiners in the United States seeking OPEC investors as partners and suppliers of oil, we have already seen a marked increase in the influence of oil-trading companies and the creation of futures markets for such energy products as heating oil.[20] The danger in the current attitudes in Washington is that top officials usually consider the small independents to be important only in terms of the domestic U.S. market and its politics. Unless this attitude changes, the United States may ignore many important questions about the relationship between its policy and the possibility of fostering beneficial innovations in energy markets. (One encouraging exception is the recent concern over incentives for smaller firms to explore for oil in the Third World.) As a first step, the government should carefully review the potential effect of futures markets on the oil trade in order to determine the implications for security objectives. It should then examine just how current policies are influencing the development of these futures markets.

Clearer thinking about opportunistic behavior also can have direct implications for the choice of policy. Although financial assistance from government for synfuels and appropriate policies for pricing are important, the key to easing the vulnerability to opportunistic behavior may lie in piecemeal experimentation with the regulatory and tax system. Ground rules aimed at reducing the costs of negotiation and bargaining concerning partnerships may be one place to start. The Reagan administration has already moved along this line by relaxing antitrust rules. This approach will allow companies to merge or form new joint ventures more flexibly.

A complementary priority for the utility industry would allow oil companies entry as equity partners and managers in the generation of electric power. (This would be a focus on prizes in the sense developed in Chapter 6.) In particular, governments could permit the oil companies to integrate vertically into the utility industry for projects involving coal, synfuels, geothermal energy, or centralized photovoltaic systems.

Such an approach has been explored elsewhere. For example, British Petroleum has received tentative approval to build electric power plants burning its North Sea gas on floating platforms in the North Sea. Indonesia has announced that it is willing to have foreign investors undertake a total package of development for geothermal power. Standard of California (Socal), for example, could drill the wells to obtain steam, build and operate the power plant, and install the transmission lines to the markets for the power. Socal would earn a profit on each phase of its investment. At the same time, vertical integration would lower its risk by allowing Socal to control more phases of the project's development, thereby reducing the chance that a technical failure by a partner will cause it to lose money. It also raises the potential size and returns on the project, thereby allowing the cost of corporate overhead to be spread over a larger financial base.

Another direction for policy is reducing the risks of changing environmental regulations. "Banking" and "bubbles" for air pollution control, which foster more marketlike allocations of resources for protecting the environment, are already much in vogue. But they do not fully reduce the risk of new costs due to changing rules.[21] And they leave largely unanswered the worries of the majors that public opinion would never permit a large oil company to "pollute equally," even though small companies, which are subjected to less public scrutiny, could do so freely. Thus it is not surprising that the Reagan administration has considered relaxing environmental regulations that are crucial to some energy projects (especially rules about air pollution and land use) rather rapidly. Such an action poses the risk of creating a political backlash later on that could make the long-term problem of accommodating environmental and energy supply needs more difficult. (There is also the acute risk that we might cause a major environmental mess if we do not err on the side of caution.)

Even if relaxation of the rules in the near future is not prudent, other types of regulatory compensation for unexpected changes in existing rules are possible. For instance, one could use collateral bonding on designated energy projects. The bonds could be a two-way obligation. Suppose that developers and the government reached an agreement on the projected costs of meeting current standards as interpreted by the scientific models used to guide their application. Then both sides could post a bond to cover changes in the costs that would result from alterations of the rules or the scientific models.[22] The government would have to pay if regulatory changes increased costs beyond some stipulated "margin of error." Similarly, if changes in the rules cut a firm's costs beyond some percentage, the firm would have to make an offsetting contribution to other programs for the abatement of pollution. Such an arrangement would limit the incentive for either party to act rashly in tampering with regulations.

In the international arena the government could consider three forms of relief for investors. First, the government could promote new ground rules for commercial transactions in international markets. The logic of Chapter 3 would lead, for example, to diplomacy's promoting a set of model coal contracts and information exchange on coal markets. The information could include full disclosure of all spot and long-term contract prices concluded in OECD markets and perhaps reporting on levels of coal stockpiles and coal shipments en route to final destinations. (The reporting system would have to protect the identity of the parties.) The standard contracts could lay out obligations of buyers and sellers about disruptions of supplies, shifts in demand, and terms of payment, to name a few. Better information and standardized contracts reduce the leeway for opportunistic behavior by making all parties privy to vital information on market conditions (including comparable contract terms).

A second approach might eliminate some of the possibilities for opportunism created by the highly specific character of energy investments. For example, in the LNG trade the United States might push for more equipment standardization through research and development and international discussions of standards.

Finally, the United States could review its policy concerning foreign tax credits for overseas energy investments. It could increase the weight accorded to the duration and frequency of a general business relationship when judging whether a U.S. firm could obtain a tax credit for its foreign oil purchases. This would give both the foreign government and the U.S. firm the option of choosing a bargain designed to build the longevity of the relationship, a development that I earlier hypothesized could build the security of the firm in particular countries. The firm could then undertake a more subtle set of trade-offs in designing a global risk strategy that balanced between good ties in one country and the overall flexibility of its global logistical and supply system.

In summary, no set of public policies can totally dispel the potential for opportunistic behavior. But policymakers can be more self-conscious about evaluating the effect of their choices on the types of risks an industry may confront. Moreover, there are some measures (such as the coal contracts, pollution bonds, or modification of criteria for foreign tax credits) that would make it harder, or less rewarding, to engage in opportunistic behavior. And other policies could raise the rewards for confronting risks (such as allowing integration into generating electricity) or lower the costs of undertaking complex transactions requiring elaborate partnerships (such as lowering the prospect of antitrust prosecution).

Of course, society must decide if the gains from these policies are worth potential losses to other goals.

More generally, analysis of energy policy must supplement highly aggregated models of market structure, potential supplies, and the dynamics of demand with more finely tuned analyses of risks of the kind discussed in this volume. We continue to be surprised by developments in the energy sector because analysts implicitly expect straightforward, rational responses to the workings of supply, demand, and political ambitions. What the chapters in this volume have suggested is that the energy market is more akin to a badly financed used-car lot in a state with strong legislation protecting consumers.[23] Let both the buyers and sellers beware!

Notes

1. There is an extensive literature on risk management by corporations that focuses on dangers to individual investments in particular countries. Moreover, it is commonplace to do detailed market analyses in order to assess threats to profits from new capacity, shifts in demand, or changing prices for inputs to production. This chapter emphasizes problems of risk related to bargaining strategies by other parties that are geared to exploit weaknesses in the global pattern of operations established by a major oil company. My analysis does not assume that the majors are risk averse. For a review of the literature on managing risks, consult Dan Haendel, *Foreign Investments and the Management of Political Risk* (Boulder, Colo.: Westview Press, 1979).

2. I draw many of the hypotheses of this chapter from the following works: David J. Teece, *Vertical Integration and Vertical Divestiture in the U.S. Oil Industry* (Stanford, Calif.: Stanford University Institute for Energy Studies, 1976); "The Multinational Enterprise: Market Failure and Market Power Considerations," *Sloan Management Review* 22 (Spring 1981):3–17; Oliver Williamson, *Markets and Hierarchies* (New York: Free Press, 1975); "Transaction-Cost Economics: The Governance of Contractual Relations," *Journal of Law and Economics* 22 (October 1979):233–261; Benjamin Klein, Robert G. Crawford, and Armen A. Alehian, "Vertical Integration, Appropriable Rents, and the Competitive Contracting Process," *Journal of Law and Economics* 21 (October 1978):297–326.

3. As noted previously, the majors' approach to organizing global activities makes them especially vulnerable to opportunistic behavior. But the conditions set out here apply to any business investor.

4. The terms for Australian investors are analyzed in the *Financial Times,* November 10, 1981, p. IV.

5. Aronson and Proctor noted in Chapter 7 that the insurance industry is proving adept at managing large new projects with the use of risk-management techniques. This development somewhat reduces the problem of opportunistic behavior due to uncertainty. But insurance is available only if the parties are

able to write a contract that is sound enough to be insurable. Thus risk management helps the parties pinpoint how to cope with risk, assuming that problems of opportunistic behavior are not serious. Moreover, insurance can be quite expensive, thus making a number of smaller energy projects unattractive.

6. The value of a reputation for reliability is one element of the asset of "goodwill" that companies are compensated for during a sale of a business to a new owner.

7. Of course, Kuwait is gambling that the legal political tradition of these nations will shield it from the worst forms of coercion, a variable listed earlier as a determinant of risk.

8. The size of a project does not necessarily determine the cost of enforcement or degree of specificity. Accordingly, size is not a determinant of likelihood of opportunistic behavior.

9. An analysis relying on the concept of opportunistic behavior treats the actors as if they were partners in a contract situation. For the purposes of this chapter I am interested in examining how the major oil companies interact with both private and public partners. Thus, I am treating a major change in regulations by a government concerning an energy project as if it constituted a form of reneging on a contract.

As students of the obsolescing bargain and the product cycle well know, risk is industry specific. As Aronson and Proctor noted in Chapter 7, the maritime industry has special insurance problems because of the complexity of its legal tradition. Moreover, Stephen Korbin has shown that the petroleum industry is the single most expropriated and nationalized industry. The reasons for a focus on the petroleum industry are a mixture of economic rewards, ease of substitution of the foreign corporation, and political salience to the mass public. I am exploring variances of risk within a single industry. Stephen Korbin, "Foreign Enterprises and Forced Divestment in LDCs," *International Organization* 34 (Winter 1980):65–80.

10. Jonathan Aronson has identified a similar function for the bank in regard to the management of foreign debt by the developing countries. Bank involvement reduces the risks of lending for private financial institutions. Jonathan David Aronson (ed.), *Debt and the Less Developed Countries* (Boulder, Colo.: Westview Press, 1979).

11. The current debate about the program of the World Bank features U.S. criticism of the bank's penchant for lending to government-owned oil corporations. My argument is that the major companies would still lose some of their market share if the private sector were the target of the loans.

Several executives of oil companies that have cooperated with the World Bank on energy projects already have argued to me that the bank's chief contribution is to enable the local NOC to pay its share of the bill. They argue that a country wishing to impose financial penalties on a foreign partner can do so by many means that would fall short of the "confrontational politics" that the bank says that it can prevent.

For a perceptive discussion of individual project risk and market share on slightly different terms, see the work of Theodore Moran, *Multinational Cor-*

porations and the Politics of Dependence (Princeton, N.J.: Princeton University Press, 1974).

12. One question for the majors may be: "Which type of NOC is the best type of steady international partner?" Is it an NOC with aggressive international plans but little domestic production or one with limited regional ambitions and a large domestic base of production?

13. For those of an academic persuasion I should note that this argument differs from the more usual thesis that countries need the majors less, therefore they value them less. Even after controlling for "need," the value assigned to a relationship may vary. Robert Axelrod, "The Emergence of Cooperation Among Egotists," *American Political Science Review* 75 (June 1981):306–318.

As I noted in Chapter 1, Saudi Arabia remained the major exception to the diversification strategy. The bargaining between Nigeria and the majors between late 1981 and early 1982 conformed to the pattern discussed here.

14. A central issue for understanding the future of the oil companies pertains to the accuracy of claims that the majors and the NOCs have inherently different preferences. If such a split truly exists, then NOCs will collaborate with one another far more frequently than with the majors. Evidence raising questions about the extent of the split can be found in L. E. Grayson, *The National Oil Companies* (New York: Wiley, 1981).

15. These large sums are primarily for hardware, a major change from the days when exploration rights were the major risk until relatively late in the project. There are two other changes in the character of investment opportunities. First, any of the really big new projects involves capital expenditures that can hurt a major company much more easily than anything in the past. Risk has increased unless efficient joint ventures and protection from risk due to changing government regulations are insured. Second, the learning curve ideally should be compressed because of regulatory risks. Fewer projects executed on a quicke schedule would be optimal in developing new resources and technologies. But the risks of doing this are substantial; if other factors compound the dangers, companies may choose to procrastinate. This discussion is drawn from Ben C. Ball, "Synfuel Supply Issues from the Commercial Pespective: New Kinds of Decisions," pp. 13–28 in International Energy Agency, *Workshops on Energy Supply and Demand* (Paris: OECD, 1978).

Some potential problems may be avoided by the current direction of synfuel projects. Economists argue that research and development works better when closely integrated to production and marketing. Edwin Mansfield, *Industrial Research and Technological Innovation* (New York: Norton, 1968). The difficulty with new technologies is often tied to meshing them with other logistical and production features of the corporation. Another is that they may not produce precisely the product that fits the companies' need. This last factor is particularly important for synthetic fuels because much of their attraction depends on how well they fill anticipated gaps in conventional supplies. Inasmuch as governments encourage the growth of nonintegrated production syndicates for synfuels, or ones without global operations, there may well be considerable time lost in selecting and testing prototypes most likely to yield the right sorts of hydrocarbons for markets in the 1990s. However, the Reagan administration policy is less likely to produce such an outcome.

16. Samuel Popkin, "Public Choice and Rural Develoment," pp. 43–79 in O. Russell and N. Nicholson (eds.), *Public Choice and Rural Development* (Baltimore: Johns Hopkins University Press, 1981).

17. Interviews with oil industry officials.

18. I am using the concept of "society" in the comparatively narrow sense of welfare economics, not in the broader perspective often employed by scholars working on problems concerning "the state and society."

19. The NSC, for example, had some able people working on energy diplomacy. But, as of 1982, it had neither the personnel nor the mandate to guide the types of analysis suggested here. One petroleum executive involved in LNG has claimed to me that the institutional gap in policymaking had already emerged by 1981 because the Department of Energy had lost power in the area and no one had replaced it.

20. Thomas Neff, "The Changing World Oil Market," pp. 23–48 in David Deese and Joseph Nye (eds.), *Energy Security* (Cambridge, Mass.: Ballinger, 1981).

21. A "bank" allows the firm to take improvements beyond mandatory levels in, for example, one of its facilities in a region and credit it toward permitted emission levels elsewhere in the region. A "bubble" sets a total level of pollutants for a region and then allows firms to buy and sell permits to "pollute" up to the total level of allowed pollutants. Richard Stewart has offered a rich list of options for reducing negotiating costs and the possibilities for opportunistic behavior in government regulation. He makes a strong case for various methods of banking and trading pollution rights, but his ideas about guaranteeing against a change in the ground rules by government seem less convincing to me. Richard B. Stewart, "Regulation, Innovation, and Administrative Law: A Conceptual Framework," *California Law Review* 69 (September 1981):1263–1377 (especially 1280–1283 and 1333–1337).

22. This idea is inspired by work of Benjamin Klein: "Transaction Cost Determinants of 'Unfair' Contractual Arrangements," *American Economic Review* 70 (May 1980):356–361. It also bears some resemblance to the elaborate network of cross-default clauses that govern the holding of debts of Third World countries by commercial banks. See the discussion by Aronson and Proctor cited in note 5. The process of setting the terms of the bonds could follow the lines of negotiations suggested by Stewart, "Regulation." I doubt that bonding would work equally well for all classes of problems. For example, it may perform better for agreements allocating clearly measurable quantities (such as some items relating to water) than for air quality problems.

23. The metaphor is inspired by George Akerlof's classic article, "The Market for 'Lemons': Quality, Uncertainty and the Market Mechanism," *Quarterly Journal of Economics* 84 (August 1970):488–500.

Conclusions

Conclusions to any edited volume are a risky business. The gaps in coverage among the individual chapters always reduce the credibility of any proposed synthesis. Nonetheless, we believe that at least seven themes emerge from the work presented here. The first pertains to the overall pattern of trade and investment in eneregy. The others relate to various dimensions of the changing relationship between the public and private sectors in the energy system.

First, the trend of world trade and foreign investment in energy does not conform to the classic categories that dominate public discussion on this topic. The increasing regulation of international trade and the growth of public corporations mandated to pursue specific government objectives in the marketplace are major departures from the liberal idea of free trade and investment. But the situation does not conform to the antithesis of liberal practices, mercantilism. Countries are not emphasizing energy self-sufficiency at all costs; but they are altering the balance of their energy trade and investment. Further, trade and investment are not becoming more regional in scope; if anything, coal and natural gas markets are showing signs of becoming global. Nor have states acquired a systematic grip over most of the investment and marketing of energy. Thus, we need new images to capture the relationship between changes in the international market for energy and the general alterations in the contours of the world trade and investment systems.

Second, the relationship between the public and private sectors has swung in favor of the public sector, but state entities often act more like private entrepreneurs than bureaucratic governmental agencies. Many of the risks involving energy trading and investment are fundamentally the same for public and private enterprises. If state enterprises benefit from the wellspring of government subsidies and from preferred access to national energy resources, the private companies reap advantages from their comparative freedom to avoid the costly commitments to particular regional markets or supply sources that governments often require from state entities. Thus, the growth of the public sector will not lead to a general revolution in the way that investment decisions are made or trading operates in the energy sector.

Even though similarities and continuities between the public and private sectors are important, it seems clear that the growing role of government regulation and of state corporations will alter the energy market in several ways. Our third conclusion is that the growth of public power has fundamentally eroded the authority of the Anglo-American majors in every major fuel market. This has an important political consequence. The effects of the political and economic priorities of the home country show up only in very subtle ways in the conduct of a global enterprise; they are nonetheless significant. (If nothing else, other governments perceive the parent countries of major global firms to be powerful.) Thus, a more diverse set of national parent governments ought to lead to a more complex hidden agenda in negotiations about the world energy trade. This change is likely to surface most clearly in a market with a strongly bilateral or regional character, such as the one for natural gas.

Fourth, another consequence of the growth of public power may emerge in the form of a renewed sensitivity to the compatibility or incompatibility of the domestic energy policies of nations. Over the past decade, for example, the OECD countries have negotiated vigorously over common standards for the rationalization of national energy policies, such as the decontrol of oil prices. But the initial agenda for these talks has largely run its course, and the next round of discussions may prove much more difficult. As Klapp pointed out, future policy decisions can directly or indirectly tilt the balance of advantages to public or private, domestic or foreign enterprises. Unlike marginal cost pricing, which most experts throughout the OECD endorsed, no widespread consensus exists about these new trade-offs. Incompatibilities in domestic policies could alter the shape of international trading in oil, gas, and coal. Moreover, different choices about how to restructure utility industries (a universal problem) could introduce major elements of uncertainty into the demand and supply sides of any set of energy forecasts. Many nations, for example, might endorse the use of coal-fired plants in principle, but different blends of utility reform will alter the likelihood of appropriate investment decisions from country to country.

Our fifth conclusion pertains to the requirement for new types of public policies. As the chapters on utilities, synfuel subsidies, and opportunistic behavior demonstrated, a major commitment by governments to intervene in the evolution of energy markets leads to new types of investment risks and opportunities. The standard repertoire of government policies—whether it be average cost pricing for utility monopolies or the use of guarantees against all losses for research and development ventures—may prove extremely inefficient in the future. For instance, almost no one has investigated how future changes in the international insurance industry might alter the types and extent of government subsidies necessary for major energy projects.

A sixth implication of these chapters concerns the transformation of private companies. As the discussions of each of the major fuels and utilities suggest, the changes in energy markets yield incentives for a major reorganization of the structure of energy corporations. Oil corporations diversify to become energy companies; their entry into coal markets opens up the possibility of vertically integrated trading in coal. Meanwhile, traditional coal suppliers must grow in size and complexity to compete on a world market. In both industries new types of exchanges (such as futures markets) grow in importance. Moreover, as the possibility of utility firms' becoming the trading networks for diverse independent sources of supply illustrates most vividly, the specialized advantages of the major firms may change greatly. The companies have responded and will continue to respond to the growth of public enterprises and regulatory fervor. The bargaining positions will inevitably continue to change. This leads to our last conclusion.

We must recognize that the interests of the commercial players (state and private) in the world market will change. OPEC national oil corporations become producers of oil in the United States. Utility firms become larger investors in the production of natural resources. Natural gas syndicates from Europe compete for the advantages of being lead partners on import deals, while continuing to operate as conventional utilities in other respects. Oil corporations acquire an interest in promoting greater sensitivity by consumers to the potential for the substitution and switching of fuels on a regular basis according to shifts in the world market. Thus they have an interest in stressing the dynamics of how one fuel's price can shape the markets for other energy options. For all firms, distinctions among producers, distributors, and consumers of energy become more blurred. Such changes in the commercial interests of the major public and private corporations eventually must influence the agenda of government regulation. In this volume we have looked at but a few examples of the implications of such changes. However, the story of the energy sector during the rest of this century may depend largely on how governments rework public policy in order to adjust to new opportunities and risks for making profit in the world energy trade.

About the Contributors

Jonathan David Aronson is an associate professor at the School of International Relations at the University of Southern California. In 1982–1983 he was a Council on Foreign Relations International Affairs Fellow in the Office of the U.S. Trade Representative. He is the author of *Money and Power: Banks and the World Monetary System* (1978) and editor of *Debt and the Less Developed Countries* (Westview, 1979).

Peter F. Cowhey is an assistant professor of political science at the University of California–San Diego. He is the author of the forthcoming *The Problems of Plenty: Energy Policy and International Politics.*

Zvi Adar is a professor in the School of Management at Tel Aviv University. He spent the 1981–1982 academic year as a visiting professor at the University of California–Davis.

Tamir Agmon is a professor in the School of Management at Tel Aviv University. He is the coeditor of *Multinationals from Small Countries* (1977). He spent the 1981–1982 academic year as a visiting professor at the University of Southern California.

Christopher Cragg was formerly a research officer for the International Business Unit at the University of Manchester Institute of Science and Technology and then at the Centre for International Studies at the London School of Economics and Politics. He was also associate editor of *Seatrade,* specializing in energy and commodity affairs.

Michael Gaffen was formerly director of international coal analysis at the U.S. Department of Energy. He is currently planning manager for a major international energy organization.

Merrie Klapp is an assistant professor of environmental studies and planning in the Department of Urban Studies and Planning at the Massachusetts Institute of Technology. She was a postdoctoral fellow jointly at the Center for International Studies at M.I.T. and at Woods Hole Oceanographic Institute.

Kermit R. Kubitz is coordinator for corporate planning at the Pacific Gas and Electric Company. He was an attorney in PG&E's legal department, where he participated in geothermal hydroelectric plant certification and regulatory approval and funding of conservation, load management, and solar programs.

Charles Rudicel Proctor is a vice-president at Marsh & McLennan, Inc. He was responsible for risk-management consulting services for Marsh & McLennan for the western United States and was involved in formalizing the coverage for launch failure and spacecraft liability insurance.

Index